Judicial tribunals
in England and Europe,
1200–1700

MANCHESTER
UNIVERSITY PRESS

Judicial tribunals in England and Europe,

1200–1700

The trial in history, volume I

edited by Maureen Mulholland
and Brian Pullan

with Anne Pullan

Manchester University Press

Manchester and New York

distributed exclusively in the USA by Palgrave

Published by Manchester University Press
Oxford Road, Manchester M13 9NR, UK
and Room 400, 175 Fifth Avenue, New York, NY 10010, USA
www.manchesteruniversitypress.co.uk

Distributed exclusively in the USA by
Palgrave, 175 Fifth Avenue, New York NY 10010, USA

Distributed exclusively in Canada by
UBC Press, University of British Columbia, 2029 West Mall,
Vancouver, BC, Canada V6T 1Z2

British Library Cataloguing-in-Publication Data
A catalogue record for this book is available from the British Library

Library of Congress Cataloging-in-Publication Data
A catalog record for this book is available from the Library of Congress

ISBN 13: 978 0 7190 6343 5

First published by Manchester University Press 2003

First digital paperback edition published 2011

Printed by Lightning Source

Contents

Tables

Contributors

Jeffrey Denton, formerly Professor of Medieval History in the University of Manchester, is now Honorary Research Fellow in the Department of History of the University of Sheffield. Among his recent works are 'Taxation and the conflict between Philip the Fair and Boniface VIII', *French History*, 11 (1997), 241–64, and 'Towards a new edition of the *Taxatio Ecclesiastica Angliae et Walliae Auctoritate Nicholai IV circa 1291'*, *Bulletin of the John Rylands University Library of Manchester*, 79 (1997), 67–79. He is the editor of *Orders and Hierarchies in Late Medieval and Renaissance Europe* (Basingstoke and London, 1999). He is working on a new edition of texts relating to the Anglo-Papal crisis of 1301–3, on a new electronic and hard-copy edition of the 1291 assessment of the value of English and Welsh ecclesiastical benefices, and on an edition of the episcopal *acta* of the bishops of Coventry and Lichfield in the thirteenth century.

R. H. Helmholz is Ruth Wyatt Rosenson Distinguished Service Professor in the Law School of the University of Chicago. His recent books include *Roman Canon Law in Reformation England* (Cambridge, 1990); *The Spirit of Classical Canon Law* (Athens, Georgia, 1996); and *The ius commune in England: Four Studies* (New York, 2001). He is now at work on a general history of the canon law and ecclesiastical jurisdiction in England for the series *The History of English Laws*, to be published by Oxford University Press.

Joseph Jaconelli is Reader in Law at the University of Manchester. He has a long-standing interest in issues of publicity and secrecy in the conduct of trials, as reflected in his articles: 'Some thoughts on jury secrecy', *Legal Studies*, 10 (1990), 91–103, and 'Rights theories and public trial', *Journal of Applied Philosophy*, 14 (1997), 169–75. His monograph on the subject, *Open Justice. A Critique of the Public Trial*, was published in 2002 by Oxford University Press. He is also the author of *Enacting a Bill of Rights: The Legal Problems* (Oxford, 1980).

Daniel Klerman is Professor of Law and History in the University of Southern California Law School. His publications include 'Settlement and the decline of private prosecution in thirteenth-century England', *Law and History Review*, 19 (2001), 1–65, and also 'Non-promotion and judicial independence', *Southern California Law Review*, 72 (1999), 455–63. An article, 'Statistical and economic methods in legal history', is to be published in *Illinois Law Review*, and another, 'Women prosecutors in thirteenth-century England', is forthcoming in *Yale Journal of Law and Humanities*. He was awarded the 2001 David Yale Prize of the Selden Society for 'distinguished contribution to the history of the laws and legal institutions of England and Wales'. He is now working on a project which explores the effects of jurisdictional competition on the development of English law.

Mary Laven is a University Lecturer at the University of Cambridge, and a Fellow of Jesus College. She is the author of *Virgins of Venice: Enclosed Lives and Broken Vows in the Renaissance Convent* (London, 2002) and of several articles on Venetian convents, including 'Sex and celibacy in early modern Venice', *The Historical Journal*, 44 (2001), 865–88. She is embarking on a new study of sociability in early modern Italy.

Maureen Mulholland is Honorary Lecturer (formerly Lecturer) in Law at the University of Manchester. She is an editor of the seventeenth and eighteenth editions and supplements of *Clerk and Lindsell on Tort* (London, respectively 1995 and 2000) and has contributed articles on English legal history to J. Cannon (ed.), *The Oxford Companion to British History* (Oxford, 1997). With M. Brazier, she has contributed a chapter on 'Droit et Sida; le Royaume Uni', to J. Foyer and L. Khaiat (eds), *Droit et Sida, comparaison internationale* (Paris, 1994), pp. 363–86, and another on 'AIDS and the law' to R. Bennet, C. Erin and J. Harris (eds), *AIDS. Ethics, Justice and European Policy* (Luxembourg, 1998), pp. 97–157. Her article 'The jury in English manorial courts' has recently appeared in J. W. Cairns and G. McLeod (eds), *The Jury in the History of the Common Law* (Oxford and Portland, Oregon, 2002), pp. 63–73.

Anthony Musson is Senior Lecturer in Law at the University of Exeter. He is the author of *Public Order and Law Enforcement: The Local Administration of Criminal Justice, 1294–1350* (Woodbridge, 1996); 'Twelve good men and true? The character of early fourteenth-century juries', *Law and History Review*, 15 (1997), 115–44; (with W. M. Ormrod) *The Evolution of English Justice: Law, Politics and Society in the Fourteenth Century* (Basingstoke, 1998); and *Medieval Law in Context: The Growth of Legal Consciousness from Magna Carta to the Peasants' Revolt* (Manchester, 2001). He is now working on two books: *English Law in the Middle Ages: A Social History*, for the Medieval Worlds series of Hambledon and London; and *Crime, Law and Society in the Later Middle Ages*, for the Medieval Texts and Sources series of Manchester University Press.

William G. Naphy is Senior Lecturer and Head of the Department of History in the School of History and History of Art at the University of Aberdeen. Among his recent publications are *Fear in Early Modern Society*, which he edited with P. Roberts (Manchester, 1997); *Plagues, Poisons and Potions: Conspiring to Spread Plague in the Western Alps, c. 1530–1640* (Manchester, 2002); 'Sodomy in early modern Geneva: various definitions, diverse verdicts', in T. Betteridge (ed.), *Sodomy and Sexual Deviance in Early Modern Europe* (Manchester, 2002), pp. 94–111; and (ed. with H. Parish) *Religion and Superstition in Reformation Europe* (Manchester, 2002). He is now working on a monograph concerning the criminalisation of sexual activity in early modern Geneva.

Brian Pullan is Emeritus Professor of Modern History in the University of Manchester. His books include *Rich and Poor in Renaissance Venice: The Social Institutions of a Catholic State, to 1620* (Oxford, 1971); *The Jews of Europe and the Inquisition of Venice, 1550–1670* (Oxford, 1983, reprint, London, 1997); and *Poverty and Charity: Europe, Italy, Venice 1400–1700* (Aldershot, 1994). He is one of the editors (with D. S. Chambers and J. Fletcher) of *Venice: A Documentary History 1450–1630* (Oxford, 1992). He is now working, with the assistance of M. Abendstern, on the recent history of the University of Manchester. One volume, *A History of the University of Manchester 1951–73* (Manchester, 2000), has appeared, and a second volume is in progress.

Acknowledgements

Earlier versions of some of the chapters in this volume were delivered at a conference on 'The Trial in History' held in Manchester on 17–19 September 1999. This conference was organised by the Department of History of the University of Manchester in association with the Faculty (now the School) of Law, and with the advice and help of members of the Wellcome Unit for the History of Medicine and of the Departments of Philosophy and of Social Anthropology. Further financial contributions in support of the conference were made by the British Academy Humanities Research Board, the University of Manchester, Messrs Eversheds, Solicitors of Manchester, and the J. K. Hyde Centre for Late Medieval and Renaissance Studies. The editors are deeply grateful to Bill Smith, the conference administrator, for his efficiency and good humour. They owe many thanks to Anne Pullan for her assistance with the editorial work. Her computing skills and her sharp eye, both for inconsistencies and for infelicities, have proved invaluable.

A companion volume, *Domestic and International Trials, 1700–2000*, edited by R. A. Melikan of St Catharine's College Cambridge, will also be published by Manchester University Press.

Abbreviations

All E.R.	All England Law Reports
A.S.V.	Archivio di Stato di Venezia
BI	Borthwick Institute of Historical Research
Burr.	Burrows Reports (contained in The English Reports)
C66	P.R.O., Chancery, Patent Rolls
Ch.	Chancery
Clem.	Clementines (the collection of decretals promulgated by Pope Clement V, 1314: see E. Friedberg, ed., *Corpus iuris canonici, pars secunda: decretalium collectiones*, Leipzig, 1922, cols 1133–1200)
Co. Litt.	*Coke on Littleton*, 1617 (Sir Edward Coke's commentary on Littleton's *Tenures*, 1481)
Co. Rep.	Reports of Sir Edward Coke
CP40	P.R.O., Common Pleas
E.R.	The English Reports
gl. ord.	*Glossa Ordinaria* (Lyons, 1556)
H.L.C.	House of Lords Cases
How.	Howard's Reports (i.e. those of B. C. Howard, who compiled reports of the judgments of the United States Supreme Court in the mid-nineteenth century)
JUST 1	P.R.O., Justices Itinerant, Assize Rolls, etc.
JUST 3	P.R.O., Justices Itinerant, Gaol Delivery Rolls
PC	Archives d'Etat de Genève, Procès Criminels
P.R.O.	Public Record Office, London
PSM	ASV, *Provveditori sopra Monasteri*
Q.B.	Queen's Bench
Q.B.D.	Queen's Bench Division
RP	*Rotuli parliamentorum* (London, House of Lords, 1783)
S.I.	Statutory Instruments

SR	*Statutes of the Realm* (London, Record Commission, 1810–1828)
U.S.	United States Supreme Court Reports
W.L.R.	Weekly Law Reports
YB	*Year Books* (Selden Society and Rolls Series)

Introduction

Maureen Mulholland

I The trial in history

Five of the contributions to this volume arise from papers delivered at the Manchester conference on the theme of the trial in history; four chapters, those of Daniel Klerman, Maureen Mulholland, Anthony Musson and Brian Pullan, have been added to them. A companion volume, *Domestic and International Trials, 1700–2000*, edited by R. A. Melikan, will be published simultaneously.

In compiling this collection, as in planning the conference, it was necessary to consider several possible approaches. Would the papers be primarily concerned with the notion of 'trial' in the abstract, or would each essay be on particular kinds of trial, or on individual trials? If the latter, would these be famous trials or typical examples of a genre? Would they concentrate on procedure and on the jurisprudence of trial, on social context and background, on politics, or on trial as ritual, as drama or as symbol?

The approach of the lawyer and legal historian to the subject of trial or trials will be different from that of the social, political or economic historian; the lawyer is particularly concerned with the nature of the court or tribunal conducting the trial, its composition, its constitutional validity, its procedure and the extent to which it applies substantive principles according to existing legal rules. For the social and economic historian, the formalities and rituals of trials are not as important in themselves as for what they reveal of the lives, the mores, and the circumstances of the participants, in such a way as to throw light on their society and their era. The prime concern for political historians will be the politics of trials and their significance in the community and in the movements of history. Happily, however, the divisions between the different approaches are not rigid and the legal historian's discipline is no longer perceived as divorced from the social, the economic or the political.

This book does not purport to give an exhaustive account of so vast a subject as 'The Trial in History'. Rather, it sets out to provide a few illuminating examples of the operation in the past of different legal systems, applied by differently constituted courts, royal and manorial, secular and ecclesiastical, which adopted different procedures, adversarial and inquisitorial. Some used juries and some did not; some looked to accusers, others to informers. The chapters in this volume discuss the principles which governed both the common law of England and the Roman and canon law of the Church and of some of the states of continental Europe. Some are written by scholars who are, by training, lawyers and members of law faculties and schools, others by historians interested in the application of the law and the functioning of the courts in past times. This collection of studies begins with a chapter by a legal theorist, Joseph Jaconelli. It explores the concept of trial, and particularly the modern notion of a fair trial, in order to analyse the assumptions which many readers will make about the nature of legal process. The issues which it raises are relevant to both volumes, but it has been placed at the beginning of Volume I as an opening conceptual analysis, against which all the cases discussed can be measured. Some meet Jaconelli's criteria for a fair trial and others do not.

Chapters 2 to 5, ranging from the thirteenth to the seventeenth century, consider criminal trials and civil litigation conducted in royal, manorial and Church courts in late medieval and early modern England. They concentrate on the structure, jurisdiction, functions, and procedures of the courts and on the roles of the judges of fact and of law, both amateur and professional, who composed them. By way of contrast, chapters 6 to 9, on the legal history of continental Europe, shift the emphasis from the judges and jurors to the prisoners arraigned before the courts, to the victims of prosecution or to the highly questionable images of them created by their enemies. These later chapters do not ignore the mentality of the judges or the procedures which they followed; to neglect such things would be to misinterpret the records which enable historians to reconstruct the lives of ordinary people or to analyse (as in chapter 6) the charges levelled at famous men. But they focus more sharply on the character and outlook of the deviants and on their efforts to defend themselves.

In its widest meaning the word 'trial' is synonymous with 'test'. In the Judaeo-Christian tradition the trials of believers are part of their relationship with God; in the Old Testament, Abraham, Job and the prophets suffered 'trials' which tested their faith and the same tradition is evident throughout Christian theology, especially in relation to suffering and ultimately to martyrdom. This meaning is still common in the expressions 'These things are sent to try us' or in the phrase 'trials and tribulations'. We commonly speak of 'trials' in the sense of tests conducted to determine the quality of something,[1] to discover the effectiveness of medicines, the mettle of athletes or the fitness of products or machinery. However, in this volume, the term 'trial' is used in its forensic sense, which, in addition to involving a test of an issue, implies a procedure or ritual to try that issue in a forum whose authority and validity are accepted as binding by the community subject to its jurisdiction. Both these meanings of trial – the test and the forensic ritual – were combined in trial by ordeal, including trial by corsned,[2] where the subject of the trial underwent a test and the outcome was deemed to be decided by divine intervention. Trial by combat was merely a different form of trial by ordeal, since the protagonists were subjected to a test of military skills, but judgment was likewise deemed to go, by divine intervention, to the victor. Although these ordeals were tests, they can legitimately be described as trials within the meaning of this collection since they took place in a forensic context, albeit a religious one, and they were conducted by representatives of authority whose jurisdiction was accepted by the participants, and whose definitive decision or judgment would be accepted as binding by them and by the society in which they functioned.[3]

One of the most striking features of medieval and early modern society was the widespread influence and consciousness of law.[4] Far from being a lawless society, medieval and early modern Europe was interwoven with a complex web of legal systems. The villein on the manor, the tradesman in the village, the feudal lord and the city merchant all inhabited a world governed by a number of different judicial systems. Throughout Christendom the jurisdiction of the Church was acknowledged overall, though this did not prevent constant battles between the ecclesiastical and secular courts, just as there were conflicts between the Church and European secular rulers, such as the great conflicts between the papacy and the holy Roman emperors and, in England, between Henry II and Thomas Becket. All classes were subject to the jurisdiction of the Church courts. Their authority extended not only to matters of discipline in faith and morals (including questions of heresy, validity of marriage, legitimacy and succession) but also to litigation between parties in complaints such as slander or breach of faith.

In England, the villein was also subject to the law and courts of the manor and to the king's justice, administered by the sheriff and later by the justices of the peace, or by the justices of oyer, terminer and gaol delivery. When he had a claim relating to land he was denied the protection of the common law but could seek the justice of the manor or, in some cases, the Church. The feudal lord could seek the justice of the king, and was also subject, at least in theory, to the criminal law and to Parliament, as well as to the jurisdiction of the Church. The tradesman and the merchant in England might find themselves arraigned before the court of the manor or the sheriff, and later the justices of the peace or the assizes, and might also be charged before the Church court with a moral transgression such as adultery or dishonesty. If such a person had a complaint he might pursue a claim for trespass, debt or defamation in the court of the manor, the church or the common law. In addition merchants and traders could bring their actions in a court of pie powder,[5] a court attached to a fair or market, or to a court of a port, such as the Tolzey Court of Bristol – one of a network of special commercial courts, much favoured by the mercantile community throughout Europe.

It was not only the Church courts which presumed to censure and to punish moral offences. All the courts of the period claimed jurisdiction over moral conduct – from the English manorial courts to the courts of great cities and states, such as those of Venice and Geneva, described in chapters 7 to 9 of this volume. In considering the relationship between law and morality, medieval and early modern courts were not affected by the dualism which now informs the legal systems of most countries with liberal democracies. The famous debate between Professor H. L. A. Hart[6] and Lord Devlin[7] in the 1960s on the division between law and morals would no doubt have seemed strange to medieval man and woman. At all levels of society, public order and State security were closely linked with Christian morality and religious orthodoxy. All the cases discussed in chapters 6 to 9 involve scandalous behaviour: heresy or the suspicion thereof; gross immorality; blatant defiance of ecclesiastical discipline; violations of sacred space or ventures into unholy space at inappropriate times; disrespect for Lent, the season *par excellence* when sins should be purged by self-denial and not compounded by self-indulgence. Some of them demonstrate how fine the distinction could be between scandalous conduct and heresy, especially where the transgressions were committed by people of great prominence who enjoyed the power to mislead by bad example (chapter 6). Should a state tolerate blasphemy, heresy, gambling, sodomy or laxity in nunneries it would risk incurring the wrath of God, which might well be expressed through visitations of plague, harvest failure or military defeat. Hence the prosecution of such excesses became a matter of protecting public safety, as well as a concern of the Church and its courts. The trial of Laura Querini, described by Mary Laven in chapter 8, demonstrates the powerful connection between the courts of the Venetian State and the Church – she is tried under canon law but her lover, if apprehended, would be tried in the courts of the State for his offence of breaking into a convent. The inquisitorial proceedings against Giorgio Moreto, described by Brian Pullan in chapter 9, show the Venetian State supporting the rules of the Church and enforcing morality as part of its carefully balanced relationship with the power of the Church.

The manorial courts, both seignoral and franchise courts, punished conduct which we would now consider purely moral offences – adultery, fornication, cheating, breaking faith – all of which were regarded as appropriate for manorial justice[8] as well as for the courts of the Church. Inevitably the overlapping of jurisdictions had consequences which were on occasions used by litigants and defendants to their own advantage. A merchant, denied a remedy under common law for breach of contract, might seek the aid of the Church courts for breach of faith or that of the mercantile court, where customs of merchants might give him a remedy. In criminal trials, choice of forum might work to the advantage of an accused person, the classic example being the use of benefit of clergy to obtain the milder punishments of ecclesiastical courts. Laura Querini's case also illustrates a division of jurisdiction according to the status of the parties; she was subject to the courts of the Church, her lover to the law of the Venetian State, and her wholehearted acceptance of guilt for their behaviour may perhaps have been more fulsome since her punishment would be milder than his.

There were, of course, conflicts of jurisdiction between the courts of Church and State and of Church and manor.[9] These conflicts were expressed in England in the statutes of *praemunire* and in disputes over jurisdiction between the common law courts and the courts of the Church – in defamation or in contract, and in the long running rivalry between common law and Chancery over injunctions and prohibitions. At a humbler level, the manorial courts, too, were jealous of their jurisdiction and punished those who sought justice from the wrong feudal lord or from the Church courts.[10] These conflicts seem to have been political rather than philosophical. The common law courts guarded their exclusive jurisdiction over freehold land and denied other courts the right to impose a death sentence. They also bitterly resented the claims of the Church courts, the mercantile courts and the court of Chancery to give remedies – especially damages – to those who sought the justice of those courts rather than of the common law, particularly where the Church courts gave remedies in cases where the common law did not. Indignation at jurisdictional conflict proceeded from the judges and officials of a court rather than from the individuals in dispute. For them, jurisdictional boundaries were unimportant compared with accessibility and effectiveness of the remedy sought. It would be too simplistic to suggest that the only motive for judges jealously guarding their jurisdiction was financial, but it must at least have been a part of the common lawyers' motivation.

II The nature, structure and systems of trial

Trial was described by Chief Justice Coke in the seventeenth century as 'the finding out by due examination of the truth of the point in issue or the question between the parties whereupon judgment may be given'.[11] As Jaconelli indicates in chapter 1, the popular concept of trial is the criminal trial. The greatest human interest is inevitably attracted by trials where the outcome will put the person on trial in jeopardy – possibly suffering loss of life or other grave penalty – and this will include trials of individuals for breaches of religious laws, where the penalty may range from penance to excommunication or death. But any analysis of trial must also include civil cases where the protagonists face each other before the court and the aphorism that 'law is the reconciliation of conflicting interests' is seen most clearly. This book refers, not only to criminal trials, but also to trials for religious offences and to civil litigation. This includes pleas of debt, trespass, slander and disputes over land heard in the manorial courts; claims of breach of faith, defamation and testamentary disputes in the Courts of the Church; and litigation between subjects in the common law courts at Westminster and on circuit. The term 'civil litigation' may be anachronistic, but these cases are all examples of disputes between individuals and are therefore arguably within the term.

Rationality

The first requirement of a fair trial analysed by Joseph Jaconelli is rationality, both of procedure and of content. The outcome should be judgment according to law in the broad sense. Different tribunals may interpret this in different ways. In the common law the rules of procedure and of evidence have developed with the aim of ensuring a fair trial and striking an appropriate balance between the interests, in the criminal courts, of State and suspect and, in civil cases, between contesting parties. There has been particular emphasis on this even-handedness in the common law, in which, even from its early days, the judge's role was that of a presiding umpire between two sides, especially in civil cases. Examples of rules of evidence developed over the centuries by the English criminal law to achieve this balance were the hearsay rule, the rule against self incrimination, the refusal to allow the prosecution to produce evidence of past convictions and the insistence that the burden of proof lies on the prosecution to establish guilt in criminal cases. Whether a trial takes place in a common law or civil law jurisdiction, a proper trial must always be directed to a judgment in the light of legal rules and principles, not made capriciously or merely to serve a particular purpose. The 'show trial' is conspicuously lacking in this requirement.[12] As Jeffrey Denton demonstrates in chapter 6, the threatened trial of Pope Boniface would have been a classic 'show trial', had it taken place.

In other trials, however, the judges and their advisers respected the standards of proof demanded by Roman and canon law. As William Naphy explains (chapter 7), Genevan courts considered it improper to convict an accused person, at least of a capital offence, unless two believable eyewitnesses testified to a criminal act or unless the accused person confessed to it. Confession became the queen of proofs in a legal system which protected the accused against condemnation on the strength of circumstantial evidence and allowed little discretion to amateur judges. To apply torture to obtain a confession might be a legitimate move, but only if certain conditions were met: there must be signposts (*indicia*) pointing to the guilt of the accused persons and amounting to partial proof thereof, or the accused must be changing their stories or contradicting themselves. As Naphy shows, 'not proven' verdicts delivered in cases of serious crime might allow accused persons to escape judgment of death, but not to avoid the severe penalty of exile meted out to those who had incurred deep suspicion but had not been formally convicted according to law.

Throughout this book questions arise about the significance in trials of amateur and professional, lay and ecclesiastical judges and of the role of other professional lawyers and lay people in the proceedings. The essays in this collection by Klerman, Mulholland, and Musson (chapters 2 to 4), are concerned with trials in medieval and early modern England and reveal that one of the notable features of English justice, then as now, was the continuous importance of lay participation in the judicial process. Indeed, even at the present day, trial in the English magistrates' court is trial by lay people, albeit with a legally qualified clerk to guide them, and many tribunals which in practice conduct trials, such as employment or disciplinary tribunals, have on their decision-making body some non-legal personnel. The chapters on late medieval English courts, whether of common law or of the manor, and even the courts of the Church in post-Reformation England,[13] reveal the importance of non-lawyers in their proceedings.

On the face of it, the judicial benches of Venetian secular courts, including that of the Provveditori sopra Monasteri (chapter 8), were entirely occupied by elected lay judges of noble rank who had no legal training and judged solely by equity. Critics of Venice sometimes represented her judges as hopelessly gullible and easily swayed by the rhetoric of vociferous and none-too-scrupulous advocates (one thinks of Voltore in Ben Jonson's Venetian play *Volpone*, whose 'soul moves in his fee'. 'This fellow', as his victim complains, 'For six sols more, would plead against his Maker.').[14] Unlike the English jurors of Daniel Klerman's chapter, Venetian judges reputedly never undertook their own inquiries or did homework of any kind, but relied entirely on evidence presented in court and argued about by advocates.[15] It should be said, however, that as a sub-commission of the Council of Ten, Venice's most powerful magistracy, the Provveditori sopra Monasteri consisted of senior and experienced magistrates who were unlikely to be ill-educated time-servers.

Another feature of late medieval and early modern English law was the development of the legal profession which, having been a purely clerical group in the formative years of the common law, gradually became a secular elite. This elite had its own identity, separated from clerical judges and lay participants by training and tradition – a development particularly fostered in the Inns of Court. Anthony Musson discusses this progress from amateurism to professionalism especially in the judiciary. The same trend can be seen in chapter 4 (Maureen Mulholland), which notes the central role of lay people in the administration of manorial justice, but also points out that the important office of steward had become the preserve of lawyers by the fourteenth century and that the power of the steward was then increased at the expense of the jury.

The development of the common law was profoundly influenced by the emergence of the legal profession, trained in the common law tradition in the Inns of Court and skilled in oral argument and in the extraordinary technicalities which developed around the forms of action. One important feature of the English system, however, was that in the formative years of the common law, the use of advocates was limited almost entirely to civil litigation and was virtually absent from criminal trials. Indeed the typical criminal trial in the common law was for centuries extremely harsh on the accused, who was not allowed counsel in felony cases until 1837.[16]

Inquisitorial procedures, on the other hand, at least in ecclesiastical courts, did not preclude the retention of advocates for the prosecution and for the defence. Professional advocates, however, played little part in the trials discussed in the later chapters of this volume. Instead, the persons on trial seem to be raising certain defences (or pleading mitigation) on their own account, but in a manner which suggests that they received some coaching outside the court room. William Naphy shows how the amateur criminal judges of Geneva were advised by a trained lawyer. In the Venetian courts, the clerks might claim to be mere executors of the orders of their superiors, or mere civil servants with no will of their own, but it was they who ran many of Venice's law courts, often interrogating witnesses and drawing up the record of the proceedings.[17] The tribunal of the Roman Inquisition in Venice, described by Brian Pullan in chapter 9, consisted of both amateur and professional judges who were present at the formal interrogation of witnesses on which the legal process depended.

The importance of the jury in the English courts provides a striking example of lay participation in the trial process. The grand jury, descended from the jury of presentment, was a fundamental aspect of communal responsibility for law and order in medieval England.[18] After the Lateran Council in 1215 had forbidden the clergy to participate in the ordeal, the English trial jury – the 'petty jury' – developed to become all-important in deciding issues of fact in the courts of the common law,[19] and its importance was to last until the present day in criminal cases. In civil cases it was to last until the twentieth century and still survives in a few cases, such as defamation actions. The concept of trial by a band of neighbours, whose local origin was reflected in the phrase 'to put oneself upon the country',[20] has been seminal in developing the Anglo-American common law trial, in which questions of fact and questions of law are analysed and separated for the jury, which has the final say in decisions of fact. It must be remembered that, despite its status as the great institution of Anglo-American law, there was another side to jury trial. It has been a proud boast of English common lawyers that torture was never part of its trial procedure, but the imposition of the barbaric procedure of the *peine forte et dure* to compel a defendant in a criminal trial either to accept trial by jury or to be pressed to death[21] can hardly be characterised by any other term. However, once that barbaric procedure became obsolete, the jury gradually achieved its status as a precious jewel of the common law[22] and became one of its most marked features. This body of neighbours which was ultimately to become the final deciding body in trials, became the backbone of the common law trial, civil as well as criminal, and is still regarded with sentimental affection by common lawyers all over the world. In England and Wales there has been a diminution in its use, especially in civil cases where it is limited to very few causes of action. Even in criminal cases its use is diminishing, but it survives and flourishes in the USA in both civil and criminal trials, as does the 'grand jury' descended from the jury of presentment.

Much has traditionally been made of the fundamental differences between the common law and the civil law, procedurally and substantively. In English jurisprudence, the term 'civil law' is used in two senses. When contrasted with 'common law', it is used to denote legal systems based on Roman law or within the Roman law tradition, including most of those in continental Europe (civil law is also a marked feature of the Scottish legal system).[23] The second meaning, common to most (if not all) legal systems, contrasts 'civil' with criminal law and procedure. Criminal law is concerned with offences against society, punishable by that society if guilt is established. Civil law is concerned with all other proceedings, especially those between individuals. The great division of trial procedures is between the adversarial mode, beloved of the common law, and the inquisitorial mode, employed in the courts of civil law jurisdictions[24] (including the ecclesiastical courts administering canon law). A historical examination of trials is a reminder that, in their origins, the common law and the civil law were both concerned with the finding of fact by the court. In seeking to discover and reveal the true facts, English law, in the king's courts, later the common law courts, and in the manorial courts, chose to use the inquest (jury), whose very name, *inquisitio*, reminds us that its function was to investigate and to reveal the true facts for the court to enable it to decide.[25] Both methods of trial are devoted to discovering the true facts so as to come to a just judgment. Perhaps the historical division between the two procedures has been exaggerated. Anthony Musson, in his chapter on the common law judges, demonstrates that they sometimes acted in an inquisitorial manner, and Daniel Klerman argues that common law juries conducted their own inquiries into the relevant facts of the case. Maureen Mulholland also shows that some of the proceedings in the manorial courts, especially the courts leet, gave to the steward what was in effect an inquisitorial role.

In both systems, common law and civil law, an important role was played by persons who were informers or accusers. In the common law, there were three ways in which a suspected criminal might be brought to trial – first, by appeal, where the person offended complained of the offence and challenged the offender before the court; secondly, by indictment; and thirdly, by information from 'approvers' or from informers, a system strengthened up to the nineteenth century by statutory payments for information. In the continental trials a similar role was played by delators – informers who denounce rather than accuse. Very often the delators, who were frequently protected by anonymity, were not themselves the victims of the alleged crime, although they might profess to be scandalised by it. If they were acting properly and not maliciously they were regarded as relieving their own consciences by passing to the court information which might be of interest to the judges as guardians of public order, Christian morality, religious orthodoxy and ecclesiastical discipline. The decision to proceed lay with the court. As J. H. Langbein has put it, the vital characteristic of inquisitorial procedure was 'officialization of all the important phases except initiation', 'the duty of governmental organs to conduct the entire proceedings *ex officio*, by virtue of office'.[26]

The English or American common lawyer, accustomed to the adversarial system of conducting proceedings, has tended to assume that this is the best method of trial, but there is an equally powerful argument to be made for an inquisitorial system,[27] where it is perhaps easier to reach the truth. In the last twenty years there has been an interesting trend towards a critical re-examination, at least by English lawyers, of the adversarial system of trial, including that revered common law institution, the jury, and a corresponding interest on the other side of the channel in varying the inquisitorial system.

Another feature of the Anglo-American common law, which is perhaps closely related to the adversarial nature of the court, has been the 'staggering orality' of its procedure. This characteristic is well illustrated in the Year Book trials described by Klerman and Musson and can even be seen in the rolls of the manorial courts described by Mulholland. This is in marked contrast to the courts of canon law and the Inquisition, described by Laven and Pullan, and to the courts of Geneva described by Naphy. In all of these legal systems the importance of written evidence, and of oral evidence transcribed by a notary, was much greater. Again, however, the division between the systems is not as great as it might seem; the oral submissions of the parties in the courts of the Church, such as those described by Richard Helmholz, were vitally important.

Inquisitorial process is typically commenced by the gathering of evidence by or under the direction of an official – an examining magistrate or 'juge d'instruction' – or a panel of judges, who then compile a dossier on which a court, often a higher court, arrives at a decision or sentence when the oral stage of the procedure is over. The oral evidence of accused persons and witnesses was nonetheless vitally important in the early stages of the Venetian trials of Laura Querini and of Giorgio Moreto, and in the courts of Geneva discussed by William Naphy. In England, although the common law courts were little affected by written evidence, the courts of the Church as well as proceedings in the conciliar courts of Chancery, Admiralty and Star Chamber – whose origins lay in the civil law and which were in their heyday in the fifteenth and early sixteenth centuries – were predominantly based on written submissions.

Openness

The second requirement, identified as essential for a proper trial, is publicity or openness.[28] Even international conventions and human rights law accept that a trial may be held *in camera* for special reasons, such as national security, or where the interests of community require a closed trial for the protection of the vulnerable, but a society which holds all its trials in this form is rightly stigmatised as failing to apply proper principles of justice. Must a proper trial be conducted in a 'court'? Jaconelli considers the meaning of the term,[29] noting that it is the character of the tribunal and its proceedings, rather than its physical context, which determine its legitimacy. Thus trials in the past have been conducted in churches, in manor houses, on the field of battle and in the open air. However, the setting of an open trial is part of its dramatic and symbolic importance. The language of the court, the costumes, the formalities and especially the ceremonial and language surrounding a trial, emphasise the authority of the court and the community in which it sits. This has a powerful psychological impact on that community as well as on those who appear before it.[30]

Openness is not only a requirement of justice being seen to be done; there are also many messages and signals given by both sides in a trial, and this very publicity may be an advantage to the prosecution or to the defendant. A trial of an individual, or group, for a criminal offence (or, where relevant, a religious one) signals to the community that the person before the court is charged with offending against society's norms and that the community will enforce those norms – with sanctions if necessary. Thus the whole ritual is designed to have a deterrent effect, but the defence may also use the trial to draw attention to a cause, a personal passion or an aspect of the law which is unsafe or unjust. Some of the great orations in history have been of this kind.[31] In Mary Laven's chapter, Laura Querini seems to have used her trial under canon law as an occasion for her apologia and to express her true feelings about the life of an early modern nun. This would, no doubt, have its effect, but would not have been widely circulated except among Church officials.

The courts described in chapters 7 to 9 indulged in various degrees of secrecy designed to conceal the full extent of scandal and to protect witnesses and informers. When promulgating sentences, the Genevan and Venetian magistrates showed some reluctance to reveal full details of the crimes committed. In Venice the commissioners in charge of convents (chapter 8) were authorised to publish in two prominent places the sentences pronounced on offenders who had illicitly entered the cloisters of Venetian nunneries. In the words of a decree of 1584, 'they shall say in general terms that [these persons were condemned] for infringing the laws about visiting female religious, but they are not to name the convent concerned (*dicendo in general per haver contrafatto alle leggi in visitar Monache senza nominar il Monasterio)'.*[32] The transcript of the trial of Giorgio Moreto indicates not only that the proceedings were conducted in private and the witnesses sworn not to disclose what had occurred, but also that the court did not generally examine the witnesses in the prisoner's presence, and that he therefore had to rely on what the interrogating judges chose to tell him. Had his case been more complex and serious, he would have received a written account of the evidence given against him, edited in such a way as to conceal the identity of the witnesses. This procedure was intended to protect informers and hostile witnesses against retaliation by the prisoners or by their friends, families and supporters, and was justified by the conviction that unless it provided such safeguards the court would never arrive at the truth about a matter so threatening as heresy.[33]

Bias

The third requirement, and in many ways the most basic to the concept of a proper trial, is the principle that there must be no bias in the tribunal which decides the issue. Freedom from bias is an essential characteristic of the judicial function.[34] The exception to this view of that function is that of the judge in a totalitarian state, such as Stalin's Russia or Hitler's Germany, where the role of the judge consisted of supporting and applying the political ideology of the State, an objective which ranked higher than the disinterested application of the law or the protection of the individual's rights. The most blatant and obvious form of bias is corruption, which is repugnant to all legal traditions, lay and religious. The figure of the corrupt judge is a classic figure of contempt and dislike, in the Bible and in literature.[35]

The prevention of other forms of bias in judges is less straightforward. The question 'what is bias?' in the context of the courts is not easy to answer. Applying the principle 'no one to be judge in his own cause (*nemo iudex in causa sua*)', the English courts have decided that two kinds of bias are objectionable. Venality and the taking of bribes clearly invalidate the proceedings, as does evidence of a financial bias in the judge. Thus in *Dimes* v. *Grand Junction Canal Company*[36] the fact that the judge, Lord Chancellor Cottenham, had shares in the Canal Company (unknown to himself), made his judgment insupportable. The least financial bias disqualifies a judge.

In the case of non-pecuniary bias the courts have developed a stricter test: if actual bias cannot be shown, was there a real likelihood of bias? If it would appear to a reasonable onlooker that there was, or might be, bias, then the decision can be attacked by way of judicial review. Justice must not only be done but must be seen to be done. The example of Lord Hoffman in the Pinochet case was a reminder of the strictness with which this rule may be interpreted today.

Although the grosser forms of prejudice can be easily perceived, what about inherent views derived from the judge's own background and experience?[37] In the trials considered in this volume there are several cases in which the judges' independence might be suspect. In the courts of the State of Venice the same judges seem to act as examining magistrates and as sentencing judges. The Venetian lay judges who took part in the trials of Laura Querini and Giorgio Moreto were not members of an independent judiciary, appointed for life, but representatives of the Council of Ten, Venice's supreme committee of public safety, and served only short terms in office. The manorial stewards in the manorial courts discussed in chapter 4, were not in any formal sense 'independent' of the manorial lord and it is perhaps surprising that so little open partiality is evident in the rolls. The judges of the common law courts (chapter 2), had a reasonably good reputation for impartiality, but it was not until 1701 that English judges achieved constitutional independence from the executive under the Act of Settlement. This provided that judges should henceforth hold office during good behaviour (*quamdiu se bene gesserint*) subject to a power of removal by the Crown on an address by both Houses of Parliament. The Act also stated that their salaries were to be fixed.

There can surely be no society in history which has avoided the effects of bias entirely – whether the grosser form of corruption or the subtler prejudice of mind, background and philosophy – and this must have been true of the medieval and early modern period. [38] Although there will undoubtedly have been prejudice and corruption at times in all the courts examined in this volume, there remained at least an aspiration to apply justice in an even handed manner (see the remarks on the judicial oath in chapter 2). However, this aspiration was hardly realised, especially in the early criminal law. [39] The reader must judge the extent to which the trials under examination here passed this test.

One of the considerations which affect the fairness of trial is the ever present influence of politics in both the micro and the macro sense. Examples of what must be seen as political were the trials in Tudor England of Thomas More, Anne Boleyn, the proceedings concerning the marriage of Henry VIII to Catherine of Aragon, and later the trials of Charles I and of the Seven Bishops. Political influence is seen at its most blatant in Jeffrey Denton's chapter where the preparations for the trial of Pope Boniface were primarily influenced by the tensions between the papacy and the French Crown, and between Boniface's own family and the rival Colonna clan. However, politics in the broad sense of the term are also evident in several of the other chapters. The trials of Giorgio Moreto and of Laura Querini were influenced by the politics of the Venetian State and its ongoing and highly charged relationship with the power of the Church. Trials in the medieval manorial courts were also imbued with political significance; the relationship between lords and their vassals was played out in the courts of the manor, as the late-medieval manor became a hotbed of social unrest and, in some places, a catalyst in the forging of new social relationships. In a broad sense all law and all legal proceedings can be regarded as political expressions, in that they consciously, or unconsciously, reflect the social and economic policies of the society in which they operate. If that society is based on (and closely linked with) a religious creed or view, then that will be expressed in its courts. Thus trials in the courts of seventeenth-century Geneva, discussed by William Naphy, were inevitably expressions of the character and moral climate of Calvinist Geneva.

Records

The accounts of the varied trials discussed in this volume depend on the records of the courts' proceedings. There are considerable variations in the fullness of these records, which reflect to some extent the differences between the two great legal traditions of the common law and the civil or Roman law. The manorial rolls, which are the sources of research on manorial justice, are plentiful and, with the 'courtkeeper's guides' published for the guidance of manorial stewards, provide a vivid picture of trials in the manorial courts. There is plenty of human interest but little detail about the way in which the courts elected their juries or reached their decisions. The records of the common law courts – which provide the sources for the chapters by Anthony Musson and Daniel Klerman – have immediacy, clarity and human interest, but complete accounts of trials are elusive. Even the Year Books, which date from the reign of Edward I, are not 'law reports' but rather sketches and notes of aspects of trials which interested the writer, for educational or reference purposes. The civilian tradition, with its emphasis on written proceedings and records, which applied both to the Church courts and the courts of secular states, provides a more accurate record, though here the record may conceal – as well as reveal – motivation, political influences from Church and State, and human instincts which are recognisable in any century.

Some chapters in this volume raise questions about the extent to which historians can use trial records to construct biographies of the people investigated, or to compose narratives of events which throw light on hidden ways of life. Or is the vision of the courts so distorted, their preoccupations so narrow, the conduct of judges so intimidating, that the transcripts can only provide evidence of the way in which courts conducted their business? Much depends on the amplitude of the records. Legal systems which depend heavily on the composition of dossiers are at an advantage over those which do not. So are systems which take a generous attitude to the kind of evidence they will admit or at least record, and are not too hostile to hearsay. As the elderly narrator says in Martin Armstrong's story 'Sombrero', 'to my mind the plain, unadorned report of this Court Martial [published in *The Sporting Magazine* for 1810], with all it implies of human suffering and inhuman cruelty, recording the very words – almost, it seems, the very intonations – of men dead and gone these hundred years, is more moving, infinitely more moving, than the finest fiction ever penned'. [40] This story itself shows how much imaginative interpretation, how much reconstruction of events and situations outside the court room, may be needed for the purpose of fleshing out the spare, dry narrative of the court's proceedings; writers of fiction enjoy far more licence than do historians. Arguments for and against the use of trial records to provide narratives are well described by Mary Laven (chapter 8). The transcript of Giorgio Moreto's trial, which provides an appendix to this book, may permit readers to try their own hands at interpreting the evidence. It may enable them to hear the voices of prisoners and witnesses, even if the judges generally hide behind the impersonal bureaucratic language and no one can tell who is asking the questions.

This volume, then, provides a few telling episodes from the history of the trial, like fragments from a grand narrative which has yet to be written, and these range from the high Middle Ages to the early modern centuries. The companion volume carries the story from the late eighteenth to the late twentieth century. It likewise asks how the trial functions, and examines the legal principles, scientific knowledge, societal norms and political practice, that contribute to the judicial process. Several chapters of the later volume are concerned with the trial in the context of the military conflicts of the twentieth century and have common grounding in the modern experience of war.

Notes

1 As in the 'trial of the pyx', a procedure formerly used to test the metal of the coinage at the Royal Mint. See chapter 1, p. 25 below.
2 Trial by 'accursed morsel', which was used primarily in cases of the clergy. The person on trial was required to swallow a piece of bread or meat in which a foreign body, such as a feather, was concealed. If he choked he was adjudged to be guilty.
3 Thus they can truly be regarded as fulfilling the present meaning of 'trial', whereas so-called 'trials' in the medieval courts of love cannot.
4 This is well described in A. Musson, *Medieval Law in Context. The Growth of Legal Consciousness from Magna Carta to the Peasants' Revolt* (Manchester and New York, 2001), especially chapters 1–3.
5 Probably so called because of the 'pieds poudrés' of the travelling traders who appeared before them. See T. Plucknett, *Concise History of the Common Law* (fifth edition, London, 1956), p. 660; W. Holdsworth, *A History of English Law* (17 vols, London, 1903–1972), I (revised 1956, reprinted 1969), pp. 526–44. These courts, attached to fairs and markets, were sometimes owned by a manorial lord. There were equivalent commercial courts throughout Europe.
6 H. L. A. Hart, *Law, Liberty and Morality* (Cambridge, 1965).
7 P. Devlin, *The Enforcement of Morals* (London and New York, 1965).
8 The manorial courts even went beyond 'offences' to prescribe good behaviour, e.g. in one of the courts in St Albans Abbey Wiiliam atte Grave is sternly admonished to 'bear himself chastely'. See A. E. Levett, *Studies in Manorial History* (Oxford, 1938), pp. 236–7.
9 See J. A. Brundage, *Medieval Canon Law* (London and New York 1995). Also R. H. Helmholz, 'Conflicts between religious and secular law: common themes in the English experience', *Cardozo Law Review*, 12 (1991), 707–28. Such conflicts were not, of course, limited to England but occurred throughout Europe. See e.g. M. E. Perry, *Crime and Society in Early Modern Seville* (Hanover, New Hampshire and London, 1980), pp. 54–67.
10 See M. Mulholland, chapter 4 in this volume.
11 Co. Litt. 124(b). Also see Section 212, Common Law Procedure Act 1852. The English courts have often had to decide whether a particular procedure is or is not a 'trial', e.g. in *Hall* v. *Brand* 12 Q.B.D. (1883).
12 Arguably, the term can apply to a legitimate and properly conducted trial which is widely publicised by the relevant authority to deter others or to emphasise the importance of the law. However, the 'show trial' is often descriptive of a trial unfairly conducted and instituted purely for propaganda purposes, such as Stalin's 'show trials' in the 1930s.
13 See R. Helmholz, chapter 5.

14 Ben Jonson, *Volpone, or the Fox*, ed. D. Cook (London, 1967), IV.ii, 122–4.

15 See the texts translated in D. Chambers and B. Pullan, with J. Fletcher (eds), *Venice: a Documentary History (1450–1630)* (Oxford, 1992), pp. 102–4.

16 See Plucknett, *Concise History*, pp. 434–5; S. F. C. Milsom, *Historical Foundations of the Common Law* (second edition, London, 1981), p. 412.

17 For examples see J. Shaw, 'The Scales of Justice. Law and the Balance of Power in the World of Venetian Guilds, 1550–1700', unpublished Ph.D. thesis, European University Institute, Fiesole, 1998, especially pp. 38–9, 46, 68.

18 Especially as provided for in the Assize of Clarendon 1166. See W. Stubbs, *Select Charters* (ninth edition, ed. H. W. C. Davis, Oxford, 1913, reprinted 1951), pp. 167–73; Plucknett, *Concise History*, pp. 112–13.

19 See Plucknett, *Concise History*, pp. 120–31; J. H. Baker, *An Introduction to English Legal History* (third edition, London, 1990), pp. 84–96, especially pp. 94–6.

20 Originally self informing – i.e. the jury spoke from their own knowledge, a completely different approach from the present rule that the jury must base their decision purely on the evidence before the court. See D. Klerman, chapter 3.

21 See Plucknett, *Concise History*, pp. 125–6.

22 For a romantic view of the jury in the common law see Lord Devlin's Hamlyn lectures, P. Devlin, *Trial by Jury* (London, 1956).

23 See especially the discussion by R. Helmholz, chapter 5.

24 An excellent analysis is given by N. Vidmar, 'A historical and comparative perspective on the common law jury' in N. Vidmar (ed.), *World Jury Systems* (Oxford, 2000), pp. 1–52.

25 . . . and whose links with the continent of Europe are strong since its true origin was probably the Frankish inquest.

26 J. H. Langbein, *Prosecuting Crime in the Renaissance: England, Germany, France* (Cambridge, Massachusetts, 1974), pp. 130–2.

27 It may be for historical reasons that the term 'inquisition' is associated in the mind of the British with religious intolerance and foreign interference.

28 See J. Jaconelli, chapter 1.

29 *Ibid.*

30 See M. Loughlin, *Sword and Scales. An Examination of the Relationship between Law and Politics* (Oxford and Portland Oregon, 2000), pp. 55–63, where the author discusses the iconography of justice.

31 E.g. the great oration by Erskine, defending Tom Paine. See T. B. and T. J. Howell (eds), *A Complete Collection of State Trials* (vols XI–XXXIII of *Cobbett's Complete Collection of State Trials*, 33 vols, London, 1809–1826), XXII, pp. 357–522.

32 Archivio di Stato, Venice, *Compilazione Leggi*, busta 288, fol. 373. Information supplied by Mary Laven.

33 Cf. B. Pullan, *The Jews of Europe and the Inquisition of Venice, 1550–1670* (Oxford, 1983), pp. 112–15. For the procedures adopted by the Roman Inquisition in Malta, see the recent work of F. Ciappara, *Society and the Inquisition in Early Modern Malta* (San Gwann, Malta, 2000), pp. 422–6.

34 See chapter 1, pp. 27–32.

35 See William Langland, *Piers Plowman*, Passus II–IV, trans. E. T. Donaldson, ed. E. D. Kirk and J. H. Anderson (New York and London, 1990), pp. 15–39; J. Lawlor, *Piers Plowman. An Exercise in Criticism* (London, 1962), pp. 21–40. Also see

A. Musson and W. M. Ormrod, *The Evolution of English Justice. Law, Politics and Society in the Fourteenth Century* (Basingstoke and London, 1999), pp. 166–8.

36 (1852) 3 H.L.C. 759.

37 For an example of this view see J. G. Griffith, *The Politics of the Judiciary* (fourth edition, London, 1991).

38 See Musson and Ormrod, *The Evolution*, pp. 38–41, pp. 166–93.

39 See Milsom, *Historical Foundations*, pp. 403–28.

40 M. Armstrong, 'Sombrero', originally published in *The Fiery Dive and Other Stories* (London, 1929); reprinted in D. L. Sayers (ed.), *Great Short Stories of Detection, Mystery and Horror*, Third Series (London, 1934), pp. 519–38.

1

What is a trial?

Joseph Jaconelli

I Three questions

To pose the question, 'What is a trial?', is to invite an answer which aims to transcend particular times, places and cultures. It is to suggest that, stripped of the rules that are peculiar to particular legal systems, those processes that are properly called 'trials' contain some inner essence. It is to claim that the proceedings against Socrates under Athenian law in 399 BC and those brought against Jesus in AD 30 under Jewish and Roman legal procedures have features in common with the televised ordeal of O. J. Simpson in a Los Angeles court-room two thousand years later.

'What is a trial?' is a question that has seldom engaged the interest of lawyers. Yet the concept of a trial is central to some of the most fundamental ideas about human rights. Imprisonment, or internment, without trial is regarded as abhorrent and capable of being justified only by the most pressing needs of wartime or national emergency. If a person is to be deprived of his liberty, it is widely felt, this should occur only as the result of a more open and formal process than the exercise of the discretion of a government official. Indeed, the use of the term 'trial' in human rights charters, particularly in those international documents to which a number of nations subscribe, raises the possibility of exploring the essence of the institution across a variety of cultures. These charters typically guarantee such rights as those to a speedy trial,[1] a fair trial,[2] a public trial,[3] trial by jury,[4] or (to quote from chapter 29 of Magna Carta) a trial conducted according to the judgment of one's peers.[5] The guarantees may be listed singly, or in combination (as, for example, with the United States Sixth Amendment's assurance of 'the right to a speedy and public trial'). In each case, however, it is the adjective (speedy, fair, public) or adjectival phrase (by jury, according to the judgment of one's peers) that bears the brunt of interpretative dispute. In regard to some of the qualifying words it is inevitably so. It would, for example, be difficult to envisage a verdict-producing process which, though qualifying as 'fair', did not amount to a 'trial'. In other cases, however, there is no necessary link between the adjective and the concept of a 'trial'. This is implicit in the comment on the guarantees of the Sixth Amendment by the US Supreme Court in *Estes v. Texas*:[6]

> Significantly, in the Sixth Amendment the words 'speedy and public' qualify the term *trial* and the rest of the Amendment defines the specific protections the accused is to have at his *trial*. Thus, the Sixth Amendment, by its own terms, not only requires that the accused have certain specific rights but also that he enjoy them at a *trial* . . .[7]

In another respect, also, the concept of a 'trial' occupies a central position in human rights charters. Some provisions of these documents, without using the word, implicitly assume the existence of the trial process. One example is the frequently encountered ban on retrospective criminal laws.[8] Such laws, unless they are brought to bear in the trial of particular individuals, scarcely embody the mischief with which they are traditionally associated. The rule against double jeopardy[9] presupposes the holding of an earlier trial. The prohibition of 'excessive bail'[10] assumes a pre-trial period, and that of 'cruel and unusual punishments'[11] limits the range of sanctions that may be inflicted on the convicted accused.[12] Other guarantees – for example, the right to cross-examine hostile witnesses, or the right to the assistance of counsel[13] – are fully intelligible only within the trial setting.

If the question of what is a trial appears not to have occasioned much controversy, two related questions – What is a 'court'? What is a 'judicial' function? – have engaged the attention of legal writers.

The first of these issues has been the subject of historical analysis.[14] The concept of a 'court', which originally was not confined to that of a court of law,[15] now reflects a number of ideas associated with the administration of justice: as a physical location (the Royal Courts of Justice situated in the Strand); as an entity that exists for the purpose of transacting business ('The court is now adjourned'); as an entity that has a continuous existence (in the description of persons as 'officers of the court'); or as the personification of the judges who sit in it ('This court takes a dim view of your conduct').[16] The unspoken assumption that courts form part of the machinery of the state scarcely required emphasis at a time when judicial authority was not fully differentiated from legislative authority and the administration of affairs in general.[17]

Once that process of differentiation started to occur, the question, 'What is a judicial function?', began to attract a substantial amount of attention. There have been many reasons why this should be so. Those written constitutions that embody the idea of the separation of powers must perforce have some understanding of what is the occasion of the exercise of 'judicial' power, in contrast to that of a 'legislative' or 'administrative' power. At the sub-constitutional level, there are various privileges associated with judicial functions. Those charged with their exercise might be exempted from civil liability for actions taken in the course of performing them. Or those who report the proceedings of a judicial body – typically the media – may enjoy immunities from forms of liability (e.g. defamation, contempt of court) that would otherwise attach to their publications. Sometimes, by contrast, there are more exacting procedural standards demanded of bodies that are classified as judicial: in particular, the duty to observe the standards of natural justice. Indeed, the rules of natural justice themselves embody in rudimentary form the standards that would be expected of any court.[18] First, the right to a hearing (*audi alteram partem*) reflects the idea of effective participation in the decision-taking process through such means as: attendance at the hearing; the making of representations; and, if necessary, legal representation. Secondly, those who adjudicate on the issue must be free of bias, or even the appearance of bias, against any of the parties ('no one to be judge in his own cause', *nemo iudex in causa sua*).

Not all occasions on which 'judicial' functions are exercised may properly be described as trials. Nevertheless, an analysis of what constitutes a judicial function will form a convenient starting point. A leading work on administrative law propounds three guidelines.[19]

First, the exercise of a judicial function ends in the making of an order that has conclusive effect. That, in itself, is not particularly helpful, but it does draw attention to the fact that the result of legal proceedings is not, as a general rule, subject to confirmation by a person or body outside the court. Certainly, the outcome may be subject to appeal to another body that is charged with judicial tasks. Once the processes of appeal are exhausted, however, there is usually some procedural bar to relitigating them, expressed in such legal doctrines as the rule against double jeopardy. This does not, of course, preclude discussion at large as to whether the correct result was reached – a question on which, in the more controversial cases, there may be vigorous debate down the years.

Secondly, does the body in question possess the trappings and procedures normally associated with a court? In other words, does it look like a court? Are matters decided by the body only when they have been initiated by parties? Does the body hold sittings? Does it do so in public? Can an adverse ruling result in the imposition of sanctions?

Thirdly, does the body resolve disputed questions of law and issues of fact? In particular, the applicable legal rules must exist prior to the facts of the dispute that give rise to the need for adjudication. This element reflects the central role of courts as institutions essential to the rule of law, forming the link between general legal norms and their application to the resolution of particular disputes.

However, the questions, 'What is a court?' and 'What is a judicial function?', are both wider and narrower than the central concern of this chapter: 'What is a trial?'

They are too wide because, in the first place, ordinary language usage appears to restrict the word 'trials' to hearings at first instance. That is, the term does not appear apposite to cover the appellate stages of proceedings, even though these are undoubtedly judicial in nature and are conducted in institutions that are clearly recognisable as courts. Hence the distinction commonly drawn between 'trial courts' and 'appellate courts'. In other words, the resolution of contested issues of fact appears to be essential to the concept of a trial. The questions are too wide in a further respect, in that the natural meaning of the word 'trial' is confined to proceedings that are criminal in nature. The word may be taken, by extension, to include those civil proceedings where an adverse judgment of the court has catastrophic consequences for an individual's general reputation and standing. Actions for defamation, clearly, are cases that may be categorised in this way. However, any type of civil case which, according to the temper of the times, will have such far-reaching consequences may properly be included in the category.[20] Prominent examples from nineteenth-century British history are those marital cases (in particular, the trial of divorce petitions) which brought great scandal on those whose conduct was condemned in the proceedings. It was cases of this type which were responsible for wrecking the political career of Charles Stewart Parnell in 1890 and, more remarkably still, that of Sir Charles Dilke several years earlier.[21]

At the opposite extreme, the concepts of 'court' and 'judicial function' are in certain respects too narrow. For, arguably, they fail to capture processes that might properly be regarded as 'trials' even though they are conducted in the legislature.

The House of Lords, as the upper house of Parliament, long conducted proceedings that were recognisable as judicial. Under chapter 29 of Magna Carta, a peer of the realm could not be tried by commoners but only by his fellow peers. The privilege, which extended to charges of treason and felony (but not misdemeanours), was last used in 1935.[22] The following year, with memories still fresh of the difficulties that could have arisen in connection with the holding of such a trial, initiatives were taken in the House of Lords to put an end to the privilege. It was not, however, until 1948 that it was abolished.[23]

In contrast, it is common to describe as the 'Trial of Queen Caroline' the proceedings brought in 1820 to dissolve Queen Caroline's marriage to King George IV and to deprive her of her title, rights and privileges.[24] Outwardly the process was legislative in nature, centring on a 'Bill of Pains and Penalties' which incorporated a divorce clause.[25] The Bill started in the House of Lords, and in due course would have proceeded to the House of Commons. In substance, however, the proceedings could be viewed as judicial. The issue was whether Queen Caroline, as alleged in the Bill's preamble, had committed adultery. To this end witnesses were called and examined; counsel were deployed to argue the case on either side; and the event was presided over by the

Lord Chancellor, Lord Eldon – although (in violation of the normal standards of judicial impartiality) he spoke and voted in favour of one side in the debate. The end to the Bill was decidedly political, withdrawn by the Government in the light of the slender majorities in the Bill's favour in the House of Lords and with the prospect of intense opposition to it when it reached the Commons.

Further instances of legislative proceedings that bear some of the characteristics of a judicial procedure are provided by Bills of Attainder and, more topically, by the impeachment process. The latter has twice been deployed, unsuccessfully, against a president of the USA: against Johnson in 1868, and Clinton in 1998–99. In both its English and American forms the impeachment procedure bears some of the traits of a trial. In particular, the accusation is framed by the lower house (the House of Commons, the House of Representatives) and the matter is tried before the upper house (the House of Lords, the Senate).[26] The provisions of the US Constitution that regulate the process of impeachment use the terminology of the criminal law. Removal from office is to take place on 'impeachment for, and conviction of, treason, bribery, or other high crimes and misdemeanours'.[27] It is also provided that 'the trial of all crimes, except in cases of impeachment, shall be by jury'.[28] In stark contrast is the provision that no person, whether a president or otherwise, is to be convicted without 'the concurrence of two thirds of the members present'.[29] Therefore, although the vocabulary of crime is used in delineating the process, the requirement of a two-thirds majority (in contrast to the requirement of simple majority or unanimity) reflects the essentially political nature of impeachment as a means of exercising control over public officials.[30]

Bills of Attainder, on the other hand, are expressly forbidden by the US Constitution, where they are mentioned in the same breath as retrospective laws.[31] In historical terms, attainder referred to the penalties incurred as a result of conviction for treason or felony, in particular the 'corruption of blood' which forbade the inheritance of land down the family line. The American conception of a Bill of Attainder, however, is of 'a legislative act which inflicts punishment without a judicial trial'.[32] Yet it is clear from their English origins that, although some Acts of Attainder were legislative substitutes for what should have been judicial proceedings, others were enacted after their subjects had been found guilty at an ordinary trial.[33]

At the other extreme, there are bodies and proceedings which, although ostensibly qualifying as 'courts' and 'trials', have procedures that are so aberrant that they come to be regarded as courts and trials in name only. Hence the use of such terms as 'kangaroo court', 'show trial' or 'Star Chamber trial' to describe travesties of due process.[34] In more marginal cases it is possible to say of a process that it ranks as a trial, albeit one that was 'unfair'. It is worth noting, however, that there does not exist a similar critical vocabulary as far as the term 'judicial function' is concerned. If a function does not merit the title 'judicial', it is simply categorised as 'legislative' or (more likely) 'administrative' in nature.[35]

As might be expected, it is revolutionary situations which provide excellent examples of procedures by reference to which the furthest limits of the institutions properly described as 'courts' or 'trials' can be explored. The legal processes employed by the Soviets are a case in point. In *The Gulag Archipelago*, Alexander Solzhenitsyn cites one N. V. Krylenko, who described the aims of the criminal courts that superseded the Tsarist codes. Krylenko is quoted as making a number of concessions: that a revolutionary tribunal was 'not that kind of court [sc. a court that is occupied with questions of guilt or innocence]';[36] alternatively, that the tribunal was 'not a court at all' since 'a tribunal is an organ of the class struggle of the workers directed against their enemies' and must act 'from the point of view of the interests of the revolution . . . having in mind the most desirable results for the masses of workers and peasants.'[37] There is, in this last remark, a frank recognition that certain bodies used by the Soviets were not merely informed by conceptions of law and procedure that were very different from those encountered in the West. Rather, they possessed no more than the outward appearance of a court.

Reference was made earlier to the scope afforded by international human rights documents, especially those to which countries throughout the world may subscribe and which are not confined to a particular continent, for exploring the essential characteristics of the trial. The International Covenant on Civil and Political Rights[38] is uniquely placed in this respect for a number of reasons. It possesses a global compass, it is concerned with the classic liberties of Western political thought (among which trial guarantees figure prominently), and it is endowed with machinery – the Human Rights Committee – for interpreting the guarantees of the treaty. In the course of checking compliance with the standards of the Covenant, the Human Rights Committee has had occasion to scrutinise tribunals that exercise special jurisdictions (styled with names such as 'Comrades Courts', 'State Security Courts' and 'Public Security Committees')[39] and also ordinary courts where the judges are required to follow revolutionary ideologies or the approved party line.[40]

Finally, it is literature which provides the best-known example of the perversion of procedures into a form scarcely recognisable as legal. Kafka's *The Trial* can be read at one level as a description of the nightmare of being subject to secret charges, before an unidentified court, with procedures that one cannot even begin to comprehend. The protagonist of the book, Joseph K., is executed after a process – perhaps that would be too formal a term to apply to the disconnected series of events around which the novel is written – which denies him the most basic information. What is the charge against him? Who is the accuser? How is K. to defend himself or his lawyer to defend him? What is the seat and who are the personnel of the court? Certainly, the vocabulary of law and legal systems is used. There has been an 'arrest': there is an 'examining magistrate': a 'lawyer' is consulted. Yet the reality falls well short of even the most extreme conceptions of legality and due process.

II Three elements

The above observations are preliminary in nature. The central aim of this section is to discuss three elements to be found in the conduct of trials. It is first necessary, however, to identify the general features of the trial process. These can be briefly stated: the accusation; the response to it of the accused; the interrogation of witnesses; argument, largely oral, on the factual and legal issues by the opposing sides, whether in person or through the medium of professional advocates;[41] the culmination of the process in the delivery of judgment of the tribunal; and, if so required, the announcement of the sanction to be inflicted.

The bodies before which trials are held will usually have general jurisdiction. A tribunal that is specialised in regard to particular categories of person or types of offence, although suspect in some circumstances, is not in itself objectionable.[42] Military personnel have traditionally been treated apart from the general courts, and courts-martial can readily be included in the category of 'trials'.[43] These are to be contrasted with procedures under disciplinary codes administered by such persons as commanding officers or prison governors.[44] Although disciplinary procedures generally will include an opportunity for the subordinate to give an account of his conduct, and are capable of culminating in the imposition of sanctions, they are essentially summary in nature and lack the tripartite tension (prosecution, accused, judge) that is characteristic of the trial.

There is, in the concept of 'trial', a strong undercurrent of the idea of a contest. The trial is necessitated by the existence of a dispute – one that is resolved by the application of the law to the facts as authoritatively found and terminated by one side or the other securing the verdict of the court. The element of dispute may be removed at the very outset of the proceedings, because either an unequivocal concession of guilt is made or there is a negotiated admission of guilt on a lesser charge. From a historical point of view this is of little concern since the famous events of the past that are commonly referred to as 'trials' have involved issues that have been sharply contested between the opposing sides.

There is considerable variety as far as the structure of courts and the methodology of trials are concerned. Some courts are staffed by professional judges, others by laymen (or any combination in between). Many judicial officials are appointed, others are elected. A commonly drawn contrast is that between the adversarial and the inquisitorial modes of trial. In the former there is an unstated association of the trial with the conduct of a game or contest, the judge remaining relatively passive (as befits a referee). It rests on the supposition that the clash between the opposing parties is more likely than other methods to produce the truth. In the inquisitorial trial, by contrast, the judge is more active – a factor which reflects the need for a judicial investigation of the circumstances in which an alleged crime has been committed. In some legal systems the alleged victim, or his family, may be joined in the proceedings (the *partie civile*) for the purpose of gaining monetary compensation from the accused. Where this facility is not available, a separate action must be brought to obtain damages, with the possibility that the two proceedings may end in contradictory pronouncements as to whether or not a person was responsible for the act in question.[45]

The word 'trial' is also deployed in a number of figurative ways. It may be used to refer to the trial, not of a person, but of an inanimate object. Such, for example, is the so-called 'trial of the pyx' held at least once a year for the purpose of determining whether coins issued by the Mint have been made in accordance with the legislative requirements.[46] A number of procedural steps are laid down by statute that are evocative of the trial of persons.[47] A 'jury' is summoned and sworn; the proceedings are attended by the officers concerned of the various departments of state; and they conclude with the publication of a 'verdict'. All this is metaphorical usage since trials proper would require the participation in the proceedings, however minimal, of the accused. For that reason those societies, largely medieval, that staged 'trials' of animals must be accounted as having held trials in a figurative sense only.[48]

More generally, the term is used in an extended sense as signifying any inquiry into an alleged crime that is conducted outside the structured setting of a courtroom and which results in the informal 'acquittal' or (more likely) 'condemnation' of an individual by public opinion. The not infrequently voiced complaint of 'trial by media' uses the word in this sense. The Court of Appeal, for example, once heard an appeal against conviction by a person who had consented to being interviewed on television in connection with events for which he was eventually charged and convicted of fraud. The purpose of the interview, the Court of Appeal had no doubt, was to expose the person as guilty. Although it rejected the appeal, the court condemned the staging of the interview as wholly improper. 'Findings' of guilt (or innocence) would be made by the public on the basis of evidence and argument in the television studio, where the interviewee did not have the benefit of counsel or any of the procedural guarantees of a trial proper. 'Trial by television', the Court of Appeal pronounced, 'is not to be tolerated in a civilized society'.[49]

The phrase 'trial within a trial'[50] is used to describe contests within a trial setting that are concerned with a specific, subsidiary issue: typically, the admissibility of an item of evidence. The first use of 'trial' in the expression is figurative, denoting a contest directed to that one matter and held in a different form (usually with the jury excluded) from the main trial event. As with the trial proper, the result of the 'trial within a trial' is victory for one side or the other.

To turn now to the central theme of this section, it is suggested that the following three elements are to be found in processes that are properly called trials.

Internal rationality

In *Bridges* v. *California*,[51] a case which raised the issue of the legality of outspoken comments reported in the press concerning a pending case, the majority judgment of the US Supreme Court pronounced:

> The very word 'trial' connotes decisions on the evidence and arguments properly advanced in open court. Legal trials are not like elections, to be won through the use of the meeting-hall, the radio, and the newspaper . . .[52]

As already noted, the idea of a trial at law – in contrast to 'trial by the media' – implies a process marked by a controlled flow of material to the judges, on the basis of which they are to reach their verdict. The selection of that material is to be rationally related to the judgment eventually recorded.[53] In modern times, however, the matching of means to end has been tempered by restraints that stem from the need to respect other values that are prized by the legal system. Both the general observation and the qualification to it require further comment.

The legal systems of the world vary considerably in the rules adopted by them in allowing or disallowing particular items of evidence. To take only one example, should the previous convictions of the accused be made available to the tribunal? Whatever the rules might be on this and other points, the failure of the trial court to follow them provides grounds for overturning a conviction. On a rare occasion, however, the verdict is quashed because the sequence of reasoning, without violating any particular rule of evidence, defies the basic ground rules of rationality for that system. A striking example is provided by a modern case in which some members of the jury in a trial for murder were led to their verdict of guilty as a result of taking soundings of a ouija board.[54]

The rationalistic matching of evidence to the question of the guilt or innocence of the accused is tempered by values associated with the liberty of the subject. This is a relatively modern phenomenon. It finds its clearest expression, at the point of drawing inferences from the evidence, in the presumption that the accused is innocent. More controversially, some legal systems impose constraints on the methods used in the fact-gathering process, thereby curbing the excesses of the investigating force. They might, for example, disallow the use at trial of evidence obtained illegally (or improperly) by the police, even in circumstances where the evidence is undoubtedly related to proof of the accused's guilt.

These observations on rationality as an aspect of trials presuppose societies where there is a sharp differentiation between social norms and legal norms, and the enforcement of the latter is attended by a distinctive formality. In some societies there exists no such distinction. Alternatively, the distinction may exist in large measure, while for the purposes of dealing with less serious misconduct a more informal court system is used, in which all aspects of a miscreant's personality and conduct might be capable of being aired.[55]

Even in the modern Anglo-American trial there exists one focal point at which considerations extraneous to the strict legal merits of a case are capable of intruding. This is the long-standing facility available to the jury to return a verdict of not guilty, even in the face of the clear guilt of the accused on the legal and factual merits, as a method of protesting against an oppressive law or its use on the occasion of a particular prosecution.[56]

Finally, a general consideration of rationality must devote some space to trial methods that, by modern lights, are extremely irrational. The medieval trial by ordeal,[57] including trial by battle,[58] springs readily to mind. However, these methods, even if not objectively true, were at least entirely rational when considered from the perspective of medieval belief systems. The processes rested on the belief, then widespread, that there existed a God who could intervene in human affairs in order to secure a just outcome. The ordeal, moreover, conferred finality on disputes in situations where the application of evidence (or, to be more precise, what is today regarded as evidence) was indeterminate.[59]

Publicity – trial as spectacle

A further element of the processes known as trials is that, as an almost invariable rule, they take place in public. This is sometimes encapsulated in the cliché: 'Not only must justice be done, it must also be seen to be done.' The incidental benefit of this aspect has been the opportunity to record the trial events for posterity. In this way written accounts have been handed down of the two most famous trials of antiquity: in the gospels, and in the works, generally known as *The Apology of Socrates*, of Plato and Xenophon.[60]

What counts as being 'in public' varies according to the media of communication available in the epoch in question. In its basic form, the rule allows for the admission to the trial of casual spectators who have no connection with the proceedings other than a wish to observe them. With the rise of the print medium, this was extended to the conferral of special facilities for the representatives of the press: both in seating specially set aside for them and in the legal privileges attaching to the publication of their reports. It was especially important that reports of trial proceedings were privileged against actions for defamation since they would inevitably result in the dissemination beyond the courtroom of allegations which were damaging to the reputation of individuals. Finally, the growth of radio and television networks in the twentieth century has created the possibility of a global audience for the most prominent trials.

Among legal theorists, Jeremy Bentham devoted some attention to the question of why trials should take place in public. Publicity was seen by Bentham as a means of keeping the otherwise errant judge up to the mark:

> [Publicity] keeps the judge himself, while trying, under trial . . . So many bystanders as an unrighteous judge (or rather a judge who would otherwise have

been unrighteous) beholds attending in his court, so many witnesses he sees of his own unrighteousness.[61]

He also saw it as a check on the dishonest witness:

> Environed as [the witness] sees himself by a thousand eyes, contradiction, should he hazard a false tale, will seem ready to rise up in opposition to it from a thousand mouths.[62]

That the process was conducted in public, however, was as true of trial by ordeal as it is of the modern trial based on the testimony of witnesses. It has been pointed out that, from the perspective of gratifying the crowds in attendance, certain ordeals had the advantage over others.[63] Trial by water yielded a quick result (as the person subject to the ordeal either sank or did not) as compared with trial by hot iron (with the three days' wait for the unbinding of the hand that had carried the iron, with the resulting dispersal and reassembling of the crowd).

Certain phases of the trial have been regarded as not regulated by the norm of publicity. The Anglo-American jury, in modern times at any rate, has pondered its verdict under conditions of secrecy – an arrangement that has never been regarded as violating the requirement of public trial.[64] Again, the substantive hearing may be held in secret for reasons that are viewed as perfectly proper: for example, where evidence impinging on issues of national security is heard, or where matters relating to children are involved.

So close is the association between the idea of a trial and that of public access that the trial which takes place behind closed doors is regarded as fundamentally defective. Secret trials have notoriously been used by tyrannical regimes as a means of disposing of their opponents.[65] Therefore it is not surprising that, with the promulgation of charters of human rights from the eighteenth century onwards, the generally accepted norm that trials were to be held in public was translated into the idea that the accused possessed a right to a public trial.[66] Departures from the standard of open access are rightly regarded with suspicion. However, trial proceedings may equally be perverted by being saturated in publicity, thereby gaining the stigma of a 'show trial'.[67]

Independence

The third element is that of the independence, or autonomy, of the process of trial, both from government and from any of the parties. It is a point that appears to overlap with, but is quite distinct from, the element of rationality.

In the light of the association of trials with the exercise of state power, it should be recognised that complete independence of governmental structures is impossible. Judges are appointed, paid, and (if the circumstances warrant it) dismissed, by government.[68] Yet, against that background, the idea of judicial independence exercises a strong hold. Landmark documents, principally the Act of Settlement 1701, are associated with the securing of that independence.

Judges are not to be distracted from the internal logic of the trial by the fear of loss of position or reduction of pay. That the courts are part of, yet separate from, the institutions of government was reflected early in the seventeenth century, in *Prohibitions del Roy*.[69] In that leading case King James I was informed that, though he might be present in his court, he could not arrogate to himself the right to judge any case. Here, again, the theme subsequently found expression in human rights charters. These documents invariably require criminal charges to be tried before (to quote the standard phrase) 'an independent and impartial tribunal'.[70] The requirement of independence from government creates particular problems in those situations in the aftermath of war where the vanquished are tried by the victors. A case in point is the 'trial' of Charles I in 1649 by a court consisting of Members of Parliament that had been brought into existence specifically for the purpose of trying the king.[71]

Not only must the process be independent of government, it must also be (and, under a more stringent test, be seen to be) independent of the parties themselves. There are cases where the connection between a party and one of the personnel trying the issue is sufficiently strong to raise doubts as to whether the judgment of the latter has been diverted from the evidence and argument presented in court. The issue of natural justice raised here (*nemo iudex in causa sua*) is one which is pursued with varying degrees of vigour in the legal systems of the world. It figures sufficiently prominently in the United States to have been the subject of a substantial specialist work.[72] It is raised relatively infrequently, by comparison, in the United Kingdom.[73]

III The functions served by trials

One approach to the question, 'What is a trial?', is to answer it, not so much by identifying the formal features of the process, but rather in terms of the functions that are served by trials.

The central purpose is to arrive at a determination, whether that the person charged is guilty or that he is to be absolved from guilt. However, subsidiary purposes are also promoted, if only incidentally, by the trial proceedings. There is an element of education as the public is schooled in the workings of the judicial system. There is also an element of deterrence as the community takes note of the punishment meted out to those found guilty. That the trial takes place in public is essential to the achievement of these aims. In the words of Jeremy Bentham:

> By publicity, the temple of justice is converted into a school of the first order, where the most important branches of morality are enforced, by the most impressive means . . .[74]

The holding of a trial presupposes that there will have been a violation of one of the most fundamental norms of conduct of society. The investigation of the circumstances of that violation forms an additional focal point of the proceedings. There is, however, an array of procedural forums – inquests and inquiries – through which that element may be pursued apart from the trial itself.

Sometimes the use of the alternative forum is necessitated by the fact that, for various reasons, a trial is not possible or feasible. The prime suspect, for example, might have died before proceedings could be instituted.[75] This was the situation after the assassination of President Kennedy. The circumstances of the murder were officially investigated in December 1963–September 1964 by a presidential commission chaired by the chief justice of the United States Supreme Court, Earl Warren. Sometimes a trial has taken place but the holding of another one is rendered impracticable either by reason of the severity of the punishment inflicted after the first event or on account of the difficulty of securing a second trial that would be fair. Both these factors account for the establishment of the Shipman inquiry. Dr Harold Shipman, a medical practitioner, was convicted in January 2000 at the Crown Court of the murder of fifteen of his patients. The terms of the inquiry, which began sitting in June 2001, were to investigate the circumstances of death of a considerably larger number of Dr Shipman's patients. In a replication of some of the features of the trial, the inquiry is being conducted in public and under the chairmanship of a High Court judge.

The investigative characteristics of a trial are to be found in the formal inquiry that is often set up in the aftermath of a disaster – though, of course, the same event may also be the focus of a number of criminal prosecutions or civil actions. In some areas (for example, maritime disasters) there is a specialist mechanism for conducting an investigation. Otherwise, a general investigatory power is contained in the Tribunals of Inquiry (Evidence) Act 1921. The tribunal that is set up under that Act possesses many of the powers that are usually associated with the jurisdiction of a court (e.g. a contempt power, the power to issue summonses for documents or witnesses). Although the tribunal itself cannot inflict punishment or make an award of damages, the report of the inquiry will often attribute blame for the event under investigation. The loss of reputation that may ensue from an adverse finding is such that the persons concerned will employ counsel to represent their interests at the hearing. In this way, where a formal investigation is held under the Merchant Shipping Act, the procedural rules stipulate that it is to be held in such a way that 'if substantial criticism is made against any person that person shall have an opportunity of making his defence either in person or otherwise'.[76]

The coroner's inquest is the most overtly judicial of the purely investigatory devices. There is a 'court', with a 'jury' that returns a 'verdict'. The nature of the proceedings is defined by the task of investigating the circumstances of an unexplained death – though, once again, the death may also form the subject of proceedings in a criminal or civil forum. The attribution of guilt is no longer one of the functions of a coroner's inquest under English law.[77] However, where the circumstances suggest that death may have occurred as a result of an illegal act, the investigation in the course of the inquest proceedings may implicate, or exonerate, particular individuals. A famous contemporary example is furnished by the 'dingo' case in Australia in the 1980s. When an infant disappeared from a camp site the parents, Lindy and Michael Chamberlain, fell under suspicion. They maintained that the baby had been dragged away by a dingo (a type of wild dog). Inquest proceedings were held, as a result of which they were pronounced blameless. The production of further evidence, however, led to the Chamberlains being indicted and convicted of murder. The balance shifted as between the competing explanations of the baby's disappearance when a royal commission produced substantial material on the propensity of dingoes to attack babies. The Chamberlains' convictions were consequently quashed. The episode vividly illustrates how the process of investigation of the circumstances of an alleged crime can be pursued in several forums – not only the trial itself, but also a coroner's inquest and (most unusually) a royal commission.[78]

IV Concluding comments

The purpose of this introductory chapter has not been to provide a stipulative definition of the word 'trial'. Any definition would be vulnerable to the production of examples to the contrary from the judicial procedures of mankind. The answer to the question, 'What is a trial?', cannot be resolved by verbal fiat. Yet something should be said about those legal proceedings which have been excluded from consideration here. Some of the most famous cases have been those where the facts were scarcely in dispute while the legal issues that dominated the argument had far-reaching consequences, not only for the parties to the case, but also (and much more significantly) for the society in which they were litigated. As is to be expected, such cases are most frequently encountered in legal systems where the courts exercise the power of constitutional review. Examples would include such decisions of the US Supreme Court as *Brown* v. *Board of Education of Topeka*,[79] in which racial segregation in the public school system was declared illegal, and also the Dred Scott case,[80] the ruling in which was responsible for precipitating the American Civil War.

Rather, the focus of this chapter has been those cases, largely criminal cases, which have been contested in courts of first instance (in contrast to appellate courts). The proceedings, even if they have also raised difficult questions of law, have at least involved disputed issues of fact and their interpretation. For the word 'trial' is fixed in the public mind with judicial procedures which, in the course of resolving those issues, decide the fortunes of particular individuals.

Notes

1 Constitution of the United States, Sixth Amendment.
2 European Convention on Human Rights, Article 6(1): 'In the determination of his civil rights and obligations or of any criminal charge against him, everyone is entitled to a fair and public hearing . . .' See, also, the Universal Declaration of Human Rights 1948, Article 10: 'Everyone is entitled in full equality to a fair and public hearing by an independent and impartial tribunal, in the determination of his rights and obligations and of any criminal charge against him.' Also, the International Covenant on Civil and Political Rights 1966, Article 14 (1): '. . . In the determination of any criminal charge against him, or of his rights and obligations in a suit at law, everyone shall be entitled to a fair and public hearing . . .'
3 Constitution of the United States, Sixth Amendment. See also the guarantees of a 'fair and public hearing' set out in n. 2, above.
4 Constitution of the United States, Seventh Amendment.
5 The original text reads: 'per legale judicium parium suorum'.
6 381 U.S. 532 (1965).
7 *Ibid.*, p. 559.
8 European Convention on Human Rights, Article 7.
9 Constitution of the United States, Fifth Amendment.
10 Constitution of the United States, Eighth Amendment.
11 *Ibid.*
12 In those documents that prohibit certain types of treatment or punishment there is no pressing need to elucidate the concept of punishment as long as the other concept (e.g. 'treatment') is sufficiently wide. The link with the institution of trial is therefore less direct. Such, for example, is the situation under the European Convention on Human Rights, Article 3: 'No one shall be subjected to torture or to inhuman or degrading treatment or punishment'.
13 Constitution of the United States, Sixth Amendment; European Convention on Human Rights, Article 6, paragraph 3(c).
14 J. H. Baker, *The Legal Profession and the Common Law: Historical Essays* (London, 1986), chapter 10 ('The changing concept of a court').
15 *Ibid.*, pp. 155–6.
16 Cf. Baker's classification of court as jurisdiction, court as an institution, and court as a corporate body.
17 *Ibid.*, p. 156.
18 For a brief account of natural justice, see P. Cane, *An Introduction to Administrative Law* (third edition, Oxford, 1996), pp. 160–92.
19 S. A. de Smith, H. Woolf and J. Jowell, *Judicial Review of Administrative Action* (fifth edition, London, 1995), pp. 1011–19.
20 It is worth recording that the *Notable British Trials* series appears to work on the same basis. Although the majority of the cases in that series are criminal prosecutions, it covers other types of case besides. There is, for example, a volume on the 'Baccarat case' of 1891: W. T. Shore (ed.), *The Baccarat Case* (London and Edinburgh, 1932). This was an action for slander, brought to refute an allegation of cheating at cards, by Sir William Gordon-Cumming. The case gained considerable attention partly because the Prince of Wales, the future Edward VII, gave evidence in the proceedings. On losing the case, Gordon-Cumming was socially ostracised.

21 Sir Charles Dilke was cited as co-respondent in a divorce suit brought in 1886. The case is remarkable because it is generally agreed among historians that he was not guilty of the charge of adultery. At the time, however, a husband could gain a divorce simply on the basis of a confession of adultery by his wife. The consequences for Dilke's career are embodied in the title of a modern biography: D. Nicholls, *The Lost Prime Minister* (London, 1995).

22 In the trial for manslaughter, in December of that year, of Lord de Clifford.

23 By the Criminal Justice Act 1948. On the early history of the institution, see L. W. Vernon Harcourt, *His Grace The Steward and Trial of Peers* (London, 1907).

24 See, for example, E. A. Smith, *A Queen on Trial: The Affair of Queen Caroline* (Dover, New Hampshire, 1993). Cf. R. A. Melikan, 'Pains and penalties procedure: how the House of Lords "tried" Queen Caroline', *Parliamentary History*, 20 (2001), 155–76. A version of this article also appears in R. A. Melikan (ed.), *Domestic and International Trials, 1700–2000* (Manchester, 2003).

25 See Smith, *Queen on Trial*, pp. 133–4 for the text of the Bill.

26 See R. Berger, *Impeachment: The Constitutional Problems* (Cambridge, Massachusetts, 1974), pp. 82–90, for an examination of the question whether impeachment is a criminal proceeding.

27 Article II, section 4.

28 Article III, section 2, clause 3.

29 Article I, section 3, clause 6.

30 The same special majority is required in the US Constitution for such clear political purposes as overriding a presidential veto of a congressional bill. It was the two-thirds majority requirement that was responsible for the narrow defeat of the impeachment process against President Johnson, by 35 to 19 votes.

31 Article I, section 9, clause 3: 'No Bill of Attainder or ex post facto Law shall be passed.'

32 E. Dumbauld, *The Constitution of the United States* (Oklahoma, 1964), p. 195. See, also, *U.S.* v. *Brown* 381 US 437 (1965), at p. 441: 'The bill of attainder, a parliamentary act sentencing to death one or more specific persons, was a device often resorted to in sixteenth, seventeenth and eighteenth century England for dealing with persons who had attempted, or threatened to attempt, to overthrow the government.' In the *Brown* case, a provision that made it a criminal offence for a member of the Communist Party to serve as an official or employee of a trade union was held to be caught by the 'Bill of Attainder' provision of the Constitution (n. 31, above).

33 D. Somervell, 'Acts of Attainder', *Law Quarterly Review*, 67 (1951), 309. Sometimes, an Act of Attainder was used to declare forfeit the estates of one who had participated in a rebellion but who, being dead, could no longer be brought to trial: *ibid.*, 306–7.

34 Of the three pejorative terms, however, 'kangaroo court' tends to be used of disciplinary proceedings of private groups and associations rather than of the court system administered by the state.

35 In the tripartite division of governmental powers, the 'administrative' category appears to function as one that is residuary, encompassing those processes that do not fit into either of the other two categories.

36 A. Solzhenitsyn, *The Gulag Archipelago 1918–1956: An Experiment in Literary Investigation* (2 vols, London, 1974), p. 308.

37 *Ibid.*

38 The Covenant entered into force in 1976, having been approved by the General Assembly of the United Nations ten years earlier.

39 See D. McGoldrick, *The Human Rights Committee: Its Role in the Development of the International Covenant on Civil and Political Rights* (Oxford, 1991), p. 399.

40 *Ibid.*, p. 401.

41 From the perspective of the accused many of these elements embody the right to a hearing (*audi alteram partem*).

42 See R. Furneaux, *Great Issues in Private Courts* (London, 1964) for an account of some notable proceedings before tribunals, many of them established under statutory authority, which have tried charges of disciplinary misconduct by members of such groups as barristers, medical practitioners and clergymen.

43 Notorious instances include those against Captain Dreyfus in France (in 1894) and Admiral Byng in England (in 1757).

44 Sometimes the misconduct in question might have been charged before the ordinary courts if the offender had not been a soldier or prisoner. Sometimes there is no equivalent penalty under ordinary law, since the provision of the disciplinary code is aimed solely at the smooth functioning of the organisation (whether armed forces or prison).

45 As happened in the case of O. J. Simpson, who, having been acquitted in the criminal proceedings, was later held liable in damages.

46 The term 'pyx' refers, not to the coins themselves, but rather to the box in which the specimen coins are contained.

47 They are set out in section 8 of the Coinage Act 1971.

48 See, generally, E. Cohen, 'Law, folklore and animal lore', *Past and Present*, no. 110 (1986), 6–37.

49 *Regina* v. *Savundranayagan and Walker* [1968] 3 All E.R. 439, p. 441H.

50 There is a monograph on the subject under the law of Malaysia and Singapore: S. A. Paul, *Trial within a Trial* (Harmonden, Kent, 1994).

51 314 U.S. 252 (1941).

52 *Ibid.*, at p. 271.

53 As with the other two features, considered below, the standard of rationality is imposed in areas of government apart from the conduct of trials. For example, it is increasingly common for the English courts, when exercising judicial review over administrative decision-making, to annul decisions on the ground of their irrationality.

54 *Regina* v. *Young (Stephen)* [1995] Q.B. 324.

55 As, for example, in the comrades' courts of Soviet Russia: see Y. Gorlizki, 'Delegalization in Russia: Soviet Comrades' Courts in retrospect', *American Journal of Comparative Law*, 46 (1998), 421–2.

56 See P. Devlin, *Trial by Jury* (London, 1956), pp. 160–5, and W. R. Cornish, *The Jury* (Harmondsworth, 1968), chapter 5.

57 R. Bartlett, *Trial by Fire and Water: The Medieval Judicial Ordeal* (Oxford, 1986).

58 *Ibid.*, chapter 6. It was abolished in England by statute in 1819.

59 *Ibid.*, pp. 157–66. See, also, D. Daube 'The scales of justice', *Juridical Review*, 63 (1951), 123–6, for the (unsubstantiated) view that the early prevalence of trial by ordeal – in which there was a clear winner and a clear loser – was conducive to the emergence of litigation that was characterised by winner-take-all outcomes.

60 In each case the *Apology* purports, rather, to recount Socrates' speech in his own defence. Of course, the extent to which these works provide accurate summaries of the trials of Jesus and Socrates, free of the interpretations of their followers, has long been controversial.

61 Jeremy Bentham, 'Rationale of judicial evidence, specially applied to English practice', in J. Bowring (ed.), *The Works of Jeremy Bentham* (11 vols, Edinburgh, 1843), VI, p. 355.

62 Jeremy Bentham, 'Draught of a code for the organization of the judicial establishment in France', in Bowring (ed.), *Works*, IV, p. 317.

63 Bartlett, *Trial*, p. 23.

64 In the United Kingdom it has been a criminal offence since the passage of the Contempt of Court Act 1981 to disclose, or even to solicit, particulars of statements, opinions, or arguments expressed, or votes cast, in the course of jury deliberations. In the USA, on the other hand, it is notorious that members of the jury in newsworthy trials are free to reveal such details, to their financial advantage, once the case is concluded.

65 H. H. Scullard, *From the Gracchi to Nero: A History of Rome 133 BC to AD 68* (fifth edition, London, 1982), p. 304, recalls the early optimism attending the emperor Nero's reign in his promising, among other things, to put an end to secret trials *intra cubiculum*.

66 For modern statements to that effect see n. 2, above. It is an idea that I have argued to be philosophically unintelligible: see J. Jaconelli, 'Rights theories and public trial'; *Journal of Applied Philosophy*, 14 (1997), 169–75.

67 To describe an event as a 'show trial' is not necessarily to conclude that the accused was wrongly convicted, or that the charge was unworthy of a civilised legal system. A good example is provided by the trial of the U2 pilot, Gary Powers, in 1960 before nearly a thousand spectators in Moscow's Hall of Columns. The trial, at one level, was entirely fair. There can be no doubt that Powers had been on a spying mission when his plane was shot down over the Soviet Union. The event can nevertheless be regarded as a show trial since its primary aim was to serve the ends of the Soviet regime at a particularly fraught stage of Cold War diplomacy.

68 In some legal systems judges are subject to popular election. But even this presupposes the existence of state rules regulating the conduct of elections.

69 (1607) 12 Co. Rep. 63: 77 E. R. 1342.

70 The phrase used in Article 10 of the Universal Declaration of Human Rights; in Article 6, paragraph 1, of the European Convention on Human Rights; and, with a slight variation, in Article 14 of the International Covenant on Civil and Political Rights.

71 A well-known account is C. V. Wedgwood, *The Trial of Charles I* (London, 1964), chapters 6 and 7.

72 R. E. Flamm, *Judicial Disqualification: Recusal and Disqualification of Judges* (Boston, Massachusetts, 1996).

73 The issue has been raised most recently, and dramatically, in the legal proceedings concerning the attempt to secure the extradition of the former dictator of Chile, General Pinochet: *Regina* v. *Bow Street Metropolitan Stipendiary Magistrate, ex parte Pinochet Ugarte (No 2)* [1999] 1 All E.R. 577. The case is particularly striking since the House of Lords set aside one of its own judgments as tainted by possible bias before rehearing the appeal in front of a differently constituted panel of judges.

74 Bentham, 'Draught', in Bowring (ed.), *Works*, IV, p. 317.
75 Rather different is the situation where the prime suspect is not apprehended. Some legal systems permit trial in those circumstances to take place *in absentia*.
76 Merchant Shipping (Formal Investigations) Rules 1985, S.I. 1985 No 1001, section 9, promulgated under the Merchant Shipping Act 1970.
77 In 1975, before the relevant change in the law, a coroner's jury returned a verdict that Lord Lucan, who had disappeared the previous year and has never been traced, was guilty of the murder of the family's nanny.
78 Lindy Chamberlain published an account of the case in *Through My Eyes: An Autobiography* (London, 1991).
79 347 U.S. 483 (1954).
80 *Dred Scott* v. *Sandford* 19 How. 393 (1857).

2

The role of amateur and professional judges in the royal courts of late medieval England

Anthony Musson

The thirteenth and fourteenth centuries witnessed a rapid expansion in the scope of royal justice in England. The growing demand for legal remedies and the need to enforce public order led to an expansion in the activities of the Westminster courts and in the increasing provision of judicial commissions (some ad hoc, others on a more regular basis) in the shires.[1] The expansion was inevitably accompanied by the need for a body of men willing and able to assist in interpreting the law and managing the complexities of litigation both in the central courts and in the sessions held in the provinces. A detailed examination of the personnel involved in royal justice would not be appropriate here, but this chapter will endeavour to provide an overview of the dynamics of the administration of justice in late medieval England and an insight into the judiciary at work.

The perception that justices engaged under royal commissions were either 'amateurs' or 'professionals' has to some extent reflected a conceptual division between 'local' and 'central' justice frequently invoked in the context of the emergence of the local magistracy and the staffing of other royal tribunals in the thirteenth and fourteenth centuries. Put at its starkest, those acting in the central courts have tended to be regarded as 'professionals', while the justices of the peace have traditionally been seen as constituting the amateur wing of the judiciary. In many ways the distinction has arisen as a result of the directions taken in historical research. Historians of the legal profession have been drawn towards the personnel of the central courts, mainly because of the quality and quantity of surviving evidence relating to the Courts of Common Pleas and King's Bench, but also out of a preconceived idea of what constituted the legal profession.[2] The distinction has been perpetuated in the significant corpus of research on the development of the justices of the peace, which has concentrated on the magistracy at the expense of the wider judicial context, and emphasises the supposed tension between the locally based men who served on judicial commissions and the 'professional' justices of the central courts.[3] It is only since the last decade or so of the twentieth century that this supposed dichotomy has been reviewed and that the significant contribution to local justice by provincially based practitioners has been recognised.[4]

This chapter offers a refocusing of the divergent historiographical trends, arguing against an artificial separation between 'central' and 'local' justice and questioning the conventional notion of a dichotomy between the 'professional' element drawn from the central courts and the 'amateur' contingent recruited from the shires. It suggests that for a variety of reasons there was a blurring of distinctions between the personnel involved in the administration of justice and that there was a broader culture to the legal profession than usually acknowledged, reflecting a considerable overlap of expertise between those traditionally labelled as 'professionals' (lawyers) or 'amateurs' (county gentry). Analysis of the personnel within the broad arena of judicial administration (not just of the central courts or the peace commissions) reveals that those (most, if not all) undertaking judicial tasks possessed a certain level of legal knowledge and justifiably ought to be credited as 'men of law'. This term is justified in contemporary practice where it appears in various parliamentary petitions and statutes (albeit somewhat ambiguously) to describe both lawyers of the central courts and county-based ones. In the later fourteenth century it was a label increasingly applied to those who were 'working justices' in the quorum at peace commissions, but who (as a result of professional demarcation on the part of central court justices) were not assize justices. In 1352, for example, it was suggested that the peace commissions in general should comprise loyal, local men who had knowledge of the law: in other words, it was assumed that the majority, if not all of the king's justices should have some understanding of legal process and administration. It is significant, therefore, that an unofficial abstract of the first chapter of the 1361 statute (now known as the Justices of the Peace Act), drawn up in about 1362, substitutes *sages de la ley* for *hommes de ley*: the implication being that it was not necessary to be a trained lawyer (*homme de ley*) merely to be 'wise' in the ways of the law (*sage de la ley*).[5]

In the thirteenth century the justices appointed to the central courts (and the eyre) came from a variety of backgrounds and possessed differing levels of experience. A dominant tendency was for the clerks of serving judges to move up to one of the benches or become eyre justices, thus creating what have been described as 'judicial dynasties'. Martin Pateshull, for example, was succeeded by his clerk, William Raleigh, who was followed by his clerks, Roger Thirkelby and Henry Bracton. Ralph Hengham and Hervey Stanton also followed this route. Hengham, a protégé of Giles Erdington (serving as his clerk from 1258), became a justice of Common Pleas in 1273.[6] Some of the justices appointed to the benches had links with the Exchequer or were members of county society with extensive experience of local justice, such as John de Cobham and Robert Malet.[7] On a number of occasions the appointed bench justices were joined or supplemented by colleagues drawn from other branches of administration. In 1234, for instance, William Raleigh, puisne judge of the King's Bench, was sometimes assisted by stewards of the royal households. Between 1258 and 1264 the chief justiciar sat in King's Bench.[8] In the later years of Edward I, senior clerks of the Common Bench occasionally heard cases alongside one or more of the justices,[9] suggesting that legal knowledge or simply administrative exigencies could hold sway over formal requirements.

A new trend in the composition of the central courts is observable from the closing decade of Edward I's reign, concomitant with changes in the structure of the legal profession. From the 1290s the justices appointed to the higher judiciary were increasingly drawn from the small group of serjeants-at-law who had by this time gained a monopoly over pleading in the central courts. This avenue of promotion to the bench was regularised during Edward II's reign, when two-thirds of serjeants followed it. In the period 1315–77 three-fifths of all king's serjeants reached the bench.[10] Experience in provincial administration continued to be a qualification for appointment to one of the benches (as in the case of Robert Baynard),[11] though after Edward III's personal assumption of power in the 1330s it became an extremely rare phenomenon.[12]

The justices of the central courts played an equally important role in provincial justice, not just through the visitations of the eyre, but through their presence on commissions of assize and gaol delivery and on ad hoc commissions of general and special oyer and terminer. From Edward II it was common to find the serjeants and justices of the central courts staffing the assize circuits. In the fourteenth century they also became associated with the peace commissions either as justices of the peace in their own right, or as members of separate commissions to try indictments, or (from 1340s) in their capacity as assize justices, as part of the quorum. Looking from one end of the spectrum, therefore, from the perspective of the central courts, there was considerable involvement and investment of personnel in 'local' justice.[13]

Like their counterparts, the county-based commissioners were not a homogenous group and had different aspirations and degrees of experience. The experience and technical knowledge of men of law operating in the provinces, however, has been seriously underestimated by historians and is seldom acknowledged. In her monograph on the royal judge William Shareshull, Bertha Putnam, for instance, dismissed the appointment in 1329 of John Annesley as Shareshull's sole colleague on the western assize circuit: 'Apparently [Annesley] was not even a serjeant-at-law; therefore in taking assizes and delivering gaols it must have been Shareshull's legal knowledge that was relied upon.' She does not consider the fact that some commissions contained no central court justices upon whose legal knowledge they could supposedly rely.[14] Local men such as Robert Madingley, Richard Rodney and Hugh Wake would not and could not have conducted assize sessions unless they had a thorough grounding in the intricacies of land law.[15] This underestimation stretches to the justices of the peace. The commissions with full powers to try offences issued after the Black Death have been seen by some historians as providing the watershed of the judicial involvement of the justices of the peace,[16] but this view negates the role played by 'men of law' in the judicial process prior to the Black Death (particularly as justices of gaol delivery in the thirteenth and early fourteenth centuries) and ignores the variety of commissions on which many of them served, whether as justices of general and special oyer and terminer, or as justices of labourers.[17]

As the fourteenth century progressed it is apparent that the increasing burden of judicial work devolving on the peace commissioners became an outlet for the experience of county-based lawyers. From the 1350s there were two developments which have considerable bearing on perception of the peace commissions. First, the personnel of the commissions increased in size over the later fourteenth and fifteenth centuries. While in earlier years the small size of commissions meant that those appointed generally acted, the expansion meant that a number of these positions were purely honorific. Secondly, the responsibility for trying offenders was concentrated in the hands of the 'quorum', a select group of named men (usually assize justices). In practice local 'men of law', such as Walter Haywode (Hampshire JP and steward to the prior of St Swithin's, Winchester) and Walter Clopton (Somerset JP and steward to the bishop of Bath and Wells) regularly entertained all manner of offences at peace sessions and duly put forward for trial indictments for felony,[18] sometimes also trying the offences that came before them.[19] Analysis of the personnel of the peace commissions in Suffolk and Gloucestershire between 1382 and 1389, when the commissions were considerably enlarged in the aftermath of the Peasants' Revolt, reveals that the expansion was chiefly the addition of lawyers active in local administration. In 1389 and 1394, the same men were formally recognised as having a distinctive role by receiving statutory sanction to act in the place of justices of assize when first trespasses, and then all cases, including felonies, were brought to judgment.[20] By the fifteenth century, the bulk of the work of the quarter sessions had fallen to this group composed of the most substantial men of legal training resident in the county.[21] This was still the case in the mid-fifteenth century, when the justices of the peace named as sitting at gaol deliveries (only ever a selection of those on the peace commission) were present 'not merely as interested onlookers' but in recognition that they were those most heavily involved in legal business in the county.[22]

A development which profoundly affected the personnel of the judiciary and influenced the identity of the legal profession was the transition from benches comprising men in holy orders to panels of non-clerical judges. Although it could be argued that the shift from clerical to lay justices represented a move towards greater professionalisation, that would be to adopt a rather superficial view of the change, since a number of influential legal figures of the late twelfth and thirteenth centuries such as Hubert Walter and Martin Pateshull and Ralph Hengham were in holy orders. The move was one that reflected the new routes of promotion that were occurring in the upper circles of the legal profession.[23]

In 1179 the Third Lateran Council prohibited ecclesiastics sitting as secular judges. In spite of the legislation, the change was extremely gradual and little serious effort was made to exclude those in holy orders. Henry II had encouraged a mixture of clerics and laymen on judicial panels and a coterie of justices who were laymen came to prominence under John, among them the influential Simon Pateshull.[24] A more vigorous campaign was waged from the early thirteenth century. Master Thomas of Chobham, for instance, in his *Summa confessorum* (c. 1216), warned against the sentencing of men to death or mutilation by clerics, urging that 'So great is the dread of human blood that even a judge who justly slays the wicked, if he enters the religious life or wishes to be made a cleric, cannot be promoted to holy orders.'[25] On a more formal level, the Fourth Lateran Council denounced the involvement of clerics in judgments of blood and much English diocesan legislation was promulgated during the early thirteenth century reflecting a similar concern. Indeed, under Henry III the involvement of clerical justices in secular cases was part of a wider campaign for the withdrawal of the clergy from secular government entirely. Arguments were put forward by Richard Grant, archbishop of Canterbury, and Robert Grosseteste, bishop of Lincoln, among others, against the intermixing of spiritual and temporal responsibilities (particularly judgments of blood), which could be held either directly as an employee of the royal courts or indirectly through the exercise of franchisal jurisdiction. The *quo warranto* inquiries reveal that several ecclesiastics possessed gallows or rights of infangthief.[26] In spite of these warnings and prohibitions, many prominent judges of the thirteenth century who were clerks in holy orders holding benefices with care of souls – among them Martin Pateshull, William Raleigh, Henry Bracton, Roger Thirkleby, Hervey Stanton and Ralph Hengham – held sessions of the general eyre and gaol delivery at which they would have been required to impose the death penalty. William Raleigh even had cases of felony adjourned for his personal hearing.[27] The role of clerks in royal justice was clearly a tenacious one.

While the spiritual prohibitions may have fallen on deaf ears, a decisive change in clerical involvement in judgments of blood came in 1299 following the royal government's Statute of Fines. The statute enacted that for criminal trials, a local knight should be associated with one of the assize justices (who under the statute had assumed jurisdiction over gaol delivery) if the other assize justice was in holy orders. Unlike the earlier ecclesiastical legislation, this particular clause was acted upon and had considerable impact on the involvement of local men of law in provincial royal justice. Irrespective of whether one of the assize justices was a cleric, local men were associated with one of the assize justices at gaol delivery.[28] The clause did not spell the end of clerical involvement in justice altogether as some chancery clerks were still commissioned to hold assizes and deliver gaols, but although they sat at assizes there is no evidence that they participated in judgments of blood.[29] The shift away from clerical involvement in gaol delivery and oyer and terminer cases was mirrored by changes in the composition of the central courts. Under Edward II, Gilbert Rothbury and Lambert Trykingham were puisne judges in holy orders, but only one of five chief justices of King's Bench (Hervey Stanton) was a cleric. By Edward III's reign clerics holding judicial positions in the central courts had virtually become a thing of the past.[30]

The peace commissions of the later fourteenth and fifteenth centuries reserved places for spiritual leaders in recognition of their place in local society. It should be emphasised, however, that these positions were purely honorific and such figures rarely, if ever, sat at actual sessions. Nevertheless there are some examples of a continued clerical involvement in lay justice, albeit under unusual circumstances. The Scottish frontier provided one such context and Bishop Appleby of Carlisle, one of the wardens of the royal march, was expected to perform his duties and turn up at court sessions in spite of his reservations at the weight of business and its suitability for a clergyman. In the context of Scottish border peace commissions, one of the first appointments to the post-1344 style 'quorum' for the march area in 1373 was the civil lawyer, Master John Appleby, dean of St Paul's Cathedral in London.[31] The presence of William Alnwick, bishop of Lincoln, at peace sessions in Bedfordshire in 1437 was probably intended to enhance the standing of the commission and impress his authority and impartiality on those who had taken part in the so-called Bedford riots.[32]

Having ascertained the character and composition of the various benches, it is necessary to consider the manner in which judges conducted the trial proceedings and the extent of their direct participation in the business before them. What role did they play in the trial itself? The justices were present to interpret the law and uphold custom of the court. Adjudication on matters of fact was primarily a matter for the jury. In what we might anachronistically (albeit conveniently) refer to as civil trials the jury were presented with a question either on the basis of the original writ initiating the proceedings or as a result of the defendant's pleadings. Their answer in some cases could conclude the proceedings without the need for a decision on the substantive legal issue.[33] In criminal trials the traditional orthodoxy maintains that the jury came to the trial already apprised of the matter since they were drawn from the neighbourhood where the offence was committed and so were able to make a decision on the details contained in the accusation.[34]

Can we discern or distinguish the activities of those county-based 'men of law' acting in a judicial capacity? It is difficult to discern any active role in the proceedings played by any of the justices since the plea rolls are silent on all but the essential details and even cast a veil of anonymity over the judgment.

In civil trials the judgment recorded in the plea rolls as issued by the justices (prefaced by the words *consideratum est* or *iudicium est*) consists either of a simple statement of the consequences of the jury's decision or more usually a repetition of the jurors' findings together with the amount of damages (calculated by the jury) and an indication of the consequences. For instance in an assize of novel disseisin held in 1317 before Lambert Trykingham, John Chaynel and Nicholas Bolingbroke at Boston (Lincolnshire) between William Clerk of Kyme and John Pylot of Lafford (in which it was alleged that the former had disseised the latter of a plot of land 243 feet by one and a half feet) the assize jury said that William was unjustly disseised, but that in fact the piece of ground measured about 226 feet by one and a half and added that William (with John's consent) had built a wall seventeen feet long, which was on his own property, not dividing it, as he had claimed. The justices then provided judgment ('it was considered that John recover his seisin') summing up the substance of the jury's answer and their award of 30*s* in damages, adding further that William was in mercy (liable to amercement) and that John would be amerced for the part of his claim that was false.[35] Sometimes the jury provided its version of the facts, but then prayed 'the learning of the court', leaving the justices to decide the legal issue.[36] The request for the court to exercise its discretion was permissible in actions of novel disseisin under the second Statute of Westminster (1285)[37] and was occasionally also broached in trespass cases where the jury were unsure of the application of the law or the issue put to them. The judges were reticent, however, about allowing juries special verdicts in many other types of action. As Chief Justice Bereford urged on one occasion in Edward II's reign, when a jury was reluctant to offer a verdict: 'Good people, tell us what you think (*Bonez gentz dites ceo qe vous scentez*).'[38]

The laconic nature of the plea roll entries is compensated to a considerable degree by the reports of cases made for private reference or teaching purposes that comprise the Year Books.[39] These unofficial accounts are an important source of information on the medieval trial and provide a much fuller picture of the royal judges in action, giving the names of the speakers, the legal discussion occurring in court and the various points of law coming from the bench.[40] The cases contained in these reports arise from proceedings held in the eyre or the Court of Common Pleas or sometimes the Court of King's Bench. As such they tend to exemplify the higher judiciary at work, rather than the county-based justices. The only insight into the work of the latter is therefore the plea rolls, from which it is difficult to gauge their individual legal input.

To what extent and to what end did the justices interact with other participants in court such as parties, counsel, witnesses, officials, members of the jury? The reports covering the central courts show how the justices interacted with the serjeants pleading before them, engaging in legal debate on points of law and procedure.[41] At times they display a sense of humour, which comes across in such a way that it is easy to imagine Bereford with a twinkle in his eye.[42] The justices could also be intimidating both to counsel and their attorneys alike and frequently no quarter was spared. In 1289, for instance, John Lovetot urged one of the serjeants to 'Answer over or we will say something you will not wish to hear.'[43] Warnings concerning pleading were frequently given,[44] though this was clearly the justices' way of managing proceedings and keeping discipline in court. In 1335 Chief Justice Herle became so exasperated by the tactics of one of the serjeants appearing before him that he urged him to 'plead your plea first and then argue: for otherwise you are driving the plough before the oxen'.[45] There is also some evidence to show that the judges' control of the proceedings was not wholly verbal: a wink, a nod, a gesture or a glance could suffice either to encourage or to warn.[46]

The nature of the proceedings and the direction that they took often necessitated interaction with the jury. Usually this would be for amplification of their answers to factual questions. Fed up with the jury's apparently evasive answers whilst hearing an assize of mort d'ancestor in 1293, Roubury bullied them into an answer by saying, 'You shall tell us in another way how he was the next heir or you shall remain shut up without eating and drinking until tomorrow morning.'[47] While such a threat may appear harsh (and perhaps was intended merely as a threat) the justices were well within their rights, since the rule regarding jury deliberations was that they should be locked up without drink or sustenance and with no human contact except a guard until their verdict was reported to the court. In 1389, when a plaintiff brought a motion for a new trial (alleging that the jury deciding his case had been in the town eating and drinking before reporting the outcome of their deliberations to the court), the judges questioned the jurors carefully on the circumstances of their apparent breach.[48]

The justices on occasion called in witnesses or questioned the plaintiff or defendant themselves, speaking directly to the individual (rather than to his or her attorney or pleader).[49] In one case, Bereford spoke directly to a witness, asking him whether he had leased the tenements as alleged and then made a quitclaim, to which the witness, Richard (the tenant), then replied.[50] Where it was alleged that the tenant had not received a summons to court, the two persons returned as summoners were examined by the court and informed of the law of the land regarding the service of valid summonses.[51] The reports dating from the late thirteenth and fourteenth centuries reveal that the justices occasionally directed their comments to 'apprentices of the bench', who were listening to and studying the proceedings from a vantage point in the courtroom (*en le cribbe*).[52] This might take the form of a mini-lecture while the serjeants were away from the bar consulting their clients,[53] or the deliberate underlining of a point made in court.[54] At one point Bereford told a serjeant that he was grateful for his challenge 'not for the sake of us who sit on the bench, but for the sake of the young men (*les joevens*) who are here'.[55]

In forming their judgment the justices sometimes needed to confer with each other or with colleagues sitting in other courts. In 1388, for instance, a particular issue was debated by the justices and the court for a long time (*et ceo mater longe temps debate par les Iustices et la court*).[56] In 1338 it is reported that 'Scot came into the common bench and asked the opinions of Shareshull, Hillary and Aldeburgh in pursuance of whose opinions the others gave judgment that the defendant should be convicted because they pleaded not guilty when they might have justified their act.'[57] Shareshull was once criticised by his companions for adjudging in haste a writ to be good, but later the justices said that they were agreed beforehand on the same judgment.[58] Advice was sometimes sought from the king's council. In 1338 Herle and all the most learned of the king's council agreed that an inquest was joined contrary to law and reason.[59] When one of the justices had been absent from court it was necessary to interrupt the proceedings to allow him to confer with his colleagues and receive an update on the case.[60] There were also occasions when it was necessary for the court to request copies of official texts which would then have to be produced in court to enable the justices to make an informed decision. This usually entailed reference to the clauses of certain statutes[61] or an inspection of entries in Domesday Book.[62]

The court was not always united in its opinion or on the most appropriate way to proceed in an action and there could be mild disagreement between the judges sitting. For example, Chief Justice Bereford, in response to his colleague John Mutford's comment that certain members of the court had said 'a great deal that runs counter to what was hitherto accounted law', concurred, but then added (perhaps markedly) 'and I will not say who they are' (presumably because they knew well enough).[63] In another case, this time from Edward III's reign, Willoughby recalled that 'a man made his plaint for common turbary to burn the turf in a messuage and to sell it at his pleasure and this cannot be said to be appendant by prescription and [yet] it was maintained'. His colleague Shareshull tried to correct him saying, 'That is not law now.' But Willoughby apparently retorted with the ultimate conversation stopper: 'One more learned than you are adjudged it.'[64]

Disturbances during sessions or offences occurring within the courtroom area 'in the presence of the justices' could lead to immediate action being taken. Pickpockets or cutpurses caught operating in the busy Westminster Hall could face immediate trial with a jury summoned from the bystanders,[65] while insulting the justices as they were about to take their seats could result in a contempt of court action. In one such case which had been brought by the King's Bench justice Robert Scardburgh against William Botevileyn and his wife, Margery, the court acted quickly, but was careful to be informed of the contempt in the correct legal manner (normally by a confession from the offender or a bill of trespass or if possible a verdict from a jury of by-standers) before proceeding to judgment. Once Margery had (finally) admitted the trespass at the bar of the court, she was re-committed to the custody of the Marshal and released on mainprise (bail).[66]

While the clerk's record of criminal trials is generally only a couple of lines offering merely the essential details, lending credence to the view that the trial itself was comparatively brief,[67] it is clear from the surviving records that the justices did not sit there wholly passive, merely awaiting and accepting the jury verdict.[68] The justices had a positive role to play and (depending upon the nature of the indictment, the type of case and the defendant's plea) needed to have a keen awareness of procedural aspects as well as of substantive matters. They were called upon to use their knowledge and experience to spot faults in the indictments that came before them. The justices might query the terms (*de forma*) of the indictment[69] as they themselves could be held to be in error if an indictment was allowed to proceed that was later found to be incompetent or imprecise.[70] The gaol delivery justices adjourned the trial of John Kykel of Thorpe in Norfolk (indicted for burglary) because his indictment did not specify any year or day and had been taken in the absence of the oath and seals of the twelve jury members.[71] In the case of Clement Gorlast of South Reppes, whose indictment (merely stating that he was a common thief of sheep) was felt to be too vague, the justices asked the jury to expand on this and name any specific thefts (which they could not).[72] Even if the accused were present in court, the justices might delay his or her trial if they did not physically have the indictment to scrutinise (because it was still in the possession of the official before whom the indictment had been made).[73] In 1330 the Norfolk gaol delivery justices, Hethersett and Reppes, quashed an indictment and allowed the two accused, John le Porter and John Nottingham, to go without day, because the court felt that an indictment endorsed by the constables of the hundred (of Brothircross in this instance) was insufficient since they did not possess the requisite authority to bring persons to trial in a judgment of blood.[74]

The gaol delivery justices also had to negotiate the intricate world of private appeals and approvers' appeals. In private appeals of felony the facts of the case were woven into a formulaic structure which had to be recited before the justices in the exact words used. The judges were required to be vigilant and slight deviations, ambiguities or procedural lapses could cause the appeal to fail on technical grounds.[75] John Pous, who appeared in court at the suit of Matilda, lately wife of William of Hoveringham of Barrow-upon-Humber, was acquitted (Matilda did not appear in court), but then asked the justices to inquire whether the appeal had been formulated maliciously. The court duly asked the jury, who found in favour of John and awarded him £10 damages.[76] When self-confessed felons (approvers) came before the justices the former generally complained that the confession had been induced by officials, or made on account of diminished responsibility, or through duress of imprisonment or even under the compulsion of the justice before whom he first appeared. It was necessary for the justices to inquire from the coroner (and seek the evidence of his rolls) as well as examine the jury as to the circumstances of the appeal.[77] In the case of a thief who had sought sanctuary in a church but was removed from there by force (on the grounds that it was never consecrated by the bishop) and then taken before the justices, the court tried to persuade him to confess and turn approver. The justices told him they believed that the verdict of the jury would go against him and he would be convicted, after which he would lose the right to speak (*postquam tu convictus es tu amittes vocem*).[78] Where an approver opted for trial by battle, which still remained an alternative to jury trial in appeals, the justices had to outline the detailed conditions relating to judicial combat.[79]

The gaol delivery rolls do not usually enter into detail about the trial other than rehearsing the indictment or accusation and providing the verdict. As with civil trials we should not be fooled by the illusion of the plea rolls into assuming that little passed between the judge and courtroom participants. The format adopted by the treatise *Placita Corone* is useful in this respect, since in providing material illustrative of gaol delivery proceedings it offers a glimpse of the matters not otherwise contained in the formal court record, such as the manner of the interrogation in chief by the justices. While it should be realised that the precedents in the volume are probably not real cases, but hybrids, and fairly stylised in their language and approach, they indicate the direction the justices should or might take in their questioning in a given scenario.[80] The criminal cases reported from the Yorkshire eyre of 1293–4 also reveal the inquisitorial approach taken by the justices and their examination of defendant, jury and other relevant parties.[81]

The gaol delivery rolls occasionally demonstrate how the justices intervened and the pattern suggests they did so when, in spite of the jury's testimony as to the facts, the circumstances of a case were still unclear or there was legitimate room for doubt or indeed the jury did not know the full story. Richard Stingyn appeared in court suspected of stealing six sheep priced at 3s. The bench asked the jury whether the sheep allegedly stolen were near his own sheep in the field. The jury replied that they were not. They were then asked whom the sheep belonged to, but they did not know. Richard was duly acquitted.[82] In cases of alleged rape or ravishment the justices often questioned the jury as to particular details omitted from their account. For instance, in a case involving the wife of Geoffrey of Stutesbury, the jury were asked if the abduction was carried out against her wish and assent.[83] In another, the justices asked how old the victim was. The jury replied that she was fifteen.[84] Where necessary, the justices would allow someone present in court to confirm or rebut the defendant's explanation of their actions. Richard Oliver of Buckenham, charged with stealing a cap and other goods, said that he had bought the cap from John Austin of South Walsham for three halfpennies in Norwich market place. John Austin appeared in court and admitted selling the cap to Oliver as the latter had claimed.[85] Robert Mateshale said he bought the sheep he was suspected of stealing from William of Shouldham, but the latter (who was present in court) denied that he had sold them to Robert.[86] The testimony of these people, therefore, was in some cases vital in determining the outcome where the jury were not able to provide the details.

When defendants refused to plead and deliberately remained mute, the justices sought the testimony of other prisoners in order to ascertain whether the accused possessed a tongue or could speak if he or she wanted to.[87] In cases of prison breach, the keeper of the gaol was required to provide details of the escape and the measures taken to recapture the prisoners.[88] There is some indication that the justices actively sought information from those jurors on the panel who had been instrumental in putting forward the original accusation. Reference to this practice comes from the trial of Chief Justice Willoughby in 1341, who, when challenged about his behaviour with respect to members of presenting and trial juries, responded by saying that speaking to those on the presenting jury, far from displaying improper motives, was in fact a reflection of standard practice. 'It is the custom for a justice to go to the indictors to encourage and inform them'.[89] The justices allowed defendants to challenge jurors even though the procedure could be used to delay the trial hearing.[90]

It was important for the gaol delivery justices to have a secure grasp of common law defences, especially self-defence and insanity. Again, enrolled cases show how they were prepared to intervene and question the jury and/or the defendant if the explanations rendered appeared inadequate or did not meet the strict legal criteria. Where self-defence was claimed the justices could press for more information as to the defendant's choice of weapon and whether there was any evidence of premeditation. Where insanity was alleged, the justices might need details on the duration of bouts of insanity and the frequency of any such attacks.[91]

In spite of (or maybe because of) the death penalty there was room for the justices to exercise discretion. This was particularly evident in cases involving young people, whose criminal liability depended upon their age at the time they committed the offence. Even though juries almost universally claimed the accused was unaware of the consequences of his or her actions, the justices still ascertained the age of young defendants. It appears, however, that there were differing views as to whether the age of criminal responsibility was twelve or fourteen.[92] It is interesting to note that a Year Book report of 1338 considers the issue of mischievous discretion, thereby revealing that criminal cases were not entirely bereft of noteworthy issues of law and procedure. It is recorded that a girl of thirteen was burned because she had killed a woman who was her mistress, which was adjudged to be treason. The argument against her being liable was based on the common law presumption that no one under age (although a precise figure was not stated) should be hanged or suffer judgment of life and limb. But, it was reported, Spigurnel had ruled that the presumption could be rebutted by evidence of malice. For where a ten-year-old child had killed his companion and concealed the body, he had demonstrated by his action that he could distinguish between evil and good and, since 'malice makes up for age' (*malitia supplet aetatem)*, he duly received the death penalty.[93] Since some children were convicted of homicide and theft we should presume the court found evidence of malice or recidivist behaviour. Discretion was also exercised in sentencing individuals when the offence for which they had been tried and convicted was less than capital. Theft of goods which was considered as felonious in the indictment could nevertheless be found by the jury to have possessed a value of less than a shilling, in other words, below the felony threshold. In some instances it was considered that the accused had already suffered sufficient punishment through a spell in prison prior to gaol delivery.[94] Even when the jury specifically tried to excuse a theft by stating that it had been committed (through necessity) out of hunger in time of famine, the defendant was sentenced to a turn in the pillory,[95] or, in another case, committed to prison for 'a night and a day until the third hour'.[96] The justices also assessed those defendants who claimed benefit of clergy, administered the reading test, checked they had the clerical habit and tonsure and that the letters patent from the ordinary were genuine.[97] In criminal trials, therefore, although the role of the judges at first blush appears to have been extremely circumscribed, there was undoubtedly scope for interaction and questioning when judges saw it as their duty to intervene.

An understanding of law and procedure could be gained from both formal- and informal training in the law. From the thirteenth century onwards this was supplemented by the medium of the written word. The increasing availability of legal literature undoubtedly helped judges and lawyers in the performance of their duties. In addition to copies of *Bracton*, which were used by various justices, treatises such as *Fleta* and *Britton* provided useful digests.[98] The most useful and practical book for men of law involved in the administration of criminal justice was the anonymous *Placita Corone* (composed during the second half of the thirteenth century), which in addition to providing precedents on appeals of felony and various defences, gives instruction on how cases should be conducted at gaol delivery.[99] It shows how the justice should interrogate prisoners and employs different methods according to the prisoner's status and degree of knowledge and using several common scenarios tries to persuade him to confess or place himself on the jury. As the modern editor of the volume puts it, '[T]hese matters were of importance to the class of unlearned magnates, civil servants and others from whom justices of oyer and terminer and gaol delivery were drawn, and also presumably to such officials as sheriffs, coroners and bailiffs who had to perform subsidiary duties connected with court hearings. On the whole it is men of this class who would have found most profit in a treatise so elementary and yet so wide in scope.'[100] Whilst this chapter argues against the implication that justices of oyer and terminer and gaol delivery were entirely 'amateurs' in the field, the number of surviving manuscripts and the spectrum of persons who might find such a treatise of practical use are important to bear in mind.

By the 1350s statute books were widely available in a handy pocket-sized form (eclipsing the roll format used from the late thirteenth century) and could be produced to order. They usually contained common law treatises (including perhaps *Placita Corone*) and a textual core of statutes from Magna Carta to the significant Edwardian legislation (especially the 1285 statutes of Westminster and Winchester) and the statutes of Edward II up to 1321.[101] While it does not necessarily follow in the medieval period that ownership meant actual use of a particular book, it is nevertheless possible that a number of men of law recorded as possessing statute books did actually thumb through the pages in the course of their judicial activities, men such as Edmund Deyncourt, John de Longueville and John de Northwode.[102] In view of the increasing number of statutes of an administrative and judicial nature pro-mulgated during Edward III's reign and the need for reference to statutes in court, it is significant that in 1362 justices of the peace requested that they be given copies of the 1361 statute.[103] Given the number of statutes and the increasing complexity of the tasks facing the justices of the peace, it is not surprising that manuals were compiled to aid them in the performance of their duties. The earliest surviving such manual, compiled in Worcestershire in *c*. 1422, is not a comprehensive account of the duties and jurisdiction of the office, but (in the words of Bertha Putnam) 'does contain almost everything that justices of the quorum and the clerk of the peace ought to know. More-over, the exclusion from the compilation of extraneous matter means that the documents form an exceedingly useful precedent or formula book easily handled, and therefore accessible for practical purposes.'[104] The compiler of the manual was probably John Weston, who was one of the 'working' justices of the peace in Worcestershire and Warwickshire and a justice of gaol deliv-ery for Worcester, Warwick and Coventry gaols in the early fifteenth century. He was a common pleader of London (1402–*c*. 1415), recorder of Coventry (1417–*c*. 1434) and in 1425 became a serjeant-at-law.[105]

The exercise of justice on a professional basis not only spawned its own sup-port literature, but also necessarily invoked ethical considerations. The extent to which they were an integral part of the psyche of justices in medieval England is difficult to discern. Certainly the oaths taken by the higher judici-ary, which after 1290 were equally applicable to all royal justices (including assize and gaol delivery justices), charged them to do equal justice to rich and poor and avoid accepting gifts or bestowing undue favour.[106] The suggestion (or accusation) that judges were open to bribery, however, was one made forcefully in much of the literary output of the period, from explicit poems such as *Song on the Venality of the King's Judges* dating from the thirteenth century,[107] to Langland's *Piers Plowman* of the fourteenth century, in which the character of Lady Meed (a symbol of venality) is closely aligned with royal justice,[108] to the fifteenth-century satire of *The London Lickpenny*, in which the litigant found that at every juncture his opportunity for justice was thwarted through lack of money.[109] The reputation of the royal judges is not helped by high profile cases such as that of Thomas Weyland, whose involvement in a murder came to light in 1289, or of Richard Willoughby, who in 1341 was accused of selling laws 'as if they had been oxen or cows', or of John Inge who, in association with John de Molyns, was found to have perverted the course of justice.[110] *An Outlaw's Song of Trailbaston*, which was inspired by the trailbaston commissions of 1305, focuses at one point on the real justices of the south-western circuit and adjudicates on their characters thus:

> The Martin and the Knoville are pious men,
> And pray for the poor that they may have safety;
> Spigurnel and Belflour are cruel men;
> If they were in my jurisdiction they would not be returned.[111]

It was the common theme of dissatisfaction that is significant and the general perception of wrongdoing that carried weight with contemporaries, even though it might itself be misguided or wrongly applicable across the board. Where judges came into court to give advice or merely to sit on cases their presence was sometimes regarded with suspicion, particularly where they appeared as a well-wisher (*benivolens*) of one of the litigants.[112] Similarly a parliamentary petition of 1401 assumes a connection between advice and interference and maintains that because of this justice was not being done in the courts.[113] It was not necessarily anything underhand, but clearly litigants noticed and drew their own conclusions. In this respect it is interesting that royal judges were prepared to admit mistakes publicly and try to make amends. Robert Tyrwhitt, for example, who had overstepped the acceptable bounds in bringing a large retinue to an arbitration, admitted in parliament that 'he ne hath noght born hym as he sholde have doon' and agreed to provide two tuns of Gascon wine, two fat oxen and twelve sheep for dinner at Melton Ross to the aggrieved party, William, Lord Roos. His speech of apology was also recorded: 'Yet for as myche I am a justice that more than an other comun man scholde have had me more discreetly and peesfully, I knowe wele that I have failled.'[114]

This chapter has provided an indication of the scope of the activities of royal justices in late medieval England. It has demonstrated that during trials juries were questioned on the facts they had presented, and matters of law and procedure were clarified. The conscientiousness of the judiciary at all levels is noticeable, even though attitudes to judges were not always entirely favourable. It has contended that the distinction 'professional' or 'amateur' is not particularly meaningful during this period and that the term 'man of law' is applicable outside the close-knit fraternity of justices operating at Westminster. The composition of judicial commissions reveals that there was a broad spectrum to the administration of justice with a proliferation of 'men of law' operating at various levels in the hierarchy of courts.

While the participatory element should be stressed, it is also possible to see a process of professional demarcation taking place over the course of the thirteenth and fourteenth centuries. Serjeants were increasingly appointed as judges of the central courts, which in turn became predominantly staffed by laymen. It was these same men who by the mid-fourteenth century were equally responsible for the operation of the assize and gaol delivery circuits. The local men of law, who had in earlier years been appointed to gaol delivery and oyer and terminer commissions (sometimes to assize commissions and occasionally to the central courts), meanwhile found their niche in the judicial work afforded by the peace commissions. The association of county-based men of law in the quorum for peace sessions after the 1380s in turn created a clear distinction between those who by the later fourteenth and fifteenth centuries viewed their place in the magistracy as a mark of political status (or a sign of honour and favour), and had no intention of becoming involved in judicial tasks, and those whose presence was required to expedite business. These lines of development not only show the avenues to the upper echelons of judicial service and highlight how the 'working justices' were selected from (and indeed descended from earlier incarnations of) the men of law of the county, but exemplify one of the most striking evolutionary features in the history of the trial.

Notes

1 The need for such commissions increased with the suspension of the general eyre in 1294.

2 For example: P. Brand, *The Origins of the English Legal Profession* (London, 1992); J. H. Baker, *The Legal Profession and the Common Law* (London, 1986). This is addressed to some extent in N. Ramsey, 'What was the legal profession?', in M. Hicks (ed.), *Profit, Piety and the Professions in Later Medieval England* (Gloucester, 1990), pp. 62–71.

3 The orthodox view is presented in B. H. Putnam, 'The transformation of the keepers of the peace into the justices of the peace, 1327–1380', *Transactions of the Royal Historical Society*, 4th series, 12 (1929), 19–48; B. H. Putnam, 'Shire officials: keepers of the peace and justices of the peace', in J. F. Willard, W. A. Morris and W. H. Dunham (eds), *The English Government at Work, 1327–1336* (3 vols, Cambridge, Massachusetts, 1940–1950), III, pp. 185–217.

4 E. Powell, 'The administration of criminal justice in late-medieval England: peace sessions and assizes', in R. Eales and D. Sullivan (eds), *The Political Context of Law* (London, 1987), pp. 48–59; A. Musson, *Public Order and Law Enforcement: The Local Administration of Criminal Justice, 1294–1350* (Woodbridge, 1996).

5 A. J. Verduyn, 'The attitude of the parliamentary commons to law and order under Edward III', unpublished D.Phil. thesis, University of Oxford, 1991, pp. 118, 284 n42.

6 R. V. Turner, *Judges, Administrators and the Common Law in Angevin England* (London, 1994), p. 199; D. J. M. Higgins, 'Judges in government and society in the reign of Edward II', unpublished D.Phil. thesis, University of Oxford, 1986, pp. 4–5.

7 T. May, 'The Cobham family in the administration of England, 1200–1400', *Archaeologia Cantiana*, 82 (1967), 1–31; D. Crook, *Records of the General Eyre*, PRO Handbooks 20 (London, 1982), pp. 139–43.

8 G. O. Sayles (ed.), *Select Cases in the Court of King's Bench*, 7 vols, Selden Society, 55, 57, 58, 74, 76, 82, 88 (London, 1936–71), I (55), pp. cxxix–cxxxiii, VII (88), pp. xliii–xliv.

9 P. Brand, 'Inside the courtroom: lawyers, litigants and justices in England in the later Middle Ages', in P. Coss (ed.), *The Moral World of the Law* (Cambridge, 2000), p. 101.

10 Brand, *Origins*, pp. 29, 108; Higgins, 'Judges in government', pp. 6–7, 10; Sayles (ed.) *Select Cases*, VII, p. xli.

11 Musson, *Public Order*, pp. 133, 159–60.

12 Sayles (ed.), *Select Cases*, VII, p. xxix: 'Then it became quite clear that the era when the benches were open to members of the civil service or to clerics or to local gentry, however talented they may have been, had come to an end by the early 1330s, if not before'.

13 R. B. Pugh, *Imprisonment in Medieval England* (Cambridge, 1968), pp. 257–60; A. Musson and W. M. Ormrod, *The Evolution of English Justice: Law, Politics and Society in the Fourteenth Century* (Basingstoke, 1998), pp. 58–62.

14 B. H. Putnam, *The Place in Legal History of Sir William Shareshull* (Cambridge, 1950), p. 21. See, for example: JUST 3/49/1 (combinations of John Thorpe, Simon Hethersett, John Fitton and Richard Walsingham). Many assize sessions in Edward II's reign contained one central court justice and one local man of law, for example: JUST 1/597, 852, 1378 (John Mutford with Hethersett and Sefoughel), 512A, 514, 515C, 515D (Lambert Trykingham with Cubbledyk or Fenton and Bolingbroke).

15 Musson, *Public Order*, pp. 1–132; for example JUST 1/97 (Cambridge), 1350 mm47, 78 (Hereford), 1350 mm43, 64d (Northants).

16 This view is espoused in R. C. Palmer, *English Law in the Age of the Black Death, 1348–1381: A Transformation of Governance and Law* (Chapel Hill, North Carolina, 1993).

17 For example: JUST 1/966 (gaol delivery sessions under general oyer and terminer/trailbaston commission to Mauley, Deyncourt, Vavasour, Insula and Sutton); JUST 1/21 (special commission – Henry Spigurnel, Geoffrey de la Lee and John de la Haye – to hear and determine *Beauflour* v. *Peyvre*); JUST 1/125 (sessions held under the statute of labourers by William Polglas and Richard Cerseaux le pier).

18 JUST 3/161.

19 JUST 3/147 m1 (Haywood), 154 m3, 3d (Musgrave).

20 R. Virgoe, 'The Crown and local government: East Anglia under Richard II', in F. R. H. Du Boulay and C. M. Barron (eds), *The Reign of Richard II: Essays in Honour of May McKisack* (London, 1971), pp. 233–5; N. Saul, *Knights and Esquires: The Gloucestershire Gentry in the Fourteenth Century* (Oxford, 1981), pp. 134–5; Powell, 'Peace sessions and assizes', pp. 55–6; S. Payling, *Political Society in Lancastrian England: The Greater Gentry of Nottinghamshire* (Oxford, 1991), pp. 177–80.

21 S. Walker, 'Yorkshire justices of the peace, 1389–1413', *English Historical Review*, 108 (1993), pp. 281–311.

22 For example: William Paston in Norfolk, Robert Caundyssh in Suffolk, John Burgoyne in Cambridge and Roger Hunte in Huntingdon. P. C. Maddern, *Violence*

and Social Order in East Anglia, 1422–1442 (Oxford, 1991), pp. 54–64; see also S. Wright, *Derbyshire Gentry in the Fifteenth Century*, Derbyshire Record Society, 8 (1983), p. 98.

23 See above; Sayles regards 'the extrusion of clerics [as] an inevitable and natural sequel to the rapid advance made by laymen trained in the law' (*Select Cases*, IV, p. xix).

24 Turner, *Judges, Administrators and Common Law*, pp. 199–204, 218–20.

25 F. Broomfield (ed.), *Summa confessorum* (Paris and Louvain, 1968), pp. 304–5, 422–5 (quotation at p. 423), cited in Turner, *Judges, Administrators and Common Law*, pp. 173–4.

26 For example: A. M. Hopkinson (ed.), *The Rolls of the 1281 Derbyshire Eyre*, Derbyshire Record Society, 27 (Chesterfield, 2000), p. 188 (no 736).

27 Turner, *Judges, Administrators and Common Lawyers*, p. 177.

28 Musson, *Public Order*, pp. 96–8. The counties forming the Midland assize circuit were an exception as the two assize justices continued to deliver the gaols for a further couple of years.

29 John Radenhale, for instance, was commissioned on the East Anglian assize circuit (*assizes:* C 66/173 m27d, m20d; 174 17d; 175 m38d m35d; *gaol delivery:* C 66/175 m35d) and is recorded as sitting for assizes at Hennowe in July and September 1331 (JUST 1/855 mm, 5, 8d). See also Thomas Sibthorpe (Musson, *Public Order*, pp. 116–17).

30 Sayles, *Select Cases*, IV, p. xix. Geoffrey Edenham may have been the same man who held a vicarage in Woodhorn in Northumberland; there were also two clerks appointed to King's Bench in 1338, though there is no evidence that they ever sat in judgment.

31 C. J. Neville, *Violence, Custom and Law. The Anglo-Scottish Border Lands in the Later Middle Ages* (Edinburgh, 1998), pp. 53–4, 56 n53, 58.

32 JUST 3/220/2; Maddern, *Violence and Social Order*, pp. 63, 220, 253–4.

33 Turner, *Judges, Administrators and Common Law*, p. 206.

34 See Klerman, below (chapter 3), for more detailed discussion on this.

35 JUST 1/514 m5 (Boston, Lincolnshire).

36 For example: M. Arnold (ed.), *Select Cases of Trespass from the King's Courts, 1307–1399*, Selden Society, 100, 103 (London, 1985, 1987), II (103), pp. 378–80, 380–1, at p. 380 (*petunt discretionem justiciarorum*).

37 *SR*, I, p. 86 (c30).

38 *YB 7 Edward II*, p. 161.

39 P. Brand, 'The beginnings of English law reporting', in C. Stebbings (ed.), *Law Reporting in England* (London, 1995), pp. 1–14.

40 Brand, 'Inside the courtroom', pp. 92–3. Even where the justices subscribe to a similar view the Year Book will provide their names, e.g. *12 & 13 Edward III*, p. 290.

41 For example: *YB 14 Edward III*, pp. 246, 252.

42 For example: *YB 3 Edward II*, pp. 79, 123.

43 P. Brand (ed.), *Early English Law Reports*, Selden Society, 111, 112 (London, 1996), II (112), p. 322.

44 See also for example: *YB 12 & 13 Edward III*, p. 350.

45 *YB 8 Edward III*, fol. 20, placita 9 at fol. 21 cited in Arnold (ed.), *Select Cases of Trespass*, ed. Arnold, I, p. xxvii.

46 For example: *YB 4 Edward II*, Part 1, p. 132.
47 *YB 21 & 22 Edward I*, p. 272. The jury acquiesced and said that he was born before the solemnisation of the marriage but after the betrothal.
48 CP 40/514 m137d cited in Arnold ed., *Select Cases of Trespass*, I, pp. xxviii–xxix; see also *YB 11 Richard II*, pp. 34–5, *YB 12 Richard II*, pp. 184–5.
49 Not all apparent interaction should be taken at face value since, as Dr Brand cautions, some early law reports ascribe dialogue to the parties rather than to the serjeants who must have spoken for them. Brand, 'Law reporting', in Stebbings (ed.), *Law Reporting*, p. 4.
50 *YB 2 & 3 Edward II*, p. 36.
51 *YB 1 & 2 Edward II*, p. 19.
52 *YB 2 & 3 Edward II*, pp. xv–xvi; P. Brand, 'Legal education in England before the Inns of Court', in J. A. Bush and A. Wijffels (eds), *Learning the Law: Teaching and the Transmission of Law, 1150–1900* (London, 1999), pp. 62–3.
53 *YB 5 Edward II*, p. 90.
54 *YB 12 & 13 Edward III*, p. 170.
55 *YB 3 Edward II*, p. 36.
56 *YB 11 Richard II*, p. 177.
57 *YB 12 & 13 Edward III*, p. 66.
58 *YB 12 & 13 Edward III*, pp. 442–4.
59 *YB 12 & 13 Edward III*, p. 298. See also *ibid.*, p. 366, *YB 11–12 Edward III*, p. 136 and Sayles (ed.), *Select Cases*, VII, pp. 79–80.
60 Brand, 'Inside the courtroom', p. 104 (see examples cited).
61 For example: *YB 1 & 2 Edward II*, p. 33; *YB 15 Edward III*, pp. 262–4.
62 *YB 1 & 2 Edward II*, p. 61; *YB 3 Edward II*, p. 45; *YB 11 & 12 Edward III*, p. 164.
63 *YB 2 & 3 Edward II*, p. xiii. The manuscript at this point has the entry 'And some people thought that he meant Stonor' (who had been taking part in a debate with counsel).
64 *YB 14 & 15 Edward III*, p. 114. 'Common turbary' is the right to dig turves.
65 Sayles (ed.), *Select Cases*, I, p. cxxxiv.
66 *YB 14 Edward III*, pp. 324–31. This case was actually far from summary, for since the bill of trespass had been drawn up and prosecuted various issues were raised (including Margery's claim that she was divorced and so could not be bound by Botevileyn's admission) and there were several adjournments while the court considered how to proceed.
67 R. B. Pugh, 'The duration of criminal trials in medieval England', in E. W. Ives and A. H. Manchester (eds), *Law, Litigants and the Legal Profession* (London, 1983), pp. 104–15; Maddern, *Violence and Social Order*, pp. 54–62.
68 At one time it was believed that the jury's control over evidence rendered redundant any need for communication between judge and jury. See for example: T. A. Green, *Verdict According to Conscience: Perspectives on the English Criminal Trial Jury, 1200–1800* (Chicago, 1985), pp. 28–33, 66–9: 'Whether the bench questioned juries at gaol delivery . . . remains unclear' (*ibid.*, p. 68 n8).
69 For example: JUST 3/117 m7d.
70 Two such instances reached the Court of King's Bench: Sayles (ed.), *Select Cases*, VI, pp. 21–5, 133.
71 JUST 3/49/2 m8d.
72 JUST 3/48 m33.

73 For example: JUST 3/48 m11d; 49/1 m2.
74 JUST 3/125 m1.
75 For a more detailed discussion see A. Musson, *Medieval Law in Context: The Growth of Legal Consciousness from Magna Carta to the Peasants' Revolt* (Manchester, 2001), pp. 154–6 and on changes in judicial policy towards appeals of felony see D. Klerman, 'Settlement and the decline of private prosecution in thirteenth-century England', *Law and History Review*, 19 (2001), 38–53.
76 JUST 3/32/1 m4.
77 For example: JUST 3/134 m64, 156 m3; *YB 30–31 Edward I*, pp. 543–5; *YB 11 & 12 Edward III*, p. 626; see also A. J. Musson, 'Turning king's evidence: the prosecution of crime in late medieval England', *Oxford Journal of Legal Studies*, 19 (1999), 467–79.
78 *YB 30–31 Edward I*, p. 541.
79 See for example the account in J. Gairdner (ed.), *Gregory's Chronicle: The Historical Collections of a Citizen of London*, Camden Society, new series, 17 (1876), pp. 199–202.
80 J. M. Kaye (ed.), *Placita Corone, or La Corone pledee devant justices*, Selden Society Supplementary Series, 4 (London, 1966), pp. xxiii, xxxv, 17–22. See Klerman, chapter 3 below, for an example of dialogue.
81 *YB 30–31 Edward I*, pp. 528–45. Although the editor says the cases were taken from the Cornish eyre of 1302, the officials and place names are specific to Yorkshire: see Brand (ed.), *Early English Law Reports*, I, p. xxii n18.
82 JUST 3/48 m20.
83 JUST 1/966 m11d.
84 JUST 3/47/3 m5.
85 JUST 3/49/1 m21. The bailiff of Blofield, Roger of Hakeford, then testified that Austin had been indicted before the sheriff for the theft of the aforesaid cap.
86 JUST 3/49/1 m38.
87 JUST 3/51/4 m7.
88 For example: JUST 3/49/1 m49.
89 *YB 14 & 15 Edward III*, p. 260. This assumes also that there were some of the indictors on the trial jury. Although this was a common feature in the days of the eyre, by the mid-fourteenth century it was not necessarily the case and, moreover, during the course of the early fourteenth century was increasingly frowned upon, culminating in the statute of 1352. It is noticeable that in the 1360s certain sheriffs when empanelling jurors assiduously excepted those who were indictors – for further discussion see A. Musson, 'Twelve good men and true? The character of early fourteenth-century juries', *Law and History Review*, 15 (1997), 135–9 and Musson, *Medieval Law in Context*, pp. 118–19.
90 JUST 3/49/1 m38; 117 m8d.
91 N. D. Hurnard, *The King's Pardon for Homicide before ad 1307* (Oxford, 1969), pp. 76–8, 92–6, 159–70.
92 Compare, for example: JUST 3/47/3 m1, 47/2 m6, 6d, 96 m3; A. W. G. Kean, 'The history of the criminal liability of children', *Law Quarterly Review*, 53 (1937), 366–8.
93 *YB 12 Edward III*, p. 627.
94 JUST 3/110 m8d.
95 JUST 3/47/2 m7.

96 JUST 3/51/4 m8.
97 For example: JUST 3/48 m20; 117 mm9d, 14.
98 These are printed in S. Thorne (ed.), *Bracton on the Laws and Customs of England* (4 vols, Cambridge, Massachusetts, 1968–1977); H. G. Richardson and G.O. Sayles (eds), *Fleta*, Selden Society, 72, 89, 99 (London, 1955–1984); F. M. Nichols (ed.), *Britton* (London, 1865).
99 *Placita Corone*, pp. ix–x.
100 *Placita Corone*, p. xxiii.
101 D. C. Skemer, 'From archives to the book trade: private statute rolls in England, 1285–1307', *Journal of the Society of Archivists*, 16 (1994), 194–9; D. C. Skemer, 'Reading the law: statute books and the private transmission of knowledge in late medieval England', in Bush and Wijffels (eds), *Learning the Law*, pp. 113–32.
102 I am grateful to Dr J. Arkenburg for allowing me to see his list of book owners (1272–1350). Deyncourt was active in Lincolnshire (e.g. JUST 3/55/2), Longueville in Northamptonshire (e.g. JUST 3/51/3) and Northwode in Kent (e.g. JUST 3/109).
103 Verduyn, 'Attitude of the parliamentary commons', p. 145.
104 B. H. Putnam, 'Early treatises on the practice of the justices of the peace in the fifteenth and sixteenth centuries', *Oxford Studies in Social and Legal History*, 7 (Oxford, 1924), 60–93.
105 *Ibid.*, pp. 73–80.
106 P. Brand, *The Making of the Common Law* (London, 1992), pp. 148–52. For the debate on compromises and influences on local justice in the later fourteenth and fifteenth centuries see Musson and Ormrod, *Evolution*, pp. 173–91.
107 P. Coss (ed.), *Thomas Wright's Political Songs* (Cambridge, 1996), pp. 224–30.
108 A. P. Baldwin, *The Theme of Government in Piers Plowman* (Woodbridge, 1981), pp. 24–34.
109 R. H. Robbins (ed.), *Historical Poems of the Fourteenth and Fifteenth Centuries* (New York, 1959), pp. 130–4.
110 See P. Brand, 'Chief justice and felon: the career of Thomas Weyland', in Eales and Sullivan (eds), *The Political Context of Law*, pp. 26–47; *YB 14 & 15 Edward III*, p. 258; N. Fryde, 'A medieval robber baron: Sir John Molyns of Stoke Poges', in R. F. Hunnisett and J. B. Post (eds), *Medieval Legal Records Edited in Memory of C. A. F. Meekings* (London, 1978), pp. 197–222.
111 R. B. Dobson and J. Taylor, *Rymes of Robin Hood: An Introduction to the English Outlaw* (revised edition, Stroud, 1997), p. 252. It is interesting that the two justices singled out for criticism were from the central courts. There are surviving plea rolls of sessions held by these justices in Wiltshire (JUST 1/1015).
112 Brand, 'Inside the courtroom', pp. 100–1.
113 *RP*, III, p. 59 [2 Henry IV no 95]: 'The Commons pray that in consideration of the very great mischiefs which occur in your Court of Chancery, because, for the discussion of all pleas relating to matters traversed in the said court, your judges of your Benches called the King's Bench and the Common Bench are drawn into the said Chancery out of their own places, in aid of the discussion of the said matters therein, to the great delay of the administration of the common law of your kingdom and to the very great damage of your lieges . . .'
114 *RP*, III, pp. 649–51.

3

Was the jury ever self informing?

Daniel Klerman[1]

For nearly two centuries, legal historians have believed that the medieval English jury differed fundamentally from the modern jury. Its members hailed from the immediate vicinity of the dispute and came to trial already informed about the facts. Jurors based their verdicts on information they actively gathered in anticipation of trial or which they learned by living in small, tight-knit communities where rumour, gossip, and local courts kept everyone informed about their neighbours' affairs. Interested parties might also approach jurors out of court to relate their side of the case. Witness testimony in court was thus unnecessary. The jurors themselves were considered the witnesses – not necessarily eye-witnesses, but witnesses in the sense that they reported facts to the judges.[2] They were self informing; they 'came to court more to speak than to listen'.[3]

The idea of the self-informing jury has provided a powerful explanation for many legal developments. Thayer and Wigmore used it to explain the late development of rules regulating oral evidence at trial. No such rules were necessary in the Middle Ages, because witness testimony was rare.[4] For Langbein, the decline of the self-informing jury in the fifteenth and sixteenth centuries explained the increasing role of justices of the peace in the prosecution of crime. In medieval times, there was no need for the government to marshal evidence against suspected criminals, because the jury knew or collected that information on its own. As early modern jurors became more ignorant of the facts, the government turned to justices of the peace to assemble the prosecution case.[5] More recently, Green explained the medieval jury's extensive discretion and power to nullify the law as a consequence of the self-informing jury. Because little evidence was presented in court, judges knew almost nothing about the facts of cases and so could not prevent jurors from deciding cases according to their own notions of culpability.[6]

Although there have long been sceptics,[7] modern doubts about the self-informing jury begin with the publication in 1988 of *Twelve Good Men and*

58

True.[8] Three of the authors in this collection questioned the extent to which jurors were self informing. McLane and Post suggested that some fourteenth-century juries may not have been self informing, while Powell argued more generally that fifteenth-century jurors heard evidence in court. For the most part, all three relied on evidence about jury composition. Some fourteenth-century jurors and most fifteenth-century jurors did not come from the village or even the hundred[9] where the crime allegedly occurred, so they were unlikely to have known about the case. The authors also put forward other arguments, including the practice of releasing a suspect if no accuser came forward to present evidence against him.[10] Such acquittals might suggest that jurors did not know enough to convict without the in-court testimony of the victim. Although McLane and Post confined their conclusions to the fourteenth century, Powell questioned whether the jury had ever been self informing.[11] 'My suspicion', he wrote, 'is that criminal trial juries were never entirely self informing in the strict sense in which the term has been interpreted, and that even in the earliest days of jury trial, accusers and witnesses had the chance to inform the jury in court'.[12] Surveying the evidence a few years later, Fisher lamented that 'the scant trial records of those early years make it hard to confirm or rebut this theory of the "self-informing" criminal jury . . .'[13]

The evidence put forward by McLane, Post and Powell is certainly provocative, but it does not prove that later medieval juries were not self informing. Even if only a few jurors were from the relevant hundred, those jurors might have known or gathered relevant information which they shared with other jurors.[14] And, as Musson put it, 'the self-informing character of trial juries was tempered,' but not negated by the evidence he uncovered that early fourteenth-century jurors sometimes heard witnesses in court.[15] Nevertheless, it is not my intention here to suggest reinterpretations of the fourteenth- and fifteenth-century evidence. Rather, I hope to address broader issues raised by Powell and Fisher. Was the jury ever self informing? Did the medieval jury hear witness in court? Could a jury be self informing and hear witnesses in court? Recent writers have not seen it necessary to present primary source evidence in favour of the idea that the medieval jury was self informing.[16] Now that serious scholars have questioned the theory, it is necessary to examine the sources afresh. The need for fresh evidence is especially acute because the modern debate has focused on the criminal jury, while earlier writers were more concerned with civil cases.[17]

This chapter will attempt to show that the thirteenth-century criminal jury was self informing. It argues that jurors came to court with extensive knowledge of the facts. They lived near the place where the crime allegedly occurred and they did not need in-court testimony to know whether a suspect was guilty. Nevertheless, jurors also probably learned from trial. The defendant undoubtedly spoke at trial and may have swayed jurors. In appeals (private prosecutions), the prosecutor, who was usually the victim, also spoke in court, and jurors could have learned from him or her.[18] Judges questioned defendants and prosecutors and spoke with jurors, and such colloquies might also have contributed to the jurors' opinions. Local officials, such as the coroner or sheriff, were present at trial, and their testimony could also have influenced the jury. Finally, although less frequently, others with information about the case might speak up at trial.

The fact that jurors learned from defendants, prosecutors, judges, officials and other witnesses might seem to contradict the idea that the jury was self informing. It could be said to confirm Powell's conjecture that 'criminal trial juries were never *entirely* self informing'.[19] Nevertheless, whereas Powell emphasised the similarity between medieval and post-medieval jurors, I emphasise the differences. Self informing is a matter of degree, but differences in degree can still be large and important. Modern jurors know practically nothing about the cases they decide, and rely exclusively on in-court testimony. In fact, those with knowledge of the parties or circumstances are routinely excluded from the jury. Early modern jurors learned most of what they needed to know in court. They may have known a little about the facts of the case or the people involved, but such knowledge did not disqualify them from service. Nevertheless, informed jurors were increasingly required to present their evidence under oath in open court.[20] Medieval jurors knew a lot and were selected for that reason. They only occasionally heard testimony, and what they learned in court was less important. To borrow a phrase from Green, there was testimony '*alongside* self informing.'[21] Although they heard witnesses, a wide gulf separates the thirteenth- and the twentieth-century jury.

As noted above, the idea of the self-informing jury is important because it helps explain developments in the history of evidence law, prosecution and jury nullification. For these purposes, it is not necessary that the jury was *entirely* self informing or that it *never* heard the testimony in court. Rather, it is enough that jurors were sufficiently well informed that regulation of in-court testimony was not seen as important, that the government did not feel the need to assist in the gathering of prosecution evidence, and that judges knew significantly less about the facts than did the jurors.

Powell implied that the term 'self informing' has usually been interpreted 'strictly' to exclude the idea that jurors learned anything from trial.[22] While there are statements in the literature to support that interpretation,[23] some of the principal proponents of the self-informing hypothesis have been more moderate. Even before modifying his views in his 1988 'Retrospective,' Green believed that '[t]he trial often may have constituted an important part of the process by which the jury informed itself or confirmed its earlier impressions.'[24] And even Maitland and Stephen noted examples of in-court testimony.[25]

This chapter focuses on the thirteenth-century criminal jury. It discusses the thirteenth century, because the sources from this period are more plentiful and because if the jury was ever self informing, it was self informing then. It marshals evidence from criminal cases, because the recent debate has focused on such cases and because Seipp has recently written on the self-informing nature of the civil jury.[26] Although this chapter focuses on the trial jury, it will also consider the presenting jury,[27] because during the thirteenth century the two juries are often difficult to distinguish and because presenting jurors usually served on the trial jury. In fact, because the presenting jury was drawn only from the hundred, while the trial jury included representatives from the four neighbouring villages, the presenting jury had access to less local knowledge than the trial jury.

I Jury composition

McLane, Post and Powell based their arguments against the self-informing jury primarily on evidence of jury composition, so it is appropriate to begin with that issue. Self-informing juries should be from the locality where the crime was allegedly committed. Ideally, they are from the villages closest to the scene of the crime. At the very least, they hail from the relevant hundred. McLane, Post and Powell showed that fourteenth- and fifteenth-century sheriffs were unable to assemble juries composed exclusively of men from the relevant hundred, much less from nearby villages.

In contrast, thirteenth-century criminal juries consisted of twelve freeholders from the hundred and twenty people from the nearest four villages. This is especially clear for the eyre.[28] All freeholders of the county and four lawful men and the reeve from every village were summoned to the eyre. The hundred bailiff and/or electors chosen by him then chose the presenting jurors from among those present at the eyre. If a case went to trial, four lawful men and the reeve from each of the nearest four villages were sworn and added to presenting juries to constitute the trial jury.[29]

The existence of separate juries for each hundred is well attested to by the structure of the eyre rolls, which divide cases by presenting district. In addition, lists of jurors, which survive for many eyres, invariably show twelve jurors for each hundred.[30] Often the plea rolls also show that representatives of the nearby villages participated in the trial jury. Although the participation of the villages was not always recorded, the failure to do so probably reflects variation in enrolling practice.[31] If the villagers were indeed absent, this would have resulted in an amercement,[32] which would have been recorded. While plea rolls record a number of 'defaults' for failure to attend the eyre as required by the summons, the number of such defaults was small, especially in comparison to the enormous number of people who were summoned.[33]

At this point it is sensible to step back and reflect on the implications of the fact that eyre jurors were not selected until the eyre itself began. Civil jurors and gaol delivery[34] jurors were summoned in advance for jury service and so could make inquiries and be informed by the parties before they left for court.[35] The four lawful men and reeve from each village, who were summoned by the sheriff to be eyre trial jurors, would have had a similar opportunity to gather evidence before the eyre, but the twelve presenting jurors, who also formed the nucleus of the trial jury, would not. Perhaps some of them could anticipate that they would be chosen to be jurors. Before the eyre even began, the hundred bailiffs might have notified those they would choose as electors, and the electors might have notified those they would choose as the remaining jurors. If so, the jurors could have discussed the cases with those who would have useful information. On the other hand, there is no evidence that jurors had advance notice they would be chosen, so they may have come to the eyre without any particular preparation. While they probably knew something about the offences and offenders from living in the relevant hundred, this may not have been sufficient. Fortunately, there were many opportunities for them to inform themselves at the eyre before trial. They could talk to representatives of the villages, to coroners, to other officials, and to other freeholders who had been summoned. Those with an interest in particular cases might also approach them to tell them their side of the story.

The discussion so far has concerned trials in eyre. Thirteenth-century suspects could also be tried at gaol delivery. Unfortunately, much less is known about gaol delivery than about the eyre. In the preface to his edition of late thirteenth-century Wiltshire gaol deliveries, Pugh concluded that suspects were frequently tried before juries from hundreds which had no apparent relationship to the crime and that the four neighbouring villages played little if any part.[36] As will be discussed below in section IV, it is not surprising that gaol delivery jurors were less local than eyre juries. Nevertheless, my own survey of early gaol delivery rolls suggests that the neighbouring villages played a role throughout the thirteenth century.[37]

II Cases without victim–prosecutor participation

One of the more convincing arguments that Post and Powell advanced against the self-informing jury theory is that defendants were frequently released without trial if no accuser came forward against them at gaol delivery.[38] There are alternative explanations for this phenomenon. Perhaps judges released such defendants because they thought that if a victim did not feel sufficiently aggrieved to come to court, the crime was not serious enough to merit trial. Nevertheless, Post and Powell were correct that this practice might imply that the victim-accuser usually presented testimony at trial and that, in the absence of such testimony, the jury lacked sufficient information to convict. It is therefore instructive to consider how similar cases were treated in the thirteenth century.

The most comparable cases were appeals (private prosecutions) in which the appellor (prosecutor) had died, had retracted his or her case, had settled with the defendant, or had decided he or she no longer wanted to prosecute. For most of the early thirteenth century, judges released defendants in such cases without trial. For a brief period around 1220 and more permanently starting in the mid-1240s, judges began routinely to put these defendants to

Table 3.1 *Jury verdicts by level of appellor participation, 1218–22 and 1246–94*

Level of appellor participation	Number in data set	% guilty
Appellor died before trial	18	33
Appellor retracted or did not prosecute	280	44
Appellor settled with defendant	89	78
Appellor prosecuted the case to jury trial	126	71

Notes: '% guilty' includes cases in which the jury said the defendant was guilty of some, but not all, of the charges brought against him. Nearly all cases in which the 'appellor settled with the defendant' were also cases in which the 'appellor retracted or did not prosecute'. For an example of such a case, see below pp. 67–8. The row labelled 'appellor prosecuted the case to jury trial' includes cases which were quashed for technical reasons, but then sent to jury trial anyway.

trial, despite the appellor's lack of interest.[39] The mere fact that such cases were put to jury trial suggests that the jury was self informing and not dependent on testimony by the victim-accuser.

Even stronger evidence comes from the verdicts rendered in such cases, which are summarised in Table 3.1. These figures come from a data set of more than a thousand eyre appeals from fourteen counties during the period 1194–1294.[40] As can be seen from the table, jurors often rendered guilty verdicts even when accuser participation was minimal. Even when the appellor had died, jurors rendered guilty verdicts a third of the time. When the appellor had retracted or did not prosecute at the eyre, the jury still convicted more than forty percent of the time. It is highly unlikely that appellors provided any evidence to the jury in such cases. On the other hand, conviction rates in such cases were lower than when the appellor prosecuted the case to jury trial. Since active participation and even testimony by the appellor is likely in such cases, it is possible that the lower conviction rates reflect the fact the jury lacked sufficient information to convict.[41] On the other hand, it is also possible that the lower conviction rate reflects the fact that many appellors retracted or failed to prosecute because they knew their cases were weak. The high conviction rate in cases which the appellor settled supports this conjecture.[42]

The evidence in this section has been confined to appeals, which were a small and decreasing proportion of cases. Comparable evidence is impossible to gather in cases prosecuted by presentment, because the records do not indicate whether the victim-accuser appeared at trial. This failure to record, however, is itself probative. If the presence of the victim-accuser were necessary, then it is likely that he or she would have been attached to attend the eyre or at least summoned to do so. In this regard, it is noteworthy that fifteenth-century sheriffs were instructed to summon 'all those who wished to prosecute prisoners' at gaol delivery,[43] but that no comparable summons to prosecutors was issued in the thirteenth century.[44]

III Trial accounts

Trial accounts are potentially the most valuable evidence in establishing whether medieval juries were or were not self informing. McLane, Post and Powell's discussions contain surprisingly few trial accounts, largely because fourteenth- and fifteenth-century sources are so uninformative. Nevertheless, with effort, even sources as arid as gaol delivery plea rolls can be coaxed to yield information on trial procedure, as Musson has demonstrated.[45] Fortunately, the thirteenth-century sources, which include treatises, plea rolls and early reports, are much more copious. Although each of these sources has its own problems, together they paint a coherent picture. Jurors came to trial already informed. Sometimes they supplemented their knowledge with testimony provided by officials and other witnesses.

Treatises

The treatise attributed to *Bracton*, probably written sometime in the late 1220s or early 1230s, contains a rather full account of a trial in eyre. I have excerpted the most relevant parts:

> We must now speak of those indicted by popular rumour . . . When because of rumour and suspicion the truth of the matter ought to be investigated by the country . . . the judge, if he is wise, ought first to inquire (if he has doubts and the jury is suspect) from what man or men the twelve jurors have learned what they put forward in their *veredictum* concerning the indicted man; having heard their answer thereon he may readily decide if any deceit or wickedness lies behind it. For perhaps one or a majority of the jurors will say that they learned the matter put forward in their *veredictum* from one of their fellow jurors, and he upon interrogation will perhaps say that he learned it from such a one, and so by question and answer the judge may descend from person to person to some low and worthless fellow, one in whom no trust must in any way be reposed. . . . [W]hen proceedings of this kind have reached the point of an inquest, in order that judgment may be reached with greater certainty and risks and doubts removed, let the justice inform the indicted man that if he suspects any of the twelve jurors he may remove him for just cause, and let the same be said of the [jurors from] the vills, as where there are deadly enmities between some of them and the indicted man, or there is a greedy desire to get his land, as was said above; if there is ground for suspicion all are to be removed, that inquiry may proceed free of all doubts. When the twelve jurors and the [jurors of] the four townships are present, those of the vills will take an oath first, each by himself or all together; lifting up their hands let them swear in these words:

'Hear this, ye justices, that we will speak the truth about what is asked of us on the king's behalf, nor will we for any reason fail to tell the truth, so help us God etc.' Then let one of the said justices speak in this way: 'Such a one, who is present, charged with the death of such a one (or some other crime) comes and denies the death and everything else and on this matter puts himself for good and ill upon the words of your mouth. . . . And therefore we tell you that on the faith that binds you to God and by the oath that you have taken you are to let us know the truth thereof, nor are you to fail in saying whether or not he is guilty of what is alleged against him . . . through fear or love or hate but with God only before your eyes, nor are you to oppress him if he be innocent of the said offence.' His discharge or condemnation will then follow, according to their verdict . . . In all crimes, major and minor, the justices, if they deem it expedient [and] for good reason, [as] where a serious crime is being concealed and the jurors intend to hide the truth through love, hatred or fear, may separate the jurors one from the other and examine each of them individually in order to establish the truth adequately.[46]

This passage is overflowing with evidence that jurors were self informing. If the judge was suspicious of the presenting jurors, he questioned them about the sources of their information. Obviously, the information on which the jurors based their presentment (accusation) was not presented in court; otherwise the judge would not have to ask about it. Once the judge was satisfied with the presentment, the defendant was allowed to challenge the jurors 'for just cause'. Note, however, the examples which *Bracton* gives for removing a juror: 'deadly enmities' and 'greedy desire to get . . . land'. Knowledge of the facts or parties was not grounds for exclusion. The jurors, including both the presenting jurors and the representatives of the four neighbouring villages, were then sworn and the judge gave them their charge. Then, without any mention of witnesses or evidence, the jurors delivered their verdict and the judge rendered the judgment: 'discharge or condemnation'. Although one can imagine many complex reasons why there is no discussion of witnesses or other evidence, surely the simplest is that witnesses and other evidence were not an ordinary or important part of trial. Finally, *Bracton*'s description of trial ends by noting that if the judge suspected that the jurors were concealing crime, they were to be examined individually. Jurors could only conceal crime, and it only made sense to question them, if they had knowledge beyond what they learned at trial.

The *Placita Corone*, a treatise most likely composed *c.* 1274–75, largely confirms *Bracton*'s account. Unlike *Bracton*, the *Placita* consists mostly of dialogues of court interactions. Most deal with appeals and show how the parties to such cases should plead. The parties themselves do most of the talking, although occasionally the judge plays a role.[47] Witnesses are conspicuously absent. In one revealing dialogue, the judge admonishes the defendant, 'Tell the truth, for if you don't we shall get to know it from the country,'[48] implying that it is 'the country' (i.e. the jury) rather than witnesses who will inform the court of what really happened.

The last part of the *Placita* is especially enlightening, because it provides four accounts of indictments tried at gaol delivery.[49] All portray trial as primarily a conversation between the judge and the accused. Unlike the appeal cases, the accuser or victim is completely absent. Instead, the judge takes on a quasi-prosecutorial role, coaxing the defendant into submitting to jury trial or badgering the defendant to confess. Once the defendant submits to jury trial, as in *Bracton*, there is nothing to report except the verdict. There is no mention of witnesses or other evidence. The following excerpt is typical:

> 'Sheriff, why has this man been taken?'
>
> 'Sir, for the death of a man whom he is supposed to have killed in self defence, as he says.'
>
> 'What is your name?'
>
> 'Sir, Thomas de N.'
>
> 'Thomas, what was the name of the man whom you killed in premeditated attack, feloniously as a felon?'
>
> 'Sir, if you please, I have never been a felon and never did mischief to living man, in premeditated attack; and so I have done nothing wrong against the man whose name you ask: who, feloniously as a felon and in premeditated attack tried to kill me on such a day, at such an hour, in such a year in my own house in such a township, for no fault on my part and solely on account of his malice.'
>
> 'Tell us the circumstances.'
>
> 'Sir, I was unwilling to lend or hire to him a horse for the purpose of riding about his business . . . And because I refused him the loan of my horse he ran at me in my own house with a Welsh knife . . . I did not at first return his blows; but when I realised that he was set on killing me I started to defend myself: that is to say I wounded him in the right arm with a little pointed knife which I carried, making no further onslaught and acting in this way only to save my own life.'
>
> 'Did he die of such wound?'
>
> 'In truth sir, I do not know.'
>
> . . .
>
> 'Thomas, you have greatly embroidered your tale and coloured your defence: for you are telling us only what you think will be to your advantage, and suppressing whatever you think may damage you, and I do not believe you have told the whole truth.'
>
> 'Sir, I have told the whole truth, and related the affair from the beginning to the end in every detail: and of this I trust God and the country both for good and evil.'
>
> And so let the inquest be held.
>
> And the jury said the same as Thomas had related. So the justice then says:

'Thomas, these good people testify by their oaths to the truth of what you have said. So our judgment is that what you did to him, you did in self defence. But we cannot release you from this prison without the king's special grace. However we will send a report of your case to the king's court and ensure that you receive his special grace.'

'Sir, I thank you.'[50]

Because this is gaol delivery, there is no presenting jury to state the accusation. It is the sheriff, therefore, who takes on this role and thus assumes a speaking part, albeit a small one. The bulk of the case involves a conversation between the judge, who seems quite hostile, and the defendant. The defendant says quite a bit, and in similar real cases, the jurors may have been influenced both by what he said and how he said it. Once the defendant has put himself on the jury, there is again no sign of testimony or evidence. The jury's verdict is reported immediately.

The description of trial in *Britton* (*c.* 1290–95) is similar to *Bracton*'s, with two principal differences. *Britton* allows the defendant to challenge jurors who have served on the presenting jury, and *Britton* says that if the jurors cannot agree and judicial questioning reveals that the jurors 'know nothing of the fact, let others be called who do know it'.[51] The first difference will be discussed in section IV below. This second difference is very strong evidence that *Britton* believed that jurors were or should have been self informing. Unfortunately, there is no corroborating evidence for this procedure.

Plea rolls

Because treatise writers are not completely reliable, it is important to compare their writing to other trial accounts. The most important are probably the eyre rolls, the official Latin record of eyre proceedings. Unfortunately, plea rolls record frustratingly little information. Often they contain only the charge, the jury verdict and miscellaneous amercements. This is especially true of thirteenth-century gaol delivery records which provide only the most skeletal information. Fortunately, for eyre plea rolls, there was wide variation in clerical practice and even a clerk who usually recorded only bare bones facts, occasionally put some life into his writing. Consider, for example, the following case from the 1247 Bedfordshire eyre:

John son of Benedict appealed Ivo Quarel, Osbert Cokel and Henry Wyncard in county court of [breach of the] king's peace, wounds and imprisonment etc. And he [John] now comes and does not want to prosecute them. Therefore let him be committed to jail and his sureties, Ayltrop Balliol and Walter son of Odo, are in mercy [fined]. And Ivo and the others come [to court]. And the jurors testify that they [John, Ivo, Osbert and Henry] have settled and they say that, in truth, the aforesaid Ivo and the others came to the property of Matthew of Leyham in Barford and fished there without Matthew's permission and contrary to his wishes. The aforesaid John came along and asked them for a pledge, and the aforesaid Ivo would not give him one, but instead struck the aforesaid John in the head with a hatchet and made two wounds each three inches long down to the crest of the head. And they [Ivo and the others] beat him badly. And afterwards they took him and bound him and put him in a boat and took him from this county [Bedfordshire] to the county of Huntingdonshire to Ivo's house at Buckden. There they dragged him with a rope to a window of Ivo's solarium and forced him to break the window with an axe. And they painted the wall near the window with the blood flowing from the wounds the aforesaid Ivo had given the aforesaid John, and they dragged him through the window and set upon him a blanket and some linen saying that he had stolen them. And they raised the hue [and cry] and caused the men who responded to the hue [and cry] to understand that eighteen thieves had come to his house, and that all except the aforesaid John had gotten away. So they put the blanket and the linen on him and took him to Huntingdon and gave him to the sheriff to be incarcerated. And he remained in prison until his tithing delivered him. Therefore let the aforesaid Ivo and the others be taken into custody. Later Ivo Quarel came and made fine for forty marks . . .[52]

What is most notable about this case is the detailed account which the jurors provided of what happened. Although it is possible that they heard testimony in court and then provided this complex narrative as a synthesis of what they heard, this seems implausible. From whom would they have heard such testimony? The appellor, although present at the eyre, did not want to prosecute and had, in fact, settled with the defendants. He is unlikely to have testified. The defendants had no incentive to provide the information. Perhaps third parties, to whom the appellor had previously related his ordeal, testified in court. Most likely, however, the jurors had informed themselves out of court, by talking to the appellor while he was still interested in pursuing the case or by talking to representatives of the relevant villages to whom the appellor might have spoken. They might also have learned from the appellor's presentation of the appeal at the county court. In this regard, it is notable that jurors are said to 'testify' (*testantur*). They were seen as witnesses themselves. It is unlikely that they were eyewitnesses. Rather, they were hearsay witnesses, synthesising and testifying as to what they heard from others before coming to court.

The jury's testimonial role is highlighted in a case from the 1227 Essex eyre. A chaplain was appealed for arson and claimed benefit of clergy. As was common in such cases, the jurors nevertheless rendered a verdict. They said that he had committed arson and 'they disclosed certain reasons for this' (*ostendunt inde certas rationes*).[53] As the theory of the self-informing jury suggests, reasons and facts were not argued to the jury. Rather, jurors offered them to the judge.

While the plea rolls generally support the idea that the jury came to court well-informed of the relevant facts, they also suggest that jurors sometimes learned from trial. Not only would trial give the defendant, the judge and the appellor (if it was an appeal) a chance to speak about the case, but other persons are occasionally mentioned in the plea rolls as providing information in open court. A homicide appeal from the 1218 Yorkshire eyre provides a particularly informative example of in-court testimony. After the principal defendant, Simon, was convicted and hanged, the record continues with proceedings against accessories. The key parts are underlined, and the original Latin of important verbs has been supplied:

> The same Jordan appeals as accessory Geoffrey of Stallingborough. <u>The sheriff, the neighbourhood, and the jurors bear witness (*testantur*) that</u> this Geoffrey came before them after Hawisa's death and said that the same Simon had many times asked him to come with him to kill Hawisa, and that on the night on which she was killed he had asked him to go with him and he said that he would not, and immediately Simon went with his daughters and killed her, and if he should wish to deny this he would prove it against him as the court shall adjudge. <u>It was attested (*testatum fuit*) by the bishop of Durham's serjeant of Howden and the 4 villages and all the neighbourhood that</u> before Geoffrey was taken they found upon him a certain jewel box and border of cloth which they well know (*noverunt*) to have belonged to Hawisa, and upon William his son they found a razor and tunic which belonged to Peter of Duffield, Hawisa's husband, who has set out to the land of Jerusalem, and <u>William said (*dixit*) that</u> Geoffrey his father entrusted them to him and Geoffrey denied (*dedixit*) this.
>
> Afterwards Geoffrey came and admitted (*cognovit*) that he was present where the aforesaid Hawisa was killed and he appeals thereof William the smith of Duffield . . .[54]

It is apparent that there were a lot of people speaking in court in this case. As would be expected, the appellor, defendant, jurors and representatives of the four villages spoke. The jurors in particular spoke at length, informing the judge of many details about the case. In addition, the sheriff and the neighbourhood (*visnetum*) joined with the jurors in reporting what Geoffrey had said to them after Hawisa's death. It is unclear exactly how this happened. While the record makes it sound as though the sheriff, the neighbourhood, and jurors spoke in unison, it is far more likely that the sheriff, one or two neighbours, and a representative of the jury spoke one after another, saying roughly the same thing. For similar reasons, the bishop of Durham's serjeant of Howden, neighbours, and representatives of the four nearby villages, probably spoke separately about finding the deceased's goods in the defendant's possession. It is not entirely clear, however, that the serjeant and neighbours spoke in open court, because, unlike the prior testimony, their words are introduced by a past tense verb – *testatum fuit* rather than *testantur*. While this change in verb tense might indicate that the testimony was communicated to jurors before the eyre, the eyre rolls are notoriously inconsistent in their use of verb tenses. Later in the same record, Geoffrey's confession is recorded in the past tense, even though it clearly happened at the eyre in open court. The record also indicates that William said that his father gave him the razor and tunic which had belonged to the deceased. Again, William probably spoke in court, although the use of the past tense might suggest otherwise.

Because the defendant confessed, there is no verdict in this case. Nevertheless, it suggests that testimony was given in open court and that in appropriate cases such testimony could have provided evidence which influenced jury verdicts. As Maitland noted, there were no rules against in-court testimony.[55] So many people were summoned to the eyre that it was inevitable that some, especially officials, would have had knowledge about criminal cases. It should not be surprising that those with knowledge wanted to speak at trial, nor that judges allowed them to do so. The fact that witnesses sometimes spoke in court does not necessarily detract from the self-informing nature of the jury. For example, in the case above, the testimony of the serjeant, neighbours, and sheriff seems duplicative.[56] Everything they said was also said by the presenting jury or four villages, who would have constituted the trial jury if the defendant had not confessed. This case thus provides a nice illustration of how witness testimony at trial is not incompatible with the idea that jurors came to trial already well informed.

Although this case shows that witnesses sometimes testified at trial, it does not prove that they were an ordinary part of criminal trials. To document the frequency and nature of such testimony, I looked for witnesses in four crown pleas eyre rolls. These rolls contain 1300 cases from different parts of England, spanning most of the century. Table 3.2 summarises the frequency of testimony, who the witness was and what he spoke about. The table suggests that testimony was quite uncommon. The plea rolls record only 80 instances of testimony in 1300 cases. That means there was testimony in only 6 per cent of the cases. Even this may exaggerate the extent to which witnesses appeared because the speaker in the overwhelming majority of such instances was not identified. Rather, the testimony is introduced by an ambiguous formula, most often 'Later it was testified that (*Postea testatum est quod*).' It is possible that such information was actually provided by the jurors, in which case it would not be properly categorised as testimony in the sense used in this chapter. The idea that such formulae were used to introduce words spoken by the jurors is supported by the 1286 Huntingdonshire eyre roll, which often uses the formula 'Later it was testified *by the jurors* that' (*Postea testatum est per juratores quod*) rather than 'Later it was testified that'.[57] This suggests that clerks writing other eyre rolls may have used 'Later it was testified that' as a shorthand for 'Later it was testified by the jurors that'. If one counted only cases which explicitly identified the person or group speaking, there were only seventeen instances of testimony. That represents testimony in barely one per cent of cases. Of course, it is possible that there were many instances of testimony which were not recorded, but given the evidence from other sources, such as treatises and reports (discussed below), this seems unlikely.

Table 3.2   *Testimony[a] in eyre plea rolls by topic and speaker, 1221–86*

	Coroner	Sheriff	County[h]	Other officials[i]	Non-officials[j]	Unidentified speaker[k]	Total
Law enforcement misconduct [b]	1	1	2	1	0	20	25
Flight[c]	0	1	0	0	0	13	14
Forfeiture[d]	0	0	0	0	0	14	14
Accusation[e]	0	0	0	0	0	9	9
Guilt[f]	1	2	0	1	0	3	7
Other[g]	4	0	1	0	2	4	11
Total	6	4	3	2	2	63	80

Notes:

[a] 'Testimony' means words spoken at trial by a speaker not identified as a judge, juror, village, appellor, defendant, attorney of a defendant, or ordinary claiming a defendant as cleric. The table counts instances of testimony. Sometimes, as in the 1218 Yorkshire case quoted above, there was more than one instance of testimony in the same case. As a result, some cases are counted twice or even three times in the table. The eighty instances of testimony occurred in only sixty-eight cases.

[b] Testimony about individuals, officials, and groups who failed to fulfil their law enforcement responsibilities, including villages that failed to pursue suspects, sureties or bailors who failed to ensure someone's presence at the eyre, and misappropriation of forfeited chattels.

[c] Testimony about whether a suspect fled or abjured and/or information about suspects who fled or abjured, including whether suspects who fled were tried and/or executed elsewhere.

[d] Testimony about whether a defendant who fled or was convicted, had chattels or lands and/or their value.

[e] Testimony which accuses someone not previously mentioned of an offence other than law enforcement misconduct. Such accusations were most often of homicide.

[f] Testimony about whether a suspect was guilty.

[g] Testimony which does not fall in any of the above categories, such as that a case was removed to the Bench in Westminster or that a neighbour was sick and thus could not attend the eyre.

[h] Means that representatives of the county court testified.

[i] Were the mayor of London and a sheriff's attorney.

[j] Means an ordinary person, i.e. one not a coroner, sheriff, other official, or representative of the county court.

[k] Means that the speaker was not identified. For example, the record might simply say 'it was testified that' (*testatum est quod*). It is possible that the jury was speaking in such instances.

Sources: D. M. Stenton (ed.), *Rolls of the Justices in Eyre . . . Gloucestershire, Warwickshire and Staffordshire, 1221, 1222* (Selden Society, 59, 1940), pp. 331–415; Meekings (ed.), *The 1235 Surrey Eyre*, II (32), pp. 379–443; Harding (ed.), *Shropshire Eyre*, pp. 196–300, 307–9; De Windt and De Windt (eds), *Royal Justice*, pp. 292–408, 476–87.

The topics of the testimony are also revealing. The overwhelming majority of the testimony was about collateral matters rather than a defendant's guilt or innocence. For example, almost a third of the testimony was about law enforcement misconduct, such as a village's failure to pursue a fleeing suspect or a pledge's failure to produce someone at the eyre. Much of the remaining testimony concerned whether a suspect had fled or abjured and/or whether such a suspect was tried and/or executed elsewhere. In addition, a substantial amount of testimony was about forfeited chattels or lands. Only sixteen instances of testimony were about matters at the core of the jury's function:

accusations of felony and the guilt or innocence of the accused. This means that testimony like that in the Yorkshire 1218 case quoted above is recorded to have occurred in barely one per cent of cases. The fact that testimony was almost always about collateral matters may help explain why it is not mentioned in other sources, such as treatises or Year Book reports.

It is also worthwhile to note the positions of those identified as speakers. The most common were officials, such as the sheriff and coroner. Since such persons were heavily involved in the law enforcement activities prior to the eyre, and since they were required to be at the eyre, it is not surprising that they often had useful information to contribute. It was extremely rare for ordinary persons to be recorded as speaking at trial. I found only two such instances in the 1300 cases examined.

One important, unresolved, issue about this testimony is whether it was sworn. Maitland thought it was not[58] and this view is supported by the lack of any mention of witness oaths in the plea rolls or treatises. Although arguments from silence are always dangerous, given the copious evidence for oaths by jurors, appellors, appellees (defendants in appeals) and compurgators, silence here is quite telling. On the other hand, the plea rolls often make use of the verb 'to testify' (*testari*), which might suggest that witnesses were sworn.

The plea roll evidence thus substantially augments our knowledge by showing that there was occasional in-court testimony. Nevertheless, such testimony seems to have been rare and largely restricted to collateral matters. In addition, it was probably provided most often by officials rather than by ordinary persons.

Year Book reports

The last few pages have focused on plea rolls, the official record of court proceedings. Toward the end of the thirteenth century, a new form of legal literature emerged – reports, often called Year Books. These were unofficial notes on cases, probably written down by lawyers for themselves and each other. The overwhelming majority of these reports deal with civil cases, but, as Seipp has noted, there was a trickle dealing with criminal cases.[59] Some of the reports provide vivid insights into the conduct of trials, because, like the *Placita Corone*, they take a dialogue form which seems to record what actually transpired in court. Unlike the *Placita*, however, the reports are about actual cases, not hypotheticals. The following case from the 1293–94 Yorkshire eyre is illustrative of the richness of some reports:

> *Judge*: Hugh, it was presented to us that you committed rape . . . how do you
> want to acquit yourself?
> *Hugh*: Lord, I request that I be able to have counsel lest I be deceived in royal
> court for lack of counsel.
> *Judge*: You ought to know that the king is a party to this case and prosecutes
> you ex officio, and in this situation the law does not allow you to have counsel

against the king ... And therefore, on the king's behalf, we order all the
pleaders who are your counsel to withdraw.
[The pleaders were removed.]
...

Judge: Do you consent to these twelve honest men, because we know that they
do not want to lie for us?
...

Hugh: I consent to my peers, but not to the twelve who accused me ...
[Hugh successfully challenged several of the jurors.]
Judge: We accuse Lord Hugh of the rape of this woman. He denied it. Asked how
he wants to acquit himself, he said 'by good country' and put himself on you
for good or bad. And therefore we order you, by virtue of your oath, to tell us
whether Lord Hugh raped this woman or not.
The twelve: We say that she was raped with force by Hugh's men.
Judge: Did Hugh consent to the deed or not?
The twelve: No.
Judge: Did they know her carnally?
The twelve: Yes.
Judge: Against the woman's will or with her consent?
The twelve: With her consent ...
Judge: Lord Hugh, because they acquit you, we acquit you.[60]

Like the accounts in the *Placita Corone*, trial was primarily a dialogue
between the judge and the defendant. The judge took a quasi-prosecutorial
role, expelling the defendant's lawyers, and, in passages omitted above, chal-
lenging his claim to clerical privilege and bullying him into submitting to jury
trial. As in *Britton*, the defendant was allowed to challenge jurors who had
served on the presenting jury. Once the jury selection process was over, the
judge immediately charged the jury. As in all of the treatises and most of the
plea roll accounts, there is no mention of witnesses. Given the lavish detail
with which other aspects of this case were recorded, it would be surprising for
the reporter to have omitted witness testimony and arguments about such
testimony, if witnesses had in fact testified. The latter part of the report is a
dialogue between the judge, who seems to have known nothing of the facts,
and the jurors, who tell him what they knew (or, perhaps, what they wanted
him to believe). The independence of jurors from what was said in court is
underlined by the fact that, while the presentment and preliminary proceedings had said nothing about accomplices, the jurors' verdict states that it was
Hugh's men, not Hugh himself, who had intercourse with the woman.

On the whole, this and other thirteenth-century reports confirm the accounts given in the treatises.[61] The testimony of witnesses is never mentioned.
Rather, trial was primarily a conversation between the judge and the defendant, and secondarily between the judge and the jury. Immediately after being
impanelled, or perhaps after some deliberation,[62] the jury rendered its verdict.

IV Explaining the decline of the self-informing jury

This chapter has tried to show that thirteenth-century jurors were self informing. By the mid-fifteenth century, however, it is clear that jurors were becoming increasingly dependent on in-court testimony. Why did the jury become less self informing? Undoubtedly, increased mobility and other social changes played a large role.[63] The essays by McLane and Post, however, suggest that fourteenth-century changes in jury composition played a part, at least in criminal cases. This timing suggests two explanations: the transition from eyre to gaol delivery[64] and the exclusion of presenting jurors from the trial jury.

The last regular eyre was held in the early 1290s. By that time, and probably several decades earlier, gaol delivery had become the principal forum in which criminal cases were heard. The rise of gaol delivery undoubtedly represented an improvement in the justice system. Eyres were held infrequently – every four years at the turn of the thirteenth century and with decreasing frequency thereafter. Decades might separate eyres toward the end of the century. Even four years was a long time to hold a homicide suspect in gaol before trial, to expect jurors to remember the facts, or to require appellors to remember the exact phrasing of their pleadings in county court. Gaol delivery sessions, which were held roughly twice a year, dramatically alleviated the problems caused by delay. Such frequent sessions, however, had at least one unanticipated effect: they made it difficult to recruit local jurors.

For eyres, recruitment of jurors was relatively easy. Although the sheriff summoned all freeholders, this was not a heavy burden, because the eyre met so infrequently. In addition, because the eyre was the forum for a wide variety of civil and criminal cases, many individuals had to attend anyway. Finally, those who served on juries would have perceived the importance of their presence, because jurors from all but the smallest hundreds would have been involved in more than a dozen cases. Even the representatives of the villages, who were specially summoned, would probably have been involved in at least a few cases.

Recruitment for gaol delivery was very different. Such sessions were held much more frequently, so summoning all freeholders and representatives from every village to each session, would have imposed a huge burden. In fact, doing so was forbidden by statute.[65] Even though gaol delivery sessions were often held at the same time as assizes for civil cases, because assize sessions were also held more frequently, fewer people had litigation to attend to. In addition, the increasing employment of attorneys and pleaders meant the parties themselves might not attend even if they had pending cases. As a result, jurors had to be specially summoned and naturally found service burdensome. In addition, because gaol delivery sessions were held so frequently, relatively few cases were heard at any one session. As a result, jurors would have felt that service was not worth the effort. If hundred jurors appeared, they likely would have had only one or two cases to try. If representatives of the village appeared, they would likely have tried only a single case. Not surprisingly, although representatives of the villages were still summoned, sheriffs seem to have given up trying to get them to attend. The plague must have aggravated these problems by drastically reducing the population – thus reducing both the pool of potential jurors and the number of suspects tried – without reducing the number of hundreds.

Not surprisingly, coroners, bailiffs, assize recognitors, and others with independent reasons to attend gaol delivery came to constitute a disproportionate fraction of jurors.[66] There were not enough of these, however, to fully staff juries of all the relevant hundreds, so judges and sheriffs had to improvise. Pugh, Post, and Powell documented the strategies they employed. Given the dynamics of juror recruitment at gaol delivery, one should not be surprised at the difficulty of assembling jurors with local knowledge. If anything, it is surprising that sheriffs were able to recruit juries that were largely hundred-based for so long. One might have thought that the system described by Powell – juries composed of men from several hundreds trying suspects from multiple hundreds – would have appeared a century earlier.

The problem created by the frequency of gaol delivery sessions was compounded by the exclusion of presenting jurors from the trial jury. As *Britton* and the Year Book report quoted above show, defendants in the late thirteenth century had the right to challenge jurors who had indicted them. In 1352, this protection was enacted into statute.[67] Although the purpose of this change was clear (to ensure a fair trial), it, like the introduction of gaol delivery, had an unintended effect: barring twelve of the most knowledgeable people, the presenting jury, from service on the trial jury.

These developments suggest that as the Middle Ages drew to a close, juries contained fewer informed members. They do not prove, however, that the late medieval jury was no longer self informing or that it relied principally on evidence presented in court by parties or witnesses. Powell pointed out that jurors from the hundred were partly replaced by officials, such as coroners, hundred bailiffs and constables. Because of their involvement in pre-trial processes, these jurors came to court with significant information about suspects.[68] In addition, fourteenth-century gaol delivery juries still consisted overwhelmingly of men from the hundred and fifteenth-century juries usually contained several from the relevant hundred. It is hard to imagine that these jurors would not have heard the local view on guilt or innocence.[69] Perhaps they were already acquainted with the suspect and the alleged crime from gossip or from discussions at local courts where the suspect may have been presented or indicted. In addition, jurors from the hundred could have discussed the case with neighbours, officials and others with relevant information about the crime and the suspect's character. Since relatively few suspects from a given hundred were tried at a gaol delivery, a juror's fact-finding burden would not have been large. In fact, a conscientious juror, cognisant that his verdict would have life or death consequences, would have been highly motivated to acquire relevant information. He could then have shared it with fellow jurors who, because they resided farther from the relevant events, could not gather evidence on their own. As noted earlier, self informing is a matter of degree. A jury with only one or a few informed jurors is less self informing than one composed exclusively of those from the immediate vicinity of the crime. It may, nevertheless, be self-informing in the sense that jury verdicts could have been based primarily on what at least one juror knew before coming to court rather than on evidence presented by parties or witnesses.

On the other hand, when juries come to contain so few members with independent information, it is easy to see how pressure would build for more in-court presentation of evidence. Jurors might be reluctant to convict based solely on the word of one of their fellows. They might want to hear themselves from those with first-hand knowledge. In addition, an accuser or witness who was unable to persuade a neighbour juror, might travel to gaol delivery himself to try to sway those who came from farther away. In this way, as jurors came less and less frequently from the hundred, prosecutors and witnesses might have come to play a larger role, and self-informed jurors a smaller one.

V Conclusion

This chapter has tried to suggest and support a moderate position: the thirteenth-century jury was self informing, but it sometimes heard witnesses at trial. As Green put it, the self-informing jury was not 'a mythical beast'.[70] Jurors were recruited from both the hundred and the neighbouring villages and thus knew an enormous amount about cases before they came to court. Sometimes they also heard testimony, but such testimony was usually unnecessary. It was frequently testimony by officials and almost always about collateral matters. As a result, what distinguishes the medieval from the modern jury is not that one heard witnesses and the other did not. Rather, it is that medieval jurors came to court with extensive knowledge about the case and the defendant. They heard testimony, but they heard much less, and what they heard was less important.

Notes

1 The author thanks Albert Alschuler, Jennifer Arlen, Paul Brand, Jamaul Cannon, David Cook, Charles Donahue, George Fisher, Christina Foster, Thomas Gallanis, Thomas Green, Ariela Gross, Richard Helmholz, Eugene Kantorovich, John Langbein, Edward McCaffery, Anthony Musson, Jennifer Murray, Christopher Stone, and David Seipp for their help, suggestions, and criticism at various stages of this project. This research was supported by a Fulbright scholarship, the National Science Foundation (Law and Social Science Program, grant no. SBR–9412044), the Social Science Research Council, and USC Law School summer research grants.

2 F. Palgrave, *The Rise and Progress of the English Commonwealth* (2 vols, London, 1832), I, pp. 243–4; H. Brunner, *Die Entstehung der Schwergerichte* (Berlin, 1872), pp. 427, 452; J. F. Stephen, *A History of the Criminal Law of England* (3 vols, London, 1883), I, pp. 255–65; F. Pollock and F. W. Maitland, *The History of English Law before the Time of Edward I* (second edition, 2 vols, Cambridge, 1988), II, pp. 622–8; J. P. Dawson, *A History of Lay Judges* (Cambridge, Massachusetts, 1960), pp. 213–27; S. F. C. Milsom, *Historical Foundations of the Common Law* (second edition, Toronto, 1981), pp. 412, 418, 421, 424; J. H. Baker, *Introduction to English Legal History* (third edition, London, 1990), pp. 88–90. See also, below, notes 3–6. For historians who disagree with this consensus, see below, notes 7, 10 and 13.

3 J. H. Langbein, 'The origins of public prosecution at common law', *American Journal of Legal History*, 17 (1973), 314.

4 J. B. Thayer, *A Preliminary Treatise on Evidence at the Common Law* (Boston, 1898), 85–136; J. H. Wigmore, *A Treatise on the Anglo-American System of Evidence* (third edition, 10 vols, Boston, 1940), I, p. 235; V, pp. 10–12. More recent research suggests that rules regulating oral testimony did not develop until the eighteenth century, and thus that the decline of the self-informing jury was a necessary condition but not the immediate cause of the emergence of evidence law. See J. H. Langbein, 'Historical foundations of the law of evidence: a view from the Ryder sources', *Columbia Law Review*, 96 (1996), 1171–2; T. P. Gallanis, 'The rise of modern evidence law', *Iowa Law Review*, 84 (1999), 499, 537–40.

5 Langbein, 'Origins', 314; J. H. Langbein, *Prosecuting Crime in the Renaissance* (Cambridge, Massachusetts, 1974), pp. 22, 43, 118–22, 204–5.

6 T. A. Green, *Verdict According to Conscience: Perspectives on the English Criminal Trial Jury 1200–1800* (Chicago, 1983), pp. 16–18.

7 M. C. Klingelsmith, 'New readings of old law', *University of Pennsylvania Law Review*, 66 (1918), 107–22; R. C. Palmer, 'Conscience and the law: the English criminal jury', *Michigan Law Review*, 84 (1986), 795–6.

8 J. S. Cockburn and T. A. Green (eds), *Twelve Good Men and True: The Criminal Trial Jury in England, 1200–1800* (Princeton, New Jersey, 1988).

9 The hundred was an administrative subdivision of the county comprising a number of villages.

10 J. B. Post, 'Jury lists and juries in the late fourteenth century', in Cockburn and Green (eds), *Twelve Good Men*, p. 76; E. Powell, 'Jury trial at gaol delivery in the late Middle Ages: the Midland Circuit, 1400–1429', *ibid.*, p. 113.

11 Powell, 'Jury trial', p. 97 ('Our hypothesis must be that by the early fifteenth century the criminal trial jury was no longer self informing in the accepted sense – *if indeed it ever had been*') (italics added).

12 *Ibid.*, pp. 115–16.

13 G. Fisher, 'The jury's rise as lie detector', *Yale Law Journal*, 107 (1997), 591–2.

14 T. A. Green, 'A retrospective on the criminal trial jury, 1200–1800', in Cockburn and Green (eds), *Twelve Good Men*, pp. 364–75; Langbein, 'Historical Foundations', 1170 n. 6; see also B. W. McLane, 'Juror attitudes toward local disorder: the evidence of the 1328 Lincolnshire trailbaston proceedings', in Cockburn and Green (eds), *Twelve Good Men*, p. 57.

15 A. Musson, *Public Order and Law Enforcement: The Local Administration of Criminal Justice, 1294–1350* (Woodbridge, 1996), p. 205.

16 See, e.g., Langbein, 'Origins', 314; Green, *Verdict*, pp. 16–17; see also twentieth-century sources cited in note 2.
17 Fisher, 'Jury's rise,' 593.
18 Women constituted more than a third of appellors. D. Klerman, 'Women prosecutors in thirteenth-century England', forthcoming in *Yale Journal of Law and Humanities*.
19 Powell, 'Jury trial', pp. 115–16 (italics added).
20 J. H. Mitnick, 'From neighbor-witness to judge of proofs: the transformation of the English civil juror', *American Journal of Legal History*, 32 (1988), 201–35.
21 Green, 'Retrospective', p. 370.
22 Powell, 'Jury trial', pp. 97, 115–16.
23 Green, *Verdict*, p. 16 ('No witnesses could come forward . . .'); Langbein, 'Historical foundations', 1170 ('The medieval jury came to court not to listen but to speak, not to hear evidence but to deliver a verdict formulated in advance.'); but see Green, *Verdict*, p. 16 n. 48, p. 18; Langbein, 'Origins', 314, quoted above, p. 58 ('*more* to speak than to listen' rather than '*not* to listen') (italics added).
24 Green, *Verdict*, p. 18.
25 F. W. Maitland, *Pleas of the Crown for the County of Gloucester . . . 1221* (London, 1884), p. xli; Stephen, *History*, pp. 259–60.
26 'Jurors, evidences, and the tempest of 1499', in J. W. Cairns (ed.), *The Dearest Birthright of the People of England* (forthcoming).
27 The presenting jury was a jury which accused persons of crime. It was the forerunner of the grand jury.
28 The eyre was a periodic session of royal justice held in the countryside to hear a wide range of civil and criminal cases.
29 C. A. F. Meekings (ed.), *The 1235 Surrey Eyre*, 2 vols, Surrey Record Society, 31, 32, 1979–83, I (31), pp. 20, 94, 97–8. Even though the representatives of the villages were sworn and associated with the presenting jurors in presenting the verdict, the sources do not always refer to them as 'jurors.' For example, plea rolls often report the verdict in a form that suggests that the villagers were not part of the jury: 'The jurors and the four neighbouring villages say on oath that . . .' See, e.g., A. Harding (ed.), *The Roll of the Shropshire Eyre of 1256*, Selden Society, 96, 1981, p. 230. See also below p. 73, where the jury is referred to as 'the twelve'. Nevertheless, because the villagers were sworn and seem to have delivered their verdict with the presenting jurors, this chapter will refer to them as part of the jury, as is common in the literature.
30 See e.g., Harding (ed.), *Shropshire Eyre*, pp. 301–6; A. R. and E. B. DeWindt (eds), *Royal Justice and the Medieval English Countryside: The Huntingdonshire Eyre of 1286, the Ramsey Abbey Banlieu Court of 1287, and the Assizes of 1287–88* (Toronto, 1981), pp. 419–21.
31 Meekings (ed.), *1235 Surrey Eyre*, I, p. 97.
32 An amercement was a monetary penalty. Today it would be called a fine.
33 See e.g. Harding (ed.), *Shropshire Eyre*, cases 514, 535, 544, 565.
34 Gaol delivery was a periodic session of royal justice in the countryside specifically to try those in jail or out on bail.
35 Pollock and Maitland, *History*, II, p. 625.
36 R. B. Pugh, *Wiltshire Gaol Delivery and Trailbaston Trials, 1275–1306*, Wiltshire Record Society, 33, 1978, pp. 18–19.

37 JUST 1/36, mm. 4–5 (Berkshire 1225 gaol delivery, seventeen cases mentioning the neighbouring vills); JUST 1/1177A, m. 4d (Suffolk 1250 gaol delivery, three cases mentioning neighbouring vills); JUST 1/1179, m. 14 (Suffolk 1254, three cases mentioning neighbouring vills); JUST 1/1179, mm. 25–25d (Norfolk and Suffolk gaol delivery 1259, thirteen cases mentioning neighbouring vills); JUST 3/18/2, m.1 (Essex 1282 gaol delivery, eight cases mentioning the neighbouring vills).

38 See above, note 10; J. G. Bellamy, *The Criminal Trial in Later Medieval England* (Toronto, 1998), pp. 103–4.

39 D. Klerman, 'Settlement and the decline of private prosecution in thirteenth-century England', *Law and History Review*, 19 (2001), 38–40, 50–3. This article did not address the treatment of appeals when the appellor died, but the same pattern appears in those cases as well.

40 *Ibid.*, 21–2.

41 No inferences should be drawn from the fact that jurors were less likely to convict when the appellor had died than when the appellor had retracted or decided not to prosecute, because the difference in conviction rates is not statistically significant.

42 For an example of such a case, see below, pp. 67–8. For a discussion of the high conviction rates in such cases, see D. Klerman, 'The selection of thirteenth-century criminal cases for trial' (unpublished manuscript).

43 Powell, 'Jury trial', p. 107; Bellamy, *Criminal Trial*, p. 103. Note, however, that Bellamy believes the purpose of this proclamation was primarily to inform appellors, not victims prosecuting their cases by indictment.

44 Meekings (ed.), *1235 Surrey Eyre*, I, p. 20; *Close Rolls of the Reign of Henry III, AD 1227–1231* (London, 1902), pp. 227, 228, 386, 388–9 (1229 and 1230 gaol deliveries); JUST 3/14/1, m. 11 (Devon 1271 gaol delivery).

45 Musson, *Public Order*, pp. 201–5.

46 S. E. Thorne (trans.), *Bracton on the Laws and Customs of England* (4 vols, Cambridge, Massachusetts, 1968–1977), II, pp. 403–6, fols 143–143b. Square brackets, parentheses and the items within them are Thorne's.

47 J. M. Kaye (ed.), *Placita Corone* or *La Corone pledee devant justices*, Selden Society, Supplementary Series, 4, 1966, pp. 8–9, 16–17.

48 *Ibid.*, p. 8.

49 *Ibid.*, pp. 17–22.

50 *Ibid.*, pp. 19–20.

51 F. M. Morgan (ed.), *Britton* (Oxford, 1865), pp. 30, 31.

52 JUST 1/4, m. 30.

53 JUST 1/229, m. 16.

54 D. M. Stenton (ed.), *Rolls of the Justices in Eyre Being Rolls of Pleas and Assizes for Yorkshire in 3 Henry III (1218–19)*, Selden Society, 56, 1937, pp. 299–301.

55 Pollock and Maitland, *History*, II, p. 628.

56 For another example of duplicative testimony, see J. G. Jenkins, *Calendar of the Roll of the Justices on Eyre, 1227*, Buckinghamshire Archaeological Society, 6, 1945, case 527.

57 De Windt and DeWindt (eds), *Royal Justice*, cases 348, 351, 352, 363, 384, 392, 528, 571, 656; but see cases 363, 388, 442.

58 Pollock and Maitland, *History*, II, p. 628.

59 D. Seipp, 'Crime in the Year Books', in C. Stubbing (ed.), *Law Reporting in Britain* (London, 1995), pp. 16–17. Seipp was kind enough to share with me his list of late thirteenth-century Year Book cases involving crime.

60 *YB 30–31 Edward I*, pp. 529–32. Contrary to the Year Book editor's suggestion, this case is from the Yorkshire eyre. D. Crook, 'Triers and the origin of the grand jury', *Journal of Legal History*, 12 (1991), 116 n. 71.

61 *YB 30–31 Edward I*, pp. 521, 528–9, 534, 535, 538–9, 541.

62 *Ibid.*, p. 541; *Britton*, p. 31.

63 Langbein, 'Origins', 315.

64 D. Crook, 'The later eyres', *English Historical Review*, 97 (1982), 241, 246–7.

65 Provisions of Westminster, 1259 (43 Henry III Provisions), *c.* 13; Statute of Marlborough, 1267 (52 Henry III Stat. Marlb.), *c.* 18.

66 Powell, 'Jury trial', pp. 88–94.

67 25 Edward III, stat. 5, c. 3.

68 Powell, 'Jury trial', pp. 88–94.

69 Green, 'Retrospective', pp. 369.

70 *Ibid.*, p. 370.

4

Trials in manorial courts
in late medieval England

Maureen Mulholland

A legal historian approaching the history of the manorial courts is aware that the comprehensive literature of the manor has been primarily concerned with the social, economic or political significance of the manor court. The rolls have been a rich source of research into the nature of medieval society, including questions of personal status, family structures, lordship, demography and social relationships, as well as the practice of agriculture and land management in the medieval English countryside.[1] For a lawyer, the study of legal institutions in themselves is a legitimate field of research, although this cannot and should not be divorced from that of the society in which they operated. Maitland himself, having a deep knowledge and understanding of the law and the instincts and skills of a historian, provided a fundamental analysis of the constitution and procedures of manorial courts in his seminal volume for the Selden Society 1889.[2] Here he affirmed the intrinsic legal importance of the courts and, in particular, stressed the significance of their procedure, since '[w]e cannot form a true notion of them unless we know how they did their ordinary work, and this we cannot know until we have mastered their common forms'.[3] It was nearly a century later that legal historians, notably John Beckerman[4] and, more recently, L. R. Poos and Lloyd Bonfield[5] restored the purely legal aspects of the court rolls to the study of legal history.

The vast range of manorial court records presents a daunting challenge to the would-be researcher. The primary sources for the manorial courts are manorial documents, consisting of account rolls, extents (surveys for valuation of the property of manors) and especially court rolls and court books. The earliest extant manorial rolls date from the thirteenth century[6] and at that stage the accounts of trial provide considerable detail. By the fourteenth century the stewards of manors were professional lawyers and it is no accident that, with the increasing professionalisation of these officials, the manorial court rolls became less informative and more formulaic. There are, nonetheless, many collections of rolls for the fourteenth and fifteenth centuries which reveal a vigorous jurisdiction whose proceedings in many respects mirrored those in developing common law courts, but which retained the informality, speed and ease of access which perhaps compensated for a lack of access to the common law courts.

Because the income of the courts was paid to the lord, the court rolls of a manor, together with extents and accounts, were primarily financial records,[7] and the steward or bailiff who compiled them was not, therefore, primarily concerned with the working of the courts. Nonetheless, the rolls provide a vivid picture of manorial legal rituals and although the late medieval rolls are less informative than those of the mid-thirteenth century, they still provide important evidence of the nature of trials in these courts – their structure, personnel and procedures, their rationale and their importance in the formulation of manorial custom and in the settlement of disputes by litigation. Although there are many variations in practice, there is considerable uniformity in the formulae used in the manorial rolls. Written in Latin, by clerks with varying degrees of skill, the rolls follow a fairly consistent procedural pattern, containing abbreviations, contractions of terms, specialised formulae and technical language, all of which became common form, constituting the legal language of the manorial system.[8]

A further valuable source of information about manorial trial procedures is the material contained in the many court keepers' guides and manuals which were produced as early as the thirteenth century. At first in manuscript, passed from one steward to another, they were later printed and circulated widely. Typical of these manuals, printed and published in the sixteenth century, are the four court guides, reproduced in 1892 in a volume edited by Maitland and Baildon and published by the Selden Society,[9] and providing important details of the procedure in a manorial court as well as an entertaining revelation of medieval community life.

The term 'court' in the medieval context, is wider than a tribunal of adjudication.[10] The court of the manor was a microcosm of the kingdom, and a little commonwealth in itself, and, like the Curia Regis of the Norman kings and their successors, executed functions which can be analysed as legislative, administrative and judicial. Like courts of the common law, which were ultimately to supersede them, the manorial courts made and developed customary law and played an important role in land transfers as well as providing for the settlement of disputes and the regulation of conduct. The evidence of the manorial rolls and court books, the court keepers' guides and the many studies of manorial jurisdiction, especially the work of Professor Beckerman[11] and Professors Poos and Bonfield,[12] demonstrate that, in hearing cases, the manorial courts were making and applying justice according to precedent, in the form of manorial custom, and adjudicating in disputes according to law. They therefore had that internal rationality which Joseph Jaconelli notes as the first requirement of a genuine trial in relation to substantive and to procedural rules.

The classic analysis of the manorial courts divides them into those which were essentially seignorial, based in the feudal relationship, and those which exercised franchisal jurisdiction whose basis lay in the delegation of royal power.[13] In the case of the seignorial courts, namely the court of the honour, the court baron and the court customary, the lord had the duty to provide a court for his vassals and the right to demand their attendance. The honour court, often called the *curia ducis* (or occasionally the *curia militum*), was a gathering of the lord's most important and powerful tenants, principally those who held by knight service, and its jurisdiction extended over a number of his manors. Although the honour was the 'head' of all the lord's manors, the honour court was the first to decline in importance as a judicial body,[14] especially when legislation in 1259 and 1267 prevented its development as a manorial court of appeal, by providing that pleas of false judgment were to be dealt with only by royal judges.

The court baron was the lord's court for a single manor for his free tenants. In addition to declaring and sometimes creating the law of the manor, it was also concerned with the interpretation and enforcement of feudal services owed to the lord, as well as with disputes between free tenants, especially over title to freehold land, at least until the late twelfth century. At that point these courts began to feel the weight of the competition of new procedures and remedies afforded to free tenants by the growth of the king's justice.

The court customary, often known as the halmote or halimote, was the court for the lord's unfree tenants, presided over by the lord's steward or his deputy, or, more commonly, by the bailiff. This court exercised 'domanial' jurisdiction, enforcing the duties of villein tenants to perform their feudal services, declaring and applying the custom of the manor in relation to the proper cultivation of the manorial land, and in particular to the rights of unfree tenants over their land, including the legal recognition of land transfers. In addition the halmote punished breaches of manorial custom, including anti-social behaviour and minor moral offences. It also dealt with civil litigation subject to the forty-shilling limit[15] imposed by the Statute of Gloucester of 1278, including pleas of trespass, debt and slander.

This categorisation of the seignorial courts into honour courts, court baron and court customary (or halmote), however, was, to a great extent, an *ex post facto* rationalisation, made in retrospect by commentators in the fifteenth and sixteenth centuries. In reality, the distinctions between the courts were far from clear cut and although in later theory the court baron was solely for free tenants and the court customary (or halmote) for unfree, the distinction was often unclear in medieval practice.

The lord's franchise jurisdiction was different in kind from his seigniorial jurisdiction over his tenants, since his entitlement to hold such a court did not belong to him by right but had to be vested in him or his ancestors by the monarch,[16] delegating some of the Crown's prerogative jurisdiction over what would now be categorised as minor criminal offences and thus permitting the lord to exercise such jurisdiction free of intervention from the king or his officers. The usual franchise jurisdiction was equivalent to that of the sheriff in the tourn – the twice-yearly session of the hundred. The common name given to hundred courts is the leet (*leta*) and sometimes *magna leta*. However, it is also often described in the rolls as *visus francpledgi/francipledgii* (view of frankpledge), since one of the first duties of these courts was originally to ensure that every male over the age of twelve was in frankpledge – i.e. a member of a tithing. The leet met twice a year and was particularly concerned with day-to-day matters relating to law and order in the manorial community and with minor crimes, especially blood letting, and breaches of the assizes of bread and beer. The leet's jurisdiction over crime did not extend to the most serious felonies, unless the franchise gave to the lord extended rights such as the rights of 'infangthief', 'outfangthief' and gallows, entitling him to hang thieves and other malefactors caught red-handed on the manor or outside it – rights which, by the middle of the fourteenth century, were reserved to the royal justices.[17] Although trial procedure differed in some respects between leet jurisdiction and seignorial jurisdiction, it is not always easy to distinguish between them, especially when the courts were dealing with conduct which was punishable both as a manorial transgression and as a leet offence.[18] Moreover, the manorial rolls reveal a constant overlap between the proceedings of the halmote and those of the court leet, both of which were often conducted at the same session. The proceedings of the two courts often appear on the same court roll.[19]

It was the procedural advantages of the king's justice which attracted free tenants and disputes over freehold land away from the lord's court to the king's court, particularly through the development of the writ. After Henry II's assertion of the principle that 'no man need answer for his freehold land without the king's writ',[20] it became necessary for the claimant in a dispute over freehold land to obtain a writ of right patent before he could compel his opponent to answer in the lord's court. Even where such a case was commenced in the lord's court, it could be removed at the parties' behest to the county court by the process of *tolt*, whence it could be removed for a hearing by the king or his justices by obtaining a writ of *pone* from the Exchequer. The introduction by Henry II of the writ of Grand Assize, available to defendants to a writ of right patent, further weakened the jurisdiction of the seignorial court over freehold land disputes, since few defendants would prefer the lottery of trial by battle in the lord's court to the rational procedure of an inquest of knights of the shire held before the royal justices. Further, the issue of *praecipe* writs by the Exchequer, even where the case was strictly for the lord's court, encouraged litigants to seek the king's rather than the lord's justice in a dispute over freehold land. The stricture in Magna Carta, to the effect that the writ *praecipe* should not issue so as to deprive a man of his court,[21] had only a minimal effect, since by the early thirteenth century the possessory assizes gave freeholders a quick and effective way of testing rights to seisin, enforced by the power of the king, through the sheriff, and tried before the royal justices by an 'inquest jury' of neighbours. These trial procedures, offered by the king's courts, were undoubtedly popular. For free tenants, whose tenure might range from the grander kind of military service – such as the provision of armour or fighting men – to the provision of a minor service such as two capons, the attraction of the king's justice to decide disputes over land was considerable. By the reign of Edward I, the remedies available from the king's courts, further strengthened by the writs of entry, had made the lord's court less and less attractive to these litigants. When the Statute of Malborough in 1267 removed the general duty of free men to attend court under pain of fine, it further undermined the jurisdiction of the manorial court, at least in relation to freehold land. Also, the monetary value to the lord of holding a court for free tenants became ever less and it seems likely that – in addition to better procedures – freeholders' increasing recourse to the king's justice can be at least partly attributed to a belief that royal justice would be more impartial and more effective than that of the manor.

The manorial court rolls show a decrease in activity of the manorial courts, both halmotes and courts baron, in the fourteenth and fifteenth centuries. But the decline of manorial jurisdiction should not be exaggerated. Numerous meetings of the court baron and of the halmote, were still being recorded in the manorial rolls and court books of the fourteenth and fifteenth centuries. The duty of the villeins to attend the manorial court continued and the manor remained the usual forum for the settlement of their disputes.[22] Further, and most importantly, until the courts of common law began to recognise and enforce title to land 'by copy of the court roll', title to land and transfers of land held by unfree tenure were dealt with solely by the court of the manor.

In the late medieval period many free tenants, too, were still being bidden to attend the manorial court.[23] This might be because, although free, they held unfree (villein) land or because they owed suit by custom of the manor or by the terms of their tenancy.[24] Even in the fourteenth century knights might still be obliged to attend the court as, for example, Robert de Nevill, knight, who in 1348 was amerced in the Wakefield manorial court for non-attendance.[25] Free tenants might also choose to avail themselves of manorial justice in minor matters, for the convenience of quick and cheap litigation. In addition, social change weakened the strict hierarchy of the countryside and manor which was affected drastically both by great cataclysms, such as the Black Death,[26] and by steady demographic, social and economic changes in town and countryside. By the fifteenth century there is little evidence in the court rolls as to which parties are free and which unfree, and theoretical procedural rules as to status no longer seemed important.[27] The main importance of the manorial courts in relation to manorial land faded after the common law courts finally recognised copyhold title[28] but the seignorial courts survived in many manors – albeit in a severely weakened form – after the fifteenth century. The leet jurisdiction was the sturdiest of all the manorial jurisdictions to survive and was still active in many manors well into the nineteenth century, though much of its work was taken over by the petty sessions of the justices of the peace.

I Trial procedure in manorial courts

This chapter is concerned specifically with the procedure of the medieval manorial courts. It is characteristic of medieval English law that the courts did not recognise a strict separation between substantive and procedural law, and that substantive law was neither separate from nor more important than procedure. In the manorial, as in the common law courts, proper procedure was not merely an adjunct to a just hearing but, as in the American doctrine of due process, was integral to it. Whether the material under examination consists of the 'dull and monotonous material' which Maitland warned was necessary for a proper understanding of the manorial courts, or the more individual cases of 'curiosities' collected by Poos and Bonfield, the procedure of the courts, as reproduced in the court rolls and court books, is worthy of study in itself. For 'any attempt to understand law in the manor court must logically include consideration of how business was brought to the tribunal, how cases proceeded once they came before the court, and by what mode of proof they were resolved'.[29]

The court baron and the halmote were originally held every three weeks, though their sittings became increasingly irregular during the fourteenth century and by the fifteenth were often held only twice yearly, at the same time as the court leet. Manorial procedure followed certain well-established forms and a typical case in the court baron or the halmote was governed in accordance with manorial law and custom, which usually prescribed the following stages.

Summons
The proceedings were commenced by summons, often announced in church on Sunday or nailed to the church door, telling the tenants and suitors of the court of the date and time of the sitting. Reasonable notice had to be given,[30] which commonly was three days' or might be as little as one day's notice.

Attendance and essoins
Since suit of court was a duty, albeit after 1267 an obligation which could generally be enforced only on unfree tenants,[31] non-attendance was a breach of feudal duty for which tenants could be amerced.[32] Virtually every court session began with amercements for non-attendance and, if the recalcitrant person failed to attend on a further occasion without excuse, the steward would order distraint or attachment of their person or their chattels. A regular aspect of the procedure of these courts was the use of 'pledging' where X's

friend or relation attended the court and acted as surety for his future attendance. The social pressures of the small community which was the manor were sufficient to ensure the court attendance of a party to litigation or even a party accused of a crime by the court's accepting another person as 'pledge'. Every manorial court roll contains a regular list of 'pledges' who were often recorded on the roll elsewhere as jurors, as affeerors or even as parties before the court in a different case. In many manors free tenants were allowed to appoint attorneys to represent them.

The custom of the manor, like the common law, allowed a party to put in a plea, known as an 'essoin', to excuse non-attendance or delay, and, if the essoin was acceptable to the court, the party concerned was excused, usually subject to a pledge that the absentee would appear at a later court to warrant or confirm that his essoin was genuine. Certain standard essoins were recognised as excusing attendance at court. In addition to the common essoin (*de malo veniendi*) which applied when the party summoned could not attend because of illness or infirmity, there were bed sickness (*de malo lecti*), serving in the king's wars (*de servitio Regis*), absence over the seas (*de ultra mare*), and absence on pilgrimage or at the Crusades (*in Terram Sanctam*), but the courts of the manor may have accepted lesser excuses. Essoins were always available to free tenants in the manor and by the fourteenth century unfree tenants could also essoin. Increasingly essoins were made by friends or relatives on behalf of absent suitors and were entered at the beginning of the roll, together with the list of amercements for non-attendance.

Election of the jury

The next stage recorded in the court rolls was the swearing-in of the suitors, pledges or jury.[33] At first, in the honour court and the court baron, the 'homage', consisting of all the suitors of the court, acted as presenters and finders of fact; later, juries were chosen from the personnel present in the court. The rolls do not explain how they were elected or on what criteria, but they were often elected from the 'chief pledges', especially in the court leet.

The functions of the jury in manorial trials were to declare – and even on occasions to create – manorial custom, to present parties to the court baron, the halmote and the leet, and sometimes to decide issues of fact before the court. This 'jury of inquest' was a procedural institution borrowed from the king's courts, and adopted with enthusiasm by the manorial courts. Here the number of jurors varied and was not limited to twelve but might be a larger or smaller number, on occasion consisting of as many as twenty-four, or even forty-eight, and as few as six.[34] This use of the jury or inquest proved popular – a popularity demonstrated by the willingness of manorial litigants, whether 'plaintiffs' or 'defendants', to pay the lord or his representative for the privilege of having a jury to decide a case. Payment would usually be a modest sum of money but occasionally might be in kind. Thus it was reported in 1249 that

Adam Moses gives half a sextary of wine to have an inquest as to whether Henry Ayulf accused him of the crime of larceny and used opprobrious and contumelious words of him. [35]

The alleged rule that there could not be a manorial jury without the presence of at least two free tenants was evidently no longer observed by the fourteenth century and manorial juries were frequently composed entirely of villeins. Indeed there were cases in several manors where free men chosen to serve on a jury objected to doing so on the grounds that they were free. [36] Generally, however, free and unfree men served as jurors together and the rolls do not seem to record that free tenants before the court objected to being tried by villeins, although in theory such an objection could be made by a free man on the ground that he should only be tried by his peers (*per paros suos*).

The duty of serving as a juror must have been onerous on occasions, since jurors could be amerced for failing to perform their duty properly (which might mean failing to present or wrongly doing so), or even for a lesser fault, as in Sandal in 1348, when the jury were amerced for putting their verdict 'in the mouth of one insufficiently knowledgeable'. They could also be punished by attaint[37] for wrongful verdicts. It is perhaps not surprising that in the manor court of Wakefield in 1316 John Swerd gave 6*d* for leave to retire from the inquest jury. [38]

It is received wisdom that the jury was a salutary counterbalance to the power of the steward in the manorial courts and that the power of the jury decreased in the fourteenth century, as the steward became more powerful, and the use of special juries, summoned to decide a question of the lord's interests, increased. However the jury was still a living and important part of manorial justice in the fourteenth and fifteenth centuries, when the rolls continue to report juries exerting their influence over the steward and instances of parties paying for an inquest to decide their case, especially in disputes involving land. [39]

In the court leet, the jury might consist of the same individuals as the halmote jury, composed of free and unfree men. Unlike the jury in the court baron and halmote, however, since the leet was exercising 'criminal' jurisdiction under powers delegated by the king, free men could be compelled to serve at the twice-yearly session of that court. The leet jury was principally a jury of presentment and by the fourteenth century such presentments were non-traversable, i.e. not open to challenge by the persons presented. This suggests that the charges, once made, were regarded as proved and therefore that 'trials' in the leet hardly fulfilled the requirements of a judicial process. [40] The rolls do not reveal whether the person charged had any opportunity to address the court or raise a defence, but even if he had no such opportunity, leet procedure was not noticeably more oppressive than the alternatives of the tourn and, from the fourteenth century, the courts of the justices of the peace.

Presentment

Presentment was at the heart of the manorial system of justice and in the sense that it initiated a case it was the equivalent of the statement of claim or writ. In the classic model of the court baron,[41] the homage (and later the jury) presented issues for the court's consideration. They also presented individuals for breaches of feudal services, though by the fourteenth century, at least in relation to free tenants, such services had usually been commuted to money payments and the court was in effect simply enforcing payments to the lord. In the halmote, tenants were presented for failing to fulfil the work which they owed on the manor as villeins and for failing to pay feudal payments or penalties such as merchet,[42] leyerwite,[43] chevage[44] or multure.[45] They were also presented for failing in their duties relating to the proper care of the manorial land, such as the neglect of weeds or ditches, or for allowing beasts to stray on to a neighbour's strip of land, or to eat or damage crops. In addition they might be presented for minor offences such as assault or slander, or for anti-social conduct such as being a 'common night walker', 'an alehouse haunter' or 'a common player at cards and tables in alehouses', or for immorality where the jurisdiction of the manor overlapped with that of church courts.

In the court leet the jury presented those accused of minor offences, especially breaches of the assizes of bread and beer and offences related to public order, such as assaults, gossiping, night prowling or leaving foul rubbish in the street. Another regular cause of presentment was an offence regarding the hue and cry – either the raising of it unnecessarily or the failure to raise it when required. As in the halmote, the presentments were made by a jury, elected by the court at the beginning of its session. This sworn body of respected members of the manor was extremely powerful in the leet, especially in the late fourteenth and in the fifteenth centuries when presentments were non-traversable.

Litigation

The common law courts were growing throughout the fourteenth and fifteenth centuries, expanding their jurisdiction over civil litigation through the development of the forms of action, but they did not provide quick, simple and accessible justice in minor local disputes. With the decline of the eyre by the fourteenth century, the ability of poor local residents to obtain justice without formality or expense declined, since they would usually lack the means to buy a writ or to cope with the technicalities of the common law, with all its complexities, without legal representation. A case in the manorial court could be commenced by a simple oral plaint or plea, whereas at common law the complainant would need to obtain the correct writ in accordance with the developing knowledge of the forms of action. The immediate and effective course for a manorial resident to recover small debts or to recover damages from a neighbour who had assaulted or slandered him was therefore to take his complaint to the three-weekly court baron or halmote, where the matter would be dealt with speedily and effectively. Although litigation in the manorial courts decreased in the later Middle Ages, it was still an important part of their work, at least until the sixteenth century; the rolls reveal many cases of minor litigation, especially in disputes over land, but also many cases of debt, trespass and slander,[46] subject to the forty-shilling limit, which was a substantial sum for an agricultural worker or peasant.[47]

Land law

The most long-lasting and significant function of the manorial courts was, perhaps, their role in dealing with land held by unfree tenure. It was a basic tenet of the common law that freehold land was the concern of the common law courts alone and that the whole paraphernalia of land actions, including the rules relating to inheritance and transfer of freehold land, were unavailable to tenants of unfree land, which was governed simply by the law and custom of the manor. Transfer of unfree land was untrammelled by the rigid formalities of the common law and was achieved in the manorial court (usually on payment of a 'fine')[48] by a simple surrender of the land into the lord's hands and a re-grant by the court on his behalf; this 'tenure by the will of the lord according to the custom of the manor' was duly entered on the court roll. By the fourteenth century a flourishing market in peasant land had developed, enhanced by the changing social and economic conditions of many peasants on the manor, whether or not technically unfree. In addition to conveyancing the manorial courts decided complex issues of title and inheritance and entry on the court rolls became proof of title. The common law did not accept title registered in this way as binding until the fifteenth century, but once that momentous step had been taken, tenure by copy of the court roll ('copyhold')[49] became a standard form of landholding in English law.

Proof

A basic issue in any trial is how the issue is to be decided. Whether the procedure is inquisitorial or adversarial, ultimately the procedural rules of a tribunal will dictate who makes the decision and by what method. Proof was all-important in medieval law courts, and much of the court's work was concerned with deciding in what ways the parties should be allowed or required to prove their case. By the twelfth century, the old Saxon trial by ordeal was no longer used and the Norman innovation of trial by battle had faded away from disputes over freehold land, after the introduction by Henry II of the Grand Assize as an alternative to battle. Trial by combat survived in the old procedure of appeal of felony, but this too had fallen into disuse after the reign of Henry II. Of the ancient methods of proof which still survived by the fourteenth century, compurgation remained as part of the machinery of the manorial courts and, as late as the fifteenth century, the rolls often reveal a party being allowed or required to 'make his law' (*fecit legem*) or to 'go to the law six (or twelve) handed',[50] but the records show that, although compurgation was still being used in the fifteenth-century manor, it had become less popular and the jury more popular as a mode of proof, particularly in issues relating to land.[51] The reasons for this are not revealed in the rolls but perhaps respect for the oath declined or the community believed that a shady character might logically be supposed to have a number of unscrupulous and unreliable friends. So in a small community such as the manor, knowledge and local prejudice would make compurgation unsatisfactory in the case of a person of poor reputation. There is also clear evidence of xenophobia in that strangers or 'foreigners', being any persons from outside the manor, were regarded with suspicion and might be unable to find local oath helpers. It seems as if the defendants could usually choose the mode of trial and that if they were unable to do so, the court would decide for them.[52] Whatever the reasons, the trial jury is frequently mentioned in the court rolls and the fact that parties before the court sought this privilege and were prepared to pay for it demonstrates its popularity as a superior mode of proof.

The use of written records or other written evidence became widespread during the fourteenth century and a typical example from the Croxley Court Book suggests a surprisingly high degree of literacy and sophistication in the twelve jurors who had to decide whether a deed of feoffment, produced by a plaintiff to prove his claim to land, was genuine.[53] The court rolls themselves became an important source of reference for the court of the manor in its later deliberations.[54]

Verdicts and sanctions

A trial on completion results in a verdict and afterwards a definitive and binding judgment. Where the manorial court gave judgment against the person presented, he or she was said to be 'in mercy' (*in misericordia*) and therefore subject to the court's sanction, usually an amercement, a monetary penalty, usually 6*d*, 12*d*, multiples of a shilling, 18*d* or often 6*s*–8*d* (1 mark). Amercements were imposed by both the halmote and the leet, but the court frequently reduced the amount or pardoned the offender on the equitable ground that he or she was poor,[55] and sometimes on other grounds such as youth or sickness. Amercements were levied for multifarious causes – for allowing beasts to stray, for failing to clear ditches, for fighting, for receiving strangers and for marrying without permission or without paying merchet. Both men and women were amerced for adultery but perhaps the most startling penalty for a modern commentator was the leyerwite – a fine levied on an unmarried woman who had had sexual relations, consensual or not, with a man. This was principally imposed on the woman but occasionally imposed also on her father. Such moral offences were also within the purview of the ecclesiastical courts.

In addition to amercements, a sanction, akin to an injunction, was an order by the court to a tenant to perform his feudal duties, e.g. to clear a ditch, to cut a hedge, to keep his pigs in, to remove weeds or to cease to co-habit with a certain woman or to harbour a 'stranger'. In cases of civil litigation, such as assault, debt or slander, the court might order payment to be made by the defendant to the plaintiff or order what was in effect specific performance, as in the case in the Wakefield manor court in 1350 when the defendant was ordered to complete the sale of a horse.[56]

In the leet, amercements were levied for anti-social behaviour, for nuisances, especially those which might be regarded as affecting community health, such as 'dumping' of carcasses or rubbish, and especially for failing to be in frankpledge and for breaking the assizes of bread and ale. The leet's punishments were often harsh, typically including stocks, pillory, tumbrel (exposure to ridicule and shame by being made to ride round in a dung cart), and, on some manors, imprisonment, but it could not take life nor could it mutilate unless the lord's grant included infangthief, outfangthief and gallows.[57] By the fourteenth century its powers had been limited by legislation, removing to the royal justices cases of burglary, robbery, theft, counterfeiting, homicide and arson. However, the leet survived long after its counterpart in the country – the sheriff's tourn – had given way to the justices of the peace as a court of lesser criminal jurisdiction. As late as the nineteenth century, courts leet were still dealing with minor offences of public order, especially where the manorial court survived to become the court of one of the towns which developed within a manor.[58]

Contempt of court

The authority of the court, symbolic of the power of the lord, was enforced by court officials, especially the steward, whose powers to punish disrespect or disobedience were extensive. The most serious contempt of court was committed by a tenant who sued in another court than that of his or her lord[59] – an easy offence to commit when there were overlapping jurisdictions, not only between different adjoining manors but also between different judicial systems. Medieval man and woman lived in a society of interlocking and co-existent legal systems,[60] each of which jealously guarded its rights. A person who had suffered a trespass might bring his case before the local court, his manorial court or, with a writ of trespass, before the common law courts, but woe betide him if he sued in a court of another lord and another manor. Conflicts might also arise where the manor court and the church court both claimed jurisdiction – as, for example, in cases of adultery or breach of faith where a judgment by the church court might result in the villein, and therefore his lord, being deprived of chattels.

In addition to jurisdictional challenges, the steward had extensive power to punish conduct regarded as insulting, disrespectful or threatening to the order of the court proceedings, e.g. by fines imposed on tenants for cursing the jury or making a noise in court. In the fourteenth and fifteenth centuries the rolls reveal a new spirit of rebelliousness and unwillingness to accept the court's authority. Thus in Wakefield manor court in 1348 the tenants from Warley were amerced 12*d* for tumult in court and at the same session the sub-bailiff was in mercy because he 'took counsel with men murmuring in court'.[61] In a fifteenth-century case, Richard Smyth and his sons were amerced £100 – a mighty penalty – for addressing opprobrious words to the steward and assaulting him.[62] In 1350–52, in a Wakefield manor court, seventy-two people failed to come to court or to essoin when summoned and even the reeve (always called the grave in Wakefield) was absent, and in many English manors the court increasingly was unable to enforce attendance or payment of rents.

Conciliation and settlement

The rolls reveal plentiful examples of manorial courts providing opportunities for alternative means of settling disputes, even where proceedings had started. Where there was litigation between A and B, the court often appointed a 'love day' at a date in the near future when the parties would be able to settle their differences and such settlement, similar to the modern practice of conciliation, frequently achieved a compromise. Sometimes, also, informal arbitration outside the court achieved an accommodation between the parties.[63] The desire of the courts to encourage such arrangements where possible has a curiously modern flavour, and reveals that the justice of the manor was more flexible than the common law.

II The personnel of the manorial court

A striking feature of the courts and of their trials was the high level of community participation – at least of the respectable members of the community. They sometimes appear in the rolls as pledges, sometimes as jurors (whether declaring custom, presenting, or deciding between two parties) and sometimes as affeerors.[64] A pledge or juror at a halmote might be presented at the next court for a manorial offence or for failing to pay a debt; a juror at the leet might be presented at another session, perhaps for breaches of the assizes of bread and ale or for a nuisance. As early as the fourteenth century, when the social distinctions between free and unfree tenants became blurred, the manorial court was attended by both villeins and free tenants together.[65] Both were subject to the same procedures and penalties and by the fifteenth century it is no longer evident from the rolls which tenants were free and which unfree. As the concept of villeinage died away gradually, without formal enactment, the court ceased to be much concerned with villeins leaving the manor, though chevage remained payable. Free and unfree tenants alike were suitors to the court, sat on juries, acted as pledges and were subject to the same trial procedures. There was still deep suspicion of 'foreigners' and 'strangers', these being persons from outside the manor, though the fourteenth and fifteenth-century rolls reveal a new kind of outsider who, although not originally from the manor, became an influential local figure in the court and in the community.[66]

The position of women before the manorial court was paradoxical. Women were often litigants or claimants before the courts, often seeking to assert their property rights to unfree land. They brought pleas of trespass and debt and were sued in their turn for the same kind of wrongs. They could not serve on juries but they brought complaints against other women and against men. A wife's consent was necessary before her husband could surrender their estate in the manorial court.[67] Yet although in some ways they were equal before the court, women were subject to particular feudal dues and disadvantages; they were liable to pay merchet if they wished to marry and amerced if they married without the necessary licence. Perhaps most startling to a modern mind is the liability of a woman who had been raped or seduced to pay leyerwite and the fact that a woman could lose her land if she was found to have committed adultery or fornication.[68]

The steward

The steward (*dapifer*, later *senescallus*) was the representative of the lord and exercised functions on his behalf. Although initially a modest appointment, the office of steward was, as early as the fourteenth century, held by important figures in local and even in national society, such as Adam de Stratton in Wiltshire, and Sir Robert Shireburn, later an M.P., in the honour court of Clitheroe, Lancashire. By the fourteenth century the steward was usually a lawyer, often using a manorial appointment as a stepping stone to higher things in the law.[69]

The estate steward was a powerful and prestigious figure who travelled round the estate, holding courts in each manor, assisted by his deputy and by the bailiff. As free tenants gradually became less significant in the manor court, the steward increasingly replaced the suitors in making decisions and in the fourteenth century he became the presiding judge in the court, though the rolls reveal that the suitors and jurors were far from being mere docile ciphers as has sometimes been suggested. Even though he was in authority and subject to few controls in the exercise of his office, other than financial accountability, he was not able to act with impunity and records of manorial hearings reveal examples of stewards being censured for oppression and injustice.[70]

The bailiff

The bailiff (*ballivus, serviens*) was a more lowly figure who bore the brunt of executing the orders of the court. He often presided in the halmote or the court baron, though not usually in the leet, in place of the steward. He had the task of summoning the suitors to the court, of taking the essoins and swearing in the jurors, and also of executing the orders of the court by distraining persons or property and collecting amercements. Unlike the steward, the bailiff was not usually a person of rank in the community though, unlike the reeve and the hayward, he was not a villein and was not obliged, as they were, to accept election by the court. He was usually paid.

The reeve and the hayward

The reeve (*prepositus*) or grave, was elected by the manorial court once a year, from the unfree tenants of the lord, and his duties were many. In return for minor favours, such as being permitted to eat at the lord's table at harvest time, he was responsible for the organisation of the manor and its agriculture. His office and that of his colleague, the hayward, were onerous and the retribution for inefficiency harsh. So in *Modus tenendi curias*,[71] Robert the reeve is sentenced to forfeit his goods and to be put in the stocks because he is always 'haunting fairs and taverns'. The office of reeve was so unwelcome that there are examples in many manorial courts of tenants paying amounts ranging from 1s to 20s to be relieved of it.[72]

Affeerors

These officials were elected annually by the court to decide the amounts to be paid to the court by way of amercements, required by Magna Carta to be assessed 'by the oaths of the honest men of the neighbourhood'.[73] Affeerors were frequently unfree tenants, but this does not seem to have prevented them from deciding amercements for free tenants, nor does there appear to be evidence of protest or appeal against the amounts fixed, a list of which appears in the margin of each court roll.

III Publicity – openness

The notion of openness is deeply ingrained in our ordinary notions of trial, and secret trials are regarded with suspicion in a free society, unless there is an overriding reason for secrecy.[74] Trials in the manorial courts fulfilled the condition of openness as they were held in the heart of the manor, in a place prescribed by manorial custom. Sometimes it was the somewhat romantic location of a tree in the manor,[75] but more usually the court would be held in the great hall of the manor house or sometimes in church.[76] Suit of court was not only a duty but also a right; hence in their essence these courts were open to all the lord's tenants. Long after the attendance of free tenants could no longer be compelled, villeins still owed suit of court and were amerced for failing to attend. Free tenants also continued to appear in the manorial court, either as tenants of unfree land or in relation to personal disputes with other tenants, including villeins, as the distinctions of status diminished. The proceedings of the manorial court continued to remain open to the inhabitants of the manor, though the fifteenth century saw the decline of manorial justice – a decline evidenced by the fact that courts ceased to be held at regular three-weekly intervals and the rolls show an increasingly long list of non-attenders, including even court officials such as the reeve.

IV Impartiality – independence and freedom from bias

The manorial court was the only realistic forum of justice for the majority of dwellers on the manor and, viewed with the eyes of the twenty-first century, that justice may seem to have been rough and its impartiality suspect. The court was, after all, the lord's court; the presiding officer, the steward, was the lord's representative and the other officials of the court were the lord's tenants and therefore beholden to him. It is tempting to see the courts of the manor as the essence of feudal oppression; how could tenants, and particularly villeins, obtain even-handed justice? Yet it is clear from the manorial records that the court and its proceedings were subject to the law and custom of the manor. The manor was not a despotism. Just as the realm was governed by the king according to law and to feudal principles, the manor was regulated by manorial law. The suitors, pledges and jury of the manor courts were fellow tenants, many of them important members of the community, and even in his most powerful period the steward could not override the judgments of the court completely. On occasion the court rose up against an unjust official and, in the case of an elected office, replaced him.[77]

Of course it would be naïve and unrealistic to assert that there was no bias, injustice or corruption; experience of human nature makes it inevitable that there would be oppression in many manors by the lord's representatives – indeed there is evidence of such conduct and of the robust response of some manorial communities. There must have been prejudice and unfairness in the judgments of the court on occasions. The rolls simply state the presentments and by the fifteenth century these were non-traversable. Further, a person of ill repute, or someone regarded as an 'outsider' or 'foreigner' probably stood little chance of a fair trial, being generally viewed with suspicion and even with hostility. However, the ideal of justice remained in the procedures of the court; it is clear from the court keeper's manuals that a party could complain if he showed that he would be prejudiced because of the jury's bias against him.[78]

V The late Middle Ages – unrest and decline

Despite the ravages of the Black Death, the manorial courts continued their sessions and the rolls reveal little of the drama and tragedy of 'the great dying', though deaths are frequently reported in the rolls when the court meets. There was, however, an increase in villeins absconding from the manor, whether because of plague or an ability to work on other manors for payment, or general social unrest. During the fourteenth century there were many outbreaks of resentment among tenants, especially villein tenants, against the lord's courts. In the abbey of Vale Royal in 1329 and 1336 the abbot was faced with two minor peasants' revolts which were typical of a wave of disturbances on many manors, such as the struggles on the manor of Thornbury, Essex in 1339.[79] The manorial rolls reveal a new spirit of defiance and of resistance to the power of the steward and his officers in a society 'seething with discontent'.[80] Whether this resentment was a symptom of a desire for personal freedom,[81] of anti-government feeling or merely of discontent with feudal burdens which were at their most onerous in the fourteenth century, resistance to the manorial court, and to manorial services, was widespread. It is not surprising that in the Peasants' Revolt in 1381 manorial court rolls were burned by the rebels as a sign of defiance.[82]

The manorial court rolls of the fifteenth century, too, reveal increasing examples of disorder and of the inability of stewards to control the proceedings or enforce the court's will. In the revolt of 1450, Jack Cade famously proposed to kill all the lawyers – a sentiment which probably also encompassed the manorial stewards of his day. The rolls demonstrate incidences of increased lawlessness – a phenomenon which may, perhaps, be linked with the increase of violence associated with fifteenth-century life, though in many manors court business seems to have continued as usual throughout the upheavals broadly associated with the Wars of the Roses. There were in the manorial courts, as in society generally, upheavals caused by disorder and quarrels between magnates and others, and manorial justice was sometimes a casualty of these power struggles. The manorial court was not only a forum for the administration of justice and the regulation of manorial society, it was also a powerful affirmation and symbol of the community of the manor and an assertion of the property rights and influence of the lord. Thus, in the Paston letters, the wife of John Paston describes her determination to hold a manorial court to assert her family's rights in the face of armed opposition from her husband's enemies.[83]

VI Language and meaning

The late medieval court rolls provide little information about the parties involved in proceedings other than their names, their occupations and the matter which brought them before the court, but there are occasionally vivid pictures of medieval manorial society. The manor is evidently a litigious society, quarrelsome, fiercely protective of land, family and custom, hierarchical, misogynistic and xenophobic. In the fourteenth and fifteenth centuries there is a new resentment of the burdens of villeinage and perhaps a new political will to express that resentment. As Mary Laven warns in her chapter, the formal language reported should not too readily be taken at face value[84] and the historian must be cautious in interpreting the meaning of the language of court rolls. For example, the regular imposition of fines for breaches of the assizes of bread and beer, despite its penal appearance, may well have been a form of licensing; brewing was an important local service (mainly performed by women) and the repeated imposition of modest fines on the same individuals suggests a tolerance of the activity rather than a desire to outlaw it. Similarly merchet may have become more a marriage licence fee than a penalty. The many cases of leyerwite may demonstrate a lawless, brutal and misogynistic society – indeed some of the cases must have involved rape in the true sense of violation – but sometimes the stories behind the case may really tell of a couple defying the wishes of the lord or of their families or of a passionate local consensual relationship. Again, the details of trespass, especially assaults and batteries, may not be literal. As in common law cases of trespass, we should be wary of deducing that the allegations of damage are literally true.[85] A look at one membrane of the fifteenth-century Dunham Massey court rolls startles the reader with details of the fierce attacks committed by several neighbours on one another. But are these true or are they conventional allegations cloaking family rivalries or property disputes?[86]

Long after the lords of the manor and their more prosperous tenants had turned to the common law courts to deal with their own litigation, the manorial courts continued to provide a cockpit for the settlement of local issues and an expression of local community values. For centuries they were the most important judicial and regulatory tribunals in the lives of the ordinary people of England, and after their decline there was little cheap, accessible justice in civil claims until the advent of the county courts in 1846, or perhaps even until the introduction of small claims procedure in the late twentieth century.

Notes

1 The development of the literature of manorial court history is well encapsulated in the editors' introduction, 'The historiography of the manor court rolls', in Z. Razi and R. Smith (eds), *Medieval Society and the Manor Court* (Oxford, 1996), pp. 1–35.
2 F. W. Maitland (ed.), *Select Pleas in Manorial and other Seignorial Courts*, Selden Society, 2, 1889.
3 *Ibid.*, p. xii.
4 J. S. Beckerman, 'Customary Law in English Manorial Courts in the Thirteenth and Fourteenth Centuries', Ph.D. thesis, University of London, 1972; J. S. Beckerman, 'Procedural innovation and institutional change in medieval English manorial courts', *Law and History Review*, 10 (1992), 197–252.
5 L. R. Poos and L. Bonfield (eds), *Select Cases in Manorial Courts, 1250–1550*, Selden Society, 114, 1998.
6 Maitland (ed.), *Select Pleas*; W. O. Ault, *Private Jurisdiction in England* (New Haven, Connecticut, 1923).
7 P. D. A. Harvey in his Introduction to *Manorial Records of Cuxham, Oxfordshire, circa 1200–1359* (London, 1976), pp. 12–57, gives a comprehensive survey of the compilation of manorial accounts, including court proceeds.

8 See P. D. A. Harvey, *Manorial Records* (London, 1984).

9 F. W. Maitland and W. P. Baildon (eds), *The Court Baron [being precedents for use in seignorial and other local courts] together with Select Pleas from the Bishop of Ely's Court of Littleport*, Selden Society, 4, 1890.

10 See J. H. Baker, 'The changing concept of a court', in his *The Legal Profession and the Common Law: Historical Essays* (London, 1986), pp. 153–69.

11 See n. 4 above.

12 Poos and Bonfield (eds), *Select Cases*.

13 Special considerations and privileges applied to those manors held by ancient demesne whose mesne lord was the monarch or his consort.

14 Though honour courts survived, on some estates (e.g. Broughton, Clitheroe).

15 Although the statute applied to trespass pleas in the communal courts, it was also applied in the manorial courts.

16 The *Quo Warranto* inquiry under Edward I and subsequent applications of the principle questioned the validity of individual lords' franchises and controlled the undue extension of private courts.

17 Though in some great estates the lord retained extensive jurisdiction.

18 Leet offences were sixty in number, manorial approximately forty, but there were overlaps between them, e.g. offences related to the hue and cry, and nuisance.

19 As in the fifteenth-century manor court rolls of Dunham Massey, Cheshire.

20 Probably not a new principle but one revived and re-asserted.

21 C. 34.

22 The whole question of the status of villeinage is complex and the fluidity of the notion of servility makes rigid categorisation impossible. See P. Hyams, 'What did Edwardian villagers understand by "law"?' in Razi and Smith (eds), *Medieval Society*, pp. 70–1.

23 Poos and Bonfield (eds), *Select Cases*, see especially the Introduction, pp. xv–cxcii.

24 In the thirteenth century a lord often stipulated that a free tenant should owe suit of court. Also lords sometimes made a special bargain with freeholders to come to 'afforce' the court for baronial business.

25 H. M. Jewell (ed.), *Court Rolls of the Manor of Wakefield 1348–50* (Leeds, 1981), pp. 20, 37.

26 Perhaps surprisingly, the manorial courts system seems to continue without a break during 1348–50, though many deaths are reported. Some rolls show an increase in villeins absconding from the manor. See Jewell (ed.) *Court Rolls*, Introduction, pp. xviii–xxi; A. E. Levett, *Studies in Manorial History* (Oxford, 1938), p. 248.

27 See below, pp. 93–4.

28 See A. W. B. Simpson, *A History of the Land Law* (Oxford, 1986), pp. 162–5.

29 Poos and Bonfield (eds), *Select Cases*, p. xxxv.

30 A 'reasonable summons' is referred to in the cartularies of Ramsey Abbey and Gloucester. Other manors required three days' notice but one day's notice was common. William Paston ordered that his tenants should be notified on Sunday about a court on the following Friday. See J. Gairdner (ed.) *The Paston Letters* (6 vols, London and Exeter, 1904), VI, p. 3, no. 938, 17 October 1478.

31 There were exceptions to this general rule, e.g. if the free tenant's duty of suit of court dated from before 1230 or was provided for in his charter.

32 An amercement was a money penalty imposed by the court.

33 See also M. Mulholland, 'The jury in English manorial courts', in J. W. Cairns and G. Mcleod (eds), *'The Dearest Birthright of the People of England.' The Jury in the History of the Common Law* (Oxford and Portland, Oregon, 2002), pp. 63–73.

34 Levett, *Studies*, p. 149.

35 Court rolls of the Abbey of Bec in Maitland, *Select Pleas*, p. 19.

36 E.g. the refusal by six men of Barnet to be sworn in as part of the inquisition, on the ground that they were free. See the Barnet Court Book, quoted by Levett in *Studies*, p. 146.

37 A procedure for trying a jury for 'false judgment' – in effect for perjury – before another, larger jury.

38 For the Sandal case see Jewell (ed.), *Court Rolls*, p. 4; for John Swerd's case, see J. Lister (ed.) *Court Rolls of the Manor of Wakefield (1315–17)*, Yorkshire Archaeological Society Record Series, 78, 1930, p. 72.

39 Poos and Bonfield, *Select Pleas*.

40 See *Colebrooke* v. *Elliott* 3 Burr.1859 [1766].

41 Maitland and Baildon (eds), *Court Baron*, *passim*.

42 An amount payable to the manorial lord by an unfree woman or her father for permission to marry.

43 Sometimes payable by the woman's father 'for inadequate guarding of his daughter ('*pro custodita sua mala*)'.

44 A payment due from a tenant for leaving the manor.

45 A toll for grinding corn at the lord's mill.

46 Damages were given for defamation and informal contracts enforced centuries before the common law. See J. P. Dawson, *A History of Lay Judges* (Cambridge, Massachusetts, 1960), p. 199.

47 C. Dyer, *Standards of Living in the Later Middle Ages* (Cambridge, 1986).

48 Here not a penalty but a monetary payment to the lord.

49 See Simpson, *History*, pp. 162–5.

50 I.e. to bring five (or eleven) 'oath helpers' with him to support his word. In some manors, villeins, women and lepers were disqualified from acting as oath helpers.

51 Juries were the usual mode of proof in the manor courts in disputes involving land. See Poos and Bonfield (eds), *Select Cases*, Introduction, p. lx.

52 Beckerman, 'Procedural innovation and institutional change', p. 214, n. 81.

53 Levett, *Studies*, p. 149.

54 Poos and Bonfield (eds), *Select Cases*, Introduction, p. lxvi.

55 E.g. Maitland, *Select Pleas*, pp. 42, 114; Jewell (ed.), *Court Rolls*, pp. 29, 109.

56 See M. Habberjam, M. O'Regan and B. Hale (eds), *Court Rolls of the Manor of Wakefield (1350–1352)* (Leeds, 1985), pp. 87–8.

57 A startling example of manorial power occurs in the court guide *Modus tenendi curias* ('The Manner of Holding Courts'), where the presenters decree that John Fox (a murderer) is to be beheaded. See Maitland and Baildon, *The Court Baron*, p. 99.

58 Such as Altrincham, Cheshire, which developed from the manor of Dunham Massey.

59 Jewell (ed.), *Court Rolls*, pp. 155–7.

60 See A. Musson, *Medieval Law in Context. The Growth of Legal Consciousness from Magna Carta to the Peasants' Revolt* (Manchester and New York, 2001), pp. 85–120, 217–27.

61 Jewell (ed.), *Court Rolls*, pp. 3–4.
62 C. Dyer, *Lords and Peasants in a Changing Society: The Estates of the Bishopric of Winchester* (Cambridge, 1980), p. 268.
63 See e.g. McIntosh, *Autonomy*, p. 198.
64 See *Affeerors*, below, p. 95.
65 In some manors a tenant could do suit by attorney.
66 Levett, *Studies*, pp. 191–2 (St Albans); Ault, *Private Jurisdiction*, pp. 315–18 (barony of Manchester).
67 Jewell (ed.), *Court Rolls*, p. 6.
68 Poos and Bonfield (eds), *Select Cases*, pp. 83, 97.
69 E.g. Robert Belknap , appointed steward of Battle Abbey in 1352, later a serjeant-at-law. See J. H. Baker, *The Common Law Tradition* (London, 2000), p. 268. Robert of Madingley (1304–10) and John of Cambridge (1328–35) were stewards who later became judges in the common law courts.
70 As in the Ramsey court. See Ault, *Private Jurisdiction*, p. 175.
71 'The manner of holding courts', in Maitland and Baildon (eds), *Court Baron*, p. 103.
72 E.g. Henry Fisher paid 6*s* 8*d* to be released from office as reeve, and John Fox and his son paid 18*d* and 2*s*, respectively, to be released from service as hayward for the Bishop of Ely's court at Littleport. See Maitland and Baildon (eds), *Court Baron*, p. 128.
73 C. 20.
74 See J. Jaconelli, Chapter 1, above.
75 As under the ash tree in the courts of the abbey of St Albans. See Levett, *Studies*, pp. 137–42.
76 A practice not approved of by the bishops. See H. S. Bennett, *The Pastons and their England: Studies in an Age of Transition* (Cambridge, 1990, reprint 1991), p. 208.
77 Ault, *Private jurisdiction*, p. 175.
78 As in Maitland and Baildon (eds), *Court Baron*, p. 63, where William denies that the jury will give him a fair hearing because of hostility towards him, 'these men have their hearts big against me and hate me much (*ils sunt les uns que ount le quer gros envers moi e mult me hoent*)'.
79 P. Franklin, 'Politics in manorial court rolls: the tactics, social composition and aims of a pre-1381 peasant movement', in Z. Razi and R. Smith (eds), *Medieval Society and the Manor Court* (Oxford, 1996), pp. 162–98: at p. 195. See also Levett, *Studies*, pp. 203–5.
80 Franklin, 'Politics', p. 162.
81 See especially the work of R. H. Hilton, including *The Decline of Serfdom in Medieval England* (second edition, London, 1983).
82 Musson, *Medieval Law*, pp. 244–6.
83 Gairdner (ed.), *Paston Letters*, IV, p. 169, no. 599, 7 August 1465.
84 See Mary Laven, below, Chapter 8.
85 E.g. in the writ of trespass the allegation that the defendant beat the plaintiff with sticks and swords and grievously wounded him so that his life was despaired of.
86 Dunham Manorial Court Rolls (1403), Grey (Stamford) of Dunham Massey Papers, John Rylands University Library of Manchester. The author acknowledges the assistance of the John Rylands Research Institute with this material.

5

Judges and trials in the English ecclesiastical courts

R. H. Helmholz

I Introduction

This chapter examines the nature of trials in the English ecclesiastical courts, paying special attention to the role played by the judges. The sources upon which it is based are: first, the formal rules of procedural law and the commentaries upon them written by the canonists and other jurists of the European *ius commune*; and second, the act books and other ancillary material from the courts themselves. In accepting the invitation to contribute to this volume, it was my hope that these two sources would illuminate each other. For the most part they do, although they leave some questions unanswered and provide some answers that are ambiguous.

This chapter concentrates its attention on the period from the mid-fifteenth century to the 1640s, when the ecclesiastical courts in England were abolished, as it turned out temporarily. Throughout this period, the Church had a system of public courts, dealing with particular areas of the law, most of which were not dealt with by the courts of the common law. In England, the customary jurisdictional divide gave to the Church the right to hear causes involving marriage and divorce, defamation, testaments and probate, tithes and other church dues, religious offences like witchcraft, heresy and blasphemy, and also crimes of the flesh like fornication, adultery and pandering.[1] Laity and the clergy alike were subject to this jurisdiction. No special jurisdiction *ratione personae* covering the clergy existed in the English courts, even though it was called for under the formal canon law,[2] and this meant that trials in the courts would have been known to a significant percentage of the English population.

II Court organisation

As in the Western Church generally, the English courts were organised by diocese. Each had its own set of courts. The number in any one diocese depended primarily on the size and the resident population, as well as the accidents of history. On the lower level, archdeacons and many other minor dignitaries also exercised *ex officio* jurisdiction, the term used to designate prosecutions for offences against the law of the church, and sometimes also instance jurisdiction, the term used to refer to litigation between private parties. However, the principal courts were those that every bishop held: a consistory court presided over by his appointee.

Above all of them stood the provincial courts of Canterbury and York, to which appeal lay from the diocesan tribunals. The system of judicial appeals from lower to higher courts meant that, before the Reformation, cases could be appealed from consistory courts, first to the provincial courts and then to the papal court in Rome. Afterwards, the Court of Delegates was normally the final court of appeal for England, although in fact it was a rare case that went beyond the Court of Arches in London, the principal court of appeal for the Province of Canterbury. In the Northern Province of York, where the number of dioceses was fewer and population smaller, the archbishop's court in York performed the same appellate role.

The ubiquity and the variety of these courts throughout England ought to be stressed in any study of ecclesiastical jurisdiction. Most English men and women would have lived in proximity to one or another of these courts, and litigation could thus be begun and conducted without making a lengthy trip to London or Westminster. In this sense, they were closer in nature to the secular local courts, discussed by Maureen Mulholland in her contribution to this volume, than they were to the courts of Kings Bench and Common Pleas. Litigants would not have had to wait long to appear before them. Most sessions of the ecclesiastical courts were held regularly, roughly speaking every three weeks throughout the year, and some more frequently still, except during the months of August and September. Most of the bishops' courts met in the cathedral of the diocese, usually in a special place devoted to that purpose. Sometimes, however, they met in one of the larger parish churches, probably for reasons of convenience. For example, the consistory court of Ely often met in Great St Mary's in Cambridge, where a large number of lawyers were to be found. A parochial venue was almost always true of most of the lower courts held by archdeacons, rural deans and other ecclesiastical dignitaries. Quite a few of the latter courts also perambulated on a regular schedule, seemingly in order to reach different parts of the diocese.

The president of each court was a judge, now called the chancellor but then known more often as the *officialis principalis*. He was served by the registrar, the man who compiled and kept the court records, and often a deputy registrar. There would always have been a staff of lawyers, called proctors, to represent the parties in civil matters, and in the larger courts there would have been several advocates, men who were expert in the law and who argued points of law for the parties.[3] Less conspicuous in the records, but usually present and undoubtedly prominent in the minds of critics, would have been a group of apparitors or summoners, the men who served the citations and other legal process that compelled parties to appear in court. They had to be present to prove that the absentees and the contumacious had in fact been lawfully summoned.

This small group of men was all there was in the way of legal professionals. There were thus fewer subordinate officials in England than would have been present in similar ecclesiastical tribunals in many parts of the Continent.[4] There was no separate group of notaries public, for example, although many English proctors would have been created notaries and done some of the work that was done elsewhere by a separate profession. There was no separate *sigillator* to guarantee the authenticity of documents. There was no *magister testamentorum*, no *receptor emendarum*. Most notably absent from English practice was the *promotor*, or *procurator fiscalis*, who prosecuted criminal matters in many courts on the Continent.

The ecclesiastical courts in England differed among themselves in how large a group of lawyers were authorised to practise at any one time. The numbers of active proctors and advocates were obviously much greater in London or York, for example, than in the court of, say, the archdeacon of Essex or even the bishop of Rochester. Some of the lesser courts had only three or four proctors serving within them, and one must assume that the number reflected the amount of litigation conducted. Moreover, no advocates at all were to be found in most of these lesser courts. It was, in any event, always a limited number of lawyers, and this was by choice. New proctors were admitted only upon the death or retirement of others.

A few of the consistory courts also employed an 'examiner general' to carry on the depositions of witnesses which provided the bedrock of proof in the spiritual forum.[5] Some courts would also have been able to call upon the bishop's 'sequestrator' to enforce appropriate orders to take revenues of churches into the bishop's hands, although it seems unlikely that these men regularly attended court sessions. Whatever the numbers, however, the organisational structure did not differ markedly from court to court. The judge would have been seated on a *cathedra*, raised above the level of the rest of the personnel during court sessions. In front of him was the registrar, perhaps with his deputy, and further forward there would have been some kind of barrier. Behind it would have stood a relatively small number of proctors and their clients.

Ecclesiastical trials

What were the trials held in the consistory courts like? It has been said that the great difference between trials using the civilian procedure characteristic of the ecclesiastical courts and trials in the English common law was that the former were written, the latter oral. There is certainly truth in this characterisation. Documents were the foundation of litigation before the ecclesiastical courts. The libel, for example, was a document that laid out the elements of the plaintiff's case. The questions (*articuli* and *interrogatoria*) to be put to the witnesses were, likewise, written out in advance. The testimony of witnesses was taken out of court, reduced to writing by the examiner and submitted to the judge for his own evaluation. A judge would not necessarily interrogate or even see a witness in person. The sentence too was a formal written document and, by the fifteenth century at the latest, each side had to produce its own sentence for use by the judge. The judge subscribed the sentence that accorded with his decision in the cause – this was the so-called *Lecta et lata* subscription – and promulgated it by reading it aloud in a formal session of the court. All these documents have survived in considerable numbers, together with a number of other written documents such as constitutions of proctors, sentences of excommunication, formal caveats and, of course, the act books themselves. They are the basis for our knowledge of what happened in litigation. This meant that court sessions can be described as meetings designed to receive the documents, with the real work of the court taking place outside the sessions of the courts themselves. This is the legitimate starting point for understanding the nature of an ecclesiastical trial. It contrasts markedly with the oral nature of the common law trials depicted, for example, in Daniel Klerman's and Anthony Musson's contributions to this volume.

However true this generalisation is as an overall matter, it is also too broad. It would be a mistake to take it for the full story. For one thing, it can give the impression that trials were secret. On the contrary, the holding of an ecclesiastical court was a public event. It was not conducted behind closed doors or simply by the exchange of papers between the parties and the judge. This openness is one reason that ecclesiastical jurisdiction would have been familiar to many men and women in England, even those with no particular interest in the canon law.

In at least five specific ways, the focus on the written documents used by the courts can give a misleading impression of the reality. First, although documents were the foundation of court procedure and were in fact handed to the court officials, there was also a good deal of speech that accompanied them. Some of it was purely formal in nature, used to introduce or to demand the introduction of documents. The treatise known as *Actor et Reus*, commonly found in archives throughout England, recorded the various stages of this colloquy and the dialogues found in it were used in practice. 'My lord', a proctor would say, 'I pray that a term should be assigned to me to propound a libel in due form of law.' The judge: 'We assign the next [term] to you for the purpose of introducing your libel, and to the adverse party to receive it.' The proctor: 'My lord, I pray that your lordship will admonish [the defendant] to appear in each and every session up until the end of the cause.'[6] So it went through to the end of the session.

This court dialogue would have been said in Latin. For some reason the English courts retained Latin for everyday usage in the courts after it had been discarded in favour of the vernacular in most parts of the Continent. The language used was, however, more than simply the picturesque formalism it now appears to have been. If a proctor failed to make a prayer or an objection at the proper time and in the proper form, the law held that the right to do so was waived. No doubt exceptions were made in practice, since there were excuses available under the law for most formal errors, but the law on the point must explain the widespread adherence to verbal formality that is so conspicuous in the records.

Second, the predominance of writing did not characterise office causes – the disciplinary cases brought against a man or woman for violation of the Church's laws. Typical examples would be prosecutions for adultery or failure to attend one's parish church. In them, the procedure was predominantly oral, although sentences of excommunication (where necessary) were supposed to be issued in writing as well. The oral nature of these trials was an inevitable result of the canon law itself, because, as in the English common law, defendants in criminal cases could not be represented by a lawyer at all, except if a question of interpreting the law arose, in which case resort to counsel was allowed. Again, as in the common law, recourse to lawyers seldom happened in criminal practice. Documents were therefore rarely used in *ex officio* matters. Most defendants could not have read them. The charge was made aloud and in the vernacular, the oaths taken similarly and the assignment of penance and negotiation about it all done orally. The records contain a mixture of formulaic Latin and common English as a result. As with the royal court plea rolls, the formal nature of the records conceals a considerable amount of discussion about the determination of criminal cases.

Third, virtually any of the documents could be omitted in practice. The *ordo iuris* was not a strait jacket. Summary procedure was authorised under the medieval canon law, and it made a difference in practice.[7] It permitted omission of all but the essential steps required to meet canonical standards of due process. By the fifteenth century, for example, the libel was almost always combined with the articles and positions into the same document. Arbitration could be used, and in fact was often assigned by judges. Where a party had introduced all his witnesses in one session, there was no need for the other two provided in the law and they were often waived in practice. All these abbreviated the trial process and dispensed with the need of some of the documents that would otherwise have been required for a trial.

Negotiation about how to proceed – since the consent of the parties might be required – of course meant that the trials were less dependent upon documents and, indeed, more informal than they otherwise would have been. In fact, the records show that many of the instance causes were disposed of without much more than oral statements by each party.[8] Many of the causes brought for 'breach of faith', for example, by which the church enforced contracts entered into together with a sworn promise to pay, were dealt with very briefly and apparently on the basis of oral statements of claim and oral responses by the parties or their proctors.[9]

Fourth, it appears that when a case called for argument about the law, this too might be done orally as well as by documentary submission. In an account of a London case from the sixteenth century, for example, the advocates for the two parties are recorded as speaking one after another, quite shortly and in answer to the point just made by the other advocate.[10] Citations to learned authorities from the *ius commune* were given and discussed by the advocates in making their argument. In other words, there was a back and forth dialogue that must have been oral, because it was too brief and spontaneous to have been part of a considered written form. The participation by advocates was thus more like a Year Book discussion in the common law (although without equivalent participation by the judges) than it was a written document to be submitted for consideration by the court.

Finally, despite the formality of the records and what can be called the initial pleading, there was a fair amount of other comment in the consistory courts and some just plain chatter. A fifteenth-century York case mentioned by the way that, 'The said official and the proctors were speaking sometimes in Latin, sometimes in English.'[11] The records regularly describe the presence of people in the courts 'in a copious multitude'. Although the phrase is formulaic, it corresponds with other evidence about the people who were present in the courts. Occasionally, the records speak of outbursts from the litigants, perhaps naturally enough when a decision went against them. Appeals could be taken *viva voce* under the law, and they were, in fact, so taken. Moreover, satires written against the ecclesiastical courts, from the fourteenth century to the seventeenth, depicted them as less than sedate. Proctors shouted, one asserted, 'not so much in order to be heard by the judge, as to keep up the noise'.[12] No doubt there was some exaggeration in the description, but it would not have been effective as satire if there were no truth whatsoever to it.[13] We must not imagine the typical meeting of a consistory court as a noiseless affair in which only formal documents and language were used, despite the famous depiction of Doctors' Commons by Charles Dickens.[14]

Role of the judge in the trials

My second subject is the role of the judges in litigation. Here, the normal starting point has been and remains a contrast between the judges of the common law courts and those within the civilian traditions. Although they were impressive to see and their intervention with juries could be decisive, common law judges came to trials ignorant of the nature of the cases. They were referees, if you like, between the two opposing counsel in civil cases, between a defendant and the victim or other prosecuting party in criminal cases. Juries decided who won or lost. By contrast, under the *ius commune* the role of a judge was far from that of a referee or spectator. The procedure was under his control and he was expected to take an active role in the investigation of facts and in moving trials ahead.[15] Issuance of the definitive sentence in any event lay with him, not with a jury, and he had the duty to make certain it was correct. There is also a good deal of truth in this widely accepted characterisation. The ultimate responsibility of decision rested upon the civilian judges who were required to review and evaluate the evidence presented by witnesses produced by the parties.

The records show that they fulfilled this responsibility in fact. Although each side submitted draft sentences, as noted above, it was up to the judges to decide between them. It is particularly noteworthy that alterations were often made to them in the course of bringing a trial to its close. Perhaps there were negotiations over the extent of liability and the wording of the sentence. However, the authoritative role of the judges appears on the sentences themselves – mostly in deletions from the wording and substitutions made above the line. This evidence demonstrates that the judges were not bound by a 'take one or the other' kind of system as one might suspect from the way in which sentences were submitted by the parties. The judges merely put the financial burden of having the sentences written out onto someone else.

As was true for the documentary nature of procedure, the 'model' of judicial activism and professional expertise taken from manuals of Continental procedure is too simple. Perhaps there is even something slightly misleading about it as a description of what went on in the English ecclesiastical courts. There were points at which the role of judges in the ecclesiastical courts can be more accurately likened to that of judges in a common law court. I know of no contemporary who made the comparison, though some observers did make a record of what the ecclesiastical court judges did in performing their role at trial.

First, the 'activist model' overestimates, by a large margin, the investigative resources at the disposal of the judges in the English spiritual courts. In truth, they had almost none. As noted above, the *promotor*, the agent employed by judges to investigate criminal matters and to conduct prosecutions in the name of the courts in many parts of the Continent, did not exist in the English ecclesiastical tribunals.[16] If an English judge wished to promote *ex officio* proceedings – and this did occasionally happen – he had to choose from among the existing proctors attached to his court to have the task done.[17] The summoners were also under his jurisdiction, but they had no legal training. Their formal responsibilities were limited to citing parties and (probably) reporting the public fame against individuals they had accumulated in carrying out that task. They would probably not have been thought suitable and the records have produced no examples where they were chosen to act as prosecutors. And, apart from the proctors, there was simply no one else.

From this paucity in personnel came a reliance on laymen, typically in the procedure of presentment by the churchwardens and 'questmen' of each parish. Laymen were chosen for a yearly term and, by the fifteenth century at the latest, churchwardens were required to answer a series of articles about what was amiss in the parish. Had the church fabric been neglected? Were the church services being performed? Were there notorious evil livers in the parish? And so forth. It was on the basis of answers provided by these laymen that most prosecutions were begun. This was, of course, inquisitorial procedure in a sense. It was conducted in the name of the court, not that of private accusers. The questions were drafted by professionals, but it was a far cry from an inquisition run by a group of trained jurists and their agents. As was true in the system of criminal prosecution in the English common law, much was left to amateurs.

Second, the 'activist model' does not fit the normal pattern of actual judicial attendance in the courts. The judges were too often absent for them to have fully performed the duties of an investigating magistrate in the civilian tradition. Francis Clerke, the London proctor who wrote a treatise on the ecclesiastical courts in the capital, remarked that the Dean of the Court of Arches, the chief civilian dignitary and judge of the highest ecclesiastical court in England, was so often occupied with diplomatic missions abroad, that he was not often in the court over which he nominally presided.[18] So spare is Clerke's description that it is impossible to know whether he meant this as a criticism of judicial conduct or not. At any rate, he did describe what one might call absenteeism from this high post.

The same absenteeism occurred among many of England's ecclesiastical court judges. For example, from the autumn of 1598 to the same time the next year, the consistory court of the diocese of Exeter was presided over by five different judges.[19] It met quite often, though sometimes for the hearing of only one or two causes, but the same judge did not always preside at consecutive sessions. It was literally true that litigants could not have been sure which judge to expect on their next appearance.[20] If the judges had had a strong group of lawyers serving under them, such absenteeism might not have had any effect on their ability to carry out the duties of an investigating magistrate. However, such a 'staff' is exactly what they lacked. There was the registrar and sometimes a deputy registrar, but, apart from the proctors, there was no one else upon whom to call.

Third, the judges in the ecclesiastical courts had neither the cohesive judicial institutions nor the ability to shape legal doctrine that their common law counterparts enjoyed. Such a role in the formulation of doctrine was not, to be sure, any part of the traditions of the *ius commune* and I do not mean to suggest any divergence between theory and practice here. Nevertheless, it is worthy of note that until the organisation of Doctors' Commons early in the sixteenth century, there was no institution like the Inns of Court in London around which judicial opinion and discussion of law and practice in the courts could coalesce. The intellectual centre of gravity in the civilian system was the university, not the courtroom, and so it remained throughout this period. In terms of the trial, this meant that the activity of the judges and the courts would not be the central focus of attention or legal development.

No equivalent to the medieval Year Books was found in the ecclesiastical system, and there were few case reports in the sixteenth and seventeenth centuries (although there were some), a time when the number of reports of common law cases exploded. When change in legal practice in the ecclesiastical forum occurred – and it did occur – it was likely to have been the work of commentators, working within university faculties or as commentators on the law. Either such commentators, or else pressure from without exerted by writs of prohibition, created the most significant changes in spiritual court practice over the years. To this extent, what the judges in the ecclesiastical courts did in the cases that came before them was less consequential than what the judges did within the traditions of the English common law. William Lyndwood, although Dean of Arches and hence the most important ecclesiastical judge in England, made his mark as the authoritative commentator on the English provincial constitutions, not as a judge.[21]

The judges: training and performance

My third subject is the professional quality of judges in the English ecclesiastical courts. Unfortunately we have no satisfactory way of evaluating that conduct overall and perhaps the best course would be simply to confess to an ignorance that is unlikely to be overcome.[22] Moreover, on some matters where more information could be obtained, such as their relations with common lawyers or their familiarity with the vast literature of the *ius commune*, we still know too little to be able to speak with confidence. However, incidental information already unearthed from the court records and the accessibility of academic comment on the subject, makes it possible to venture three statements about the quality of the work by the judges who conducted the trials in ecclesiastical courts.

First, there is the question of their formal qualifications. If we examine the pages of the *Summa aurea* of Hostiensis (d. 1271),[23] one of the most famous and accessible of the academic commentators on the medieval canon law, in search of the qualifications required of judges, we find five listed:

1 Condition. Judges could not be of servile condition.
2 Sex. Women could not hold the office.
3 Discretion. Judges must be *compos mentis*.
4 Age. Judges must be at least twenty years old.
5 Fame. Judges must not be excommunicated or notorious heretics.

It is not a long list. The number of requirements for judging that might have been mentioned but were not, may stand out more prominently than the requirements that were. The exclusions of women and the unfree are what one expects for the Middle Ages and, apart from them, it does not appear that the formal disqualifications were particularly onerous. It is noteworthy that neither holy orders nor a university education was required according to this thirteenth-century author's review of the texts of the *Corpus iuris canonici*. Although the canon law elsewhere excluded laymen from taking cognisance over *spiritualia*, a prohibition that would have excluded the possibility of laymen judging some, but not all, of the causes that came before the ecclesiastical courts in England.[24] The formal canon law also excluded inferiors from judging their superiors and, under one understanding, this too might have required that judges be in holy orders when cases involving the clergy came before them.[25] However, no specific legal training is found among the requirements for judicial office. No requirement of having passed an examination appears and the age limit, to put it mildly, would have excluded very few men from taking a judicial seat. It was only provincial legislation in England that required advocates (and therefore judges) to have attended university lectures in the law and to have taken a degree.[26]

What was the situation in fact? We can say little about many things, the age of judges, for example. Judging by women was what might be called a 'non-issue'. But some things we can say. Almost all the judges before the Reformation seem to have been clerics and most, but not all, of the pre-1640 judges seem to have been university graduates in law.[27] A Tudor statute allowed laymen and married men to exercise spiritual jurisdiction if they held a doctorate in civil law,[28] and it seems eventually to have become the rule that only laymen so trained could act as judges. The principal exception to it was that the holder of the ecclesiastical office, a bishop or an archdeacon, could himself exercise jurisdiction if he chose, and this sometimes happened in practice. If it had not indeed been true during the thirteenth century, the status of university graduate came to be required for acting regularly as a judge in the ecclesiastical forum. It is true that on occasion men who held degrees in theology, sometimes even only the M.A., were appointed to act as surrogates to the principal judges in the spiritual courts, and sometimes these men acted as judges for considerable lengths of time. But these were exceptions. For the most part, acting as a judge in an ecclesiastical court was a 'career path' down which many graduates of the law faculties at Oxford and Cambridge passed.[29]

Second, there is the question of the fees paid to the justice and the attendant question of judicial integrity. Like many office-holders in the *Ancien Regime*, the judges of England's ecclesiastical courts depended upon court fees for their basic incomes. And the records of individual trials that were fully recorded, customarily included the payment of court fees, of which judges took a share.[30] Litigants paid for libels, for commissions to examine witnesses, for sentences, for documents of appeal; indeed they paid for all the paper produced during trials. Part of the money paid for these items went to the judges. Such fees were not necessarily illegal under the medieval *ius commune*.[31] It was a question of whether or not they constituted bribery and would pervert the course of justice, though some critics regarded the line as too thin to be workable and therefore one that was not worthy of respect.[32]

It is also true that there were checks under the law designed to prevent bribery and partiality. The prohibitions against corruption were oft stated in the law and the oaths ecclesiastical lawyers were obliged to take routinely would have reminded them of their professional responsibilities.[33] No canonist endorsed more than the taking of a 'moderate sum' for expenses on the part of court officials, and the *ius commune* provided no blanket immunity from liability or prosecution to its judges. They might have been proceeded against for deliberate error or peculation. If they asserted jurisdiction when they possessed none, their acts were a nullity in law. And, of course, it is important to remember that their judicial actions were always subject to appeal to a higher court to an extent those of common law judges were not. These protective devices must have caught some takers of bribes and may have frightened others into compliance with the law.

Nonetheless, the continuing criticism of the ecclesiastical court system as venal in nature cannot have been altogether mistaken. Although much of it was directed against the proctors and the summoners attached to the courts, some of the blame (if that is the right word) must be laid at the door of the judges. One of the more unattractive features of the system was that in *ex officio* cases, defendants were obliged to pay court fees even if they were (as we would say) acquitted.[34] The fees mounted up. They made many judges wealthy. It was considered surprising and worthy of remark, for example, that Sir Daniel Dun, Dean of Arches between 1598 and 1616, was not a rich man when he died. Virtually every matter treated in the courts in which Dun took part, ended in a payment being assessed against the parties. We may say, if we like, that the ecclesiastical courts shared this characteristic with virtually every court system in medieval and early modern Europe. And it is true that we have not wholly solved the problem today. Still, these defences should not cause us to overlook the important part that 'revenue raising' played in early trials in the ecclesiastical forum.

Third, the granting of considerable discretion to judges under the *ius commune* is worth noting because of the decisive effect it had on the conduct of many trials. Its endorsement in the texts must explain some of the apparent variations (and even inconsistencies) in procedure that are found in contemporary act books. For instance, excommunication for contumacy was not automatic in the ecclesiastical courts; it lay in the discretion of the judges.[35] Some of the practices that led to criticism levelled at the judges, as in allowing too easy commutation of penance in return for the payment of money, were endorsed within the canon law itself. They were within the discretion of the presiding officer, who was directed to take account of all the relevant factors. The judges would have defended their actions by citing the discretion they were supposed to exercise under the law.

Legal historians have probably not yet paid enough attention to the existence and extent of discretion that was commonly vested in medieval judges. It was crucial for the conduct of trials. In comparison with legal rules, however, it is harder to talk about the actual exercise of discretion. By the nature of the concept, elaboration and satisfactory generalisation elude historians.

However, the commentators of the *ius commune* commented frequently that matters had, in the end, to be left 'to the discretion of a good judge',[36] and on this point the evidence of the records, and that of the commentaries, are at one. For example, the number of compurgators assigned in compurgation was left for the judge to decide. So was the pace of litigation. Reliance on judicial discretion in these matters is obviously what happened in practice, for the records repeatedly show variation and choice on the part of those in charge. Even the weight assigned to particular evidence was left largely to judicial evaluation, although again there were limits and many rules for guidance of judges contained in treatises like the huge treatise on the law of proof by *Mascardus*.[37] W. G. Naphy's contribution to this volume is suggestive of its importance in the evaluation of criminal conduct in other legal arenas, and it is suggestive for the courts of the Church as well. The *ius commune* set its face against any requirement that judges explain their reasons in giving sentences,[38] and that too was a measure of the considerable discretion given to them under the existing law.

III Conclusion

Our knowledge of trials in the ecclesiastical courts before 1640 and of the role in judges in conducting them is imperfect. We do not know much, for example, about how long most trials lasted. We do not even know whether it is correct, strictly speaking, to use the modern term 'trial' to describe proceedings before the courts of the church. Much of the procedure was purely formal in character and some of the most important decisions, like the negotiations over the wording of each sentence, were made away from the public record. There is a real distance between what happened in the ecclesiastical courts and what we commonly think of as a trial. Added to this uncertainty is the difficulty caused by the physical disappearance of the courts where ecclesiastical trials once took place. Only in Chester cathedral has a consistory court physically outlasted the disappearance of the greater part of ecclesiastical jurisdiction during the nineteenth century. Depictions of the courts in action are also few and far between.[39] Perhaps more could be done to find them, but so far no one has made a systematic effort.

Despite gaps in the surviving evidence, much can be recovered, and it appears that these ecclesiastical proceedings fit comfortably within the definition of a trial given by Joseph Jaconelli at the outset of this volume. Proceedings were open. Trials were public events. They were available to all whose claims (or offences) fitted within the division of jurisdiction that prevailed in England. They were in no sense the exclusive preserve of the clergy. Proceedings in them followed the rules set down by the sophisticated procedural system of the European *ius commune*, although this system always left room for many adjustments in customary practice. The ecclesiastical courts were presided over by judges trained in the law at the universities, men who were following a recognised career path. It will not do, of course, to make these courts into ideals of justice or to describe their judges as paragons of impartiality. Both have attracted criticism in every period of their existence.[40] The early modern and medieval courts continue to do so among historians today.[41] No doubt not all of the criticism is misplaced, but it is fair to conclude that proceedings held before the English ecclesiastical courts, were not 'Kafkaesque' perversions of what trials should be.

Notes

1 For general accounts of the court organisation, see A. H. Thompson, *The English Clergy and Their Organization in the Later Middle Ages* (Oxford, 1947), pp. 40–71: W. Stubbs, 'Report on Ecclesiastical Courts, 1883', Historical Appendix No. I to Vol. I (*Parliamentary Papers*, 1883, Vol. 24). For specific dioceses, see B. Woodcock, *Medieval Ecclesiastical Courts in the Diocese of Canterbury* (Oxford, 1952), pp. 6–29; R. A. Marchant, *The Church Under Law: Justice, Administration, and Discipline in the Diocese of York, 1560–1640* (Cambridge, 1969); R. M. Haines, *The Administration of the Diocese of Worcester in the First Half of the Fourteenth Century* (London, 1965), pp. 104–14; C. A. Ritchie, *The Ecclesiastical Courts of York* (Arbroath, 1956); M. Aston, *Thomas Arundel, A Study of Church Life in the Reign of Richard II* (Oxford, 1967), pp. 53–82; F. S. Hockaday, 'The Consistory Court of the Diocese of Gloucester', *Transactions of the Bristol and Gloucestershire Archaeological Society*, 46 (1924), 195–287.
2 An obvious exception to the rule that jurisdiction was not based upon personal status in England was the jurisdiction of the university courts; see, e.g., A. Shepard, 'Legal learning and the Cambridge University courts, c. 1560–1640', *Journal of Legal History*, 19 (1998), 62–74.
3 For an overview of the profession, with references to earlier literature, see R. O'Day, *The Professions in Early Modern England, 1450–1800. Servants of the Commonweal* (Harlow, 2000), pp. 151–61, and from a different perspective, D. R. Coquillette, *The Civilian Writers of Doctors' Commons, London* (Berlin, 1988), pp. 22–44.
4 Compare the situation in France, described in A. Lefebvre-Teillard, *Les Officialités à la veille du Concile de Trente* (Paris, 1973), pp. 33–8, and P. Fournier, *Les Officialités au Moyen-Age* (Paris, 1880), pp. 29–31.
5 E.g., Mr Richard Burgh was styled examiner general in a York Act book (1417): Borthwick Institute of Historical Research (hereinafter BI), Cons.AB.1, fol. 50.
6 See, e.g., Cambridge University Library, MS. Dd.10.36 (late sixteenth-century formulary), fol. 29 r.–v., containing a simple version of the dialogue.
7 See Clem. 5.11.2; 2.1.1; see also R. H. Helmholz, *Marriage Litigation in Medieval England* (Cambridge, 1974), pp. 120–2.
8 This was not unlawful; see *gl. ord.* AD X 2.3.1 s. v. *libellum reclamationis*.
9 See Woodcock, *Medieval Ecclesiastical Courts*, pp. 84, 89–92.
10 Doyle v. Waynman, Bodleian Library Oxford, Tanner MS. 280, fols 307–12.
11 BI, CP.F 132 (1421).
12 See *The Proctor and the Parator* (place of publication unknown, 1641). No pagination.

13 This was also a European phenomenon; see A. Steins, 'Der ordentliche Zivilprozeß nach den Offizialatsstatuten', in *Zeitschrift für Rechtsgeschichte, Kanonistische Abteilung*, 59 (1973), 190–262, at, 201.

14 *David Copperfield* (Penguin edition) (Harmondsworth, 1966. First edition, 1850), p. 330: 'such a cosey, dosey, old fashioned, time-forgotten, sleepy-headed little family party'.

15 See, e.g., P. Stein, *Roman Law in European History* (Cambridge, 1999), p. 59; P. Ourliac, 'L'Office du juge dans le droit canonique classique', in *Mélanges offerts à Pierre Hébraud* (Toulouse, 1982), p. 638.

16 R. M. Wunderli, *London Church Courts and Society on the Eve of the Reformation* (Cambridge, Massachusetts, 1981), p. 37.

17 E.g., Ex officio contra Mawger and Mawger (Diocese of York 1599), BI, CP.G.3048, brought for sexual relations and marrying outside of the church. William Fethergill, one of the court proctors, was assigned as the promotor of the cause.

18 Francis Clerke, *Praxis in curiis ecclesiasticis*, tit. 2 (London, 1684), pp. 4–5. The work was written in the 1590s and circulated widely in manuscript before its publication.

19 Taken from Devon Record Office, Exeter, MS. Act book CC 784C; the judges were Matthew Sutcliffe, LL. D., Richard Rutter, M. A., Nicholaus Wyatt, LL. B., Evan Morrice, LL. D. and Edward Peard, LL. B. The number of their appearances as judge recorded in the Act book was, respectively, eleven, five, five, forty-six and three. The Commissary court of London between 24 November 1599 and 22 March 1600, met before five judges, Thomas Ridley, LL. D., Thomas Pope, LL. D., John Amy, LL. D., Thomas Crompson, LL. D., and Edward Burton, M. A. See London Guildhall, MS. Act book 9064/15, fols 21–42v, but the first two were by far the most frequent. The consistory court of Ely meeting in Great St Mary's, Cambridge between April 1628 and April of the next year, was presided over by four different judges, Thomas Eden, LL. D., the official principal, and three surrogates, Robert King, M. A., George Eden, M. A., and Thomas Lake, M. A. See Cambridge University Library, EDR D/2/42, fols 1–160. On the other hand, in the Canterbury commissary court for 1475, John Parmenter, Leg. Lic., was the only judge recorded as having acted. See Canterbury Cathedral Archives, MS. Act book Y.1.12, fols 44–111.

20 BI C/C/AB.3, fol. 41 (1531), the *officialis principalis* delegated four different men to act as judges in his stead during his absence from the court: Henry Barbet, LL. D., Thomas Fox, Thomas Marsar, and John Altman.

21 On Lyndwood, see B. E. Ferme, *Canon Law in Late Medieval England: A Study of William Lyndwood's 'Provinciale' with particular reference to Testamentary Law* (Rome, 1996).

22 Even a list of the men who served as judges in the consistory courts is to be greatly desired. None exists, although the very top of the profession, the advocates and judges in London, has been well served; see B. Levack, *The Civil Lawyers in England, 1603–1641: A Political Study* (Oxford, 1973) and G. D. Squibb, *Doctors' Commons: A History of the College of Advocates and Doctors of Law* (Oxford, 1977).

23 Henricus de Segusio (Hostiensis), *Summa aurea* (Venice, 1581), Lib. I, tit. *De officio ordinarii*, no. 2.

24 *Ibid.*, X 2.1.2. Panormitanus understood this as meaning that laymen could exercise jurisdiction in such cases only if the power was committed to them by the pope. See his *Commentaria in libros Decretalium* (Lyons, 1517) AD X 1.6.43, no. 4.

25 *C. 2. q. 7 c.* 10.

26 See Council of Lambeth (1281), in F. M. Powicke and C. R. Cheney (eds), *Councils & Synods with other Documents relating to the English Church* (2 vols, Oxford, 1964). II (AD 1205–1313), pp. 917–18.

27 E. Nys, *Le Droit romain, le droit des gens et le Collège des Docteurs en droit civil* (Brussels, 1910) p. 105.

28 37 Hen. VIII, *c.* 17 (1545).

29 See A. L. Browne, 'The medieval officials-principal of Rochester', *Archaeologia Cantiana*, 53 (1940), pp. 29–61. See generally, P. Brand, *The Origins of the English Legal Profession* (Oxford 1992), pp. 145–6.

30 See Woodcock, *Medieval Ecclesiastical Courts*, pp. 136–7; R. A. Marchant, *The Church under the Law: Justice, Administration and Discipline in the Diocese of York, 1560–1640* (Cambridge, 1969), p. 246.

31 See, e.g., Panormitanus, *Commentaria*, AD X 3.1.10, no. 10; William Durantis, *Speculum iudiciale* (Basel, 1575, repr. Aachen, 1975), Lib. 4, Pt. 4, tit. *De magistris*.

32 See, e.g., Dante, *The Divine Comedy: Paradiso*, Canto 9, lines 127–35, (ed.) C. S. Singleton (Princeton, New Jersey, 1975), pp. 102–03. See generally, J. A. Yunck, *The Lineage of Lady Meed: The Development of Medieval Venality Satire* (Notre Dame, Indiana, 1963).

33 See Brand, *Origins*, pp. 152–4; J. A. Brundage, 'The medieval advocate's profession', *Law and History Review*, 6 (1988), 439–64.

34 See, e.g., G. R. Quaife, *Wanton Wenches and Wayward Wives: Peasants and Illicit Sex in Early Seventeenth Century England* (New Brunswick, New Jersey, 1979), p. 196.

35 Noted, e.g., in British Library MS. Harl. 3190 (seventeenth-century account of civil law in England), fol. 31: 'If anyone fails to appear when summoned to judgment, he shall be subject to excommunication at the discretion of the judge (*Si quis in iudicium vocatus non venerit pro arbitrio iudicis est excommunicandus*).'

36 See, e.g., *gl. ord.* AD Sext 1.3.11, s.v. *paucis*; and see generally R. M. Fraher, 'Conviction according to conscience: the medieval jurists' debate concerning judicial discretion and the law of proof', *Law and History Review*, 7 (1989), 32–40.

37 Josephus Mascardus (d. 1588), *Conclusiones probationum omnium quae in utroque foro quotidie versantur* (Frankfurt, 1593).

38 See P. Godding, 'Jurisprudence et motivation des sentences, du moyen âge à la fin du 18ᵉ siècle', in C. Perelman and P. Foriers (eds), *La motivation des décisions de justice* (Brussels, 1978), pp. 37–67, esp. pp. 42–50; A. Wijffels, 'Le Juge et le jugement dans la tradition du ius commune européen', in R. Jacob (ed.) *Le juge et le jugement dans les traditions juridiques européennes* (Paris, 1996), pp. 167–79.

39 That found as the frontispiece in Squibb, *Doctors' Commons*, p. ii, taken from R. Ackermann, *Microcosm of London* (1808), has been much used; it depicts a more formal institution than most diocesan courts would have been.

40 See, e.g., M. Haren, *Sin and Society in Fourteenth-Century England: A Study of the Memoriale Presbiterorum* (Oxford, 2000), pp. 14–16.

41 See, e.g., G. R. Elton, *The Tudor Constitution* (second edition, Cambridge, 1982), pp. 218–21: 'fear and dislike' of the courts; P. Williams, *The Tudor Regime* (Oxford, 1979), pp. 259–62: 'weak and feeble machinery'.

6

The attempted trial of
Boniface VIII for heresy[1]

Jeffrey Denton

Despite strenuous efforts by the French Crown and its allies over a period of eight years Boniface VIII was not ultimately tried. Legal procedures for a trial were put in motion in 1303, in an attempt to summon the pope before a General Council of the Church; and later, after his death in October 1303, as the accusations continued to grow, there was a protracted quest to persuade the new French pope, Clement V, to condemn Boniface posthumously. Over the period 1303 to 1311 the accusations against the pope developed and became more elaborate until the legal processes, first against the person of the pope and then against his memory, were abandoned following a political agreement. The posthumous stages of the whole affair were soon very largely forgotten, indeed became shrouded in secrecy as an embarrassing episode in both papal and French history,[2] but the conflict during the last stages of Boniface's life, beginning in 1301 and culminating in the attempts to bring him to trial in 1303, produced masses of documentation and political treatises[3] that were of continuing significance for the French monarchy and the French state and, indeed, for the future of the papacy. It was the first time in European history that such a welter of detailed evidence was produced by an attempt to defame or indict a supreme political leader. The surviving evidence is not always easy to interpret and has at times been wildly misinterpreted. This chapter will concentrate on the evidence of 1303: specifically, the sets of complaints against the pope of March and June 1303 which constituted the first stages in the planned legal process and from which the later accusations very largely stemmed.

What were the charges contained in the initial trial texts of March and June 1303? We now have the benefit of Jean Coste's excellent critical editions of all the complaints against Boniface.[4] The March text[5] was a set of carefully prepared propositions by the knight and lawyer William de Nogaret, presented to Philip IV and his council. It constituted a trenchant defence of the Church, beginning, like a sermon, with the claim that events foreseen by St Peter, 'glorious prince of apostle', had come to pass: 'But there were false prophets also among the people, even as there shall be false teachers among you' 'by reason of whom the way of truth shall be evil spoken of. And through covetousness shall they with feigned words make merchandise of you' 'following the way of Balaam the son of Bosor who loved the ways of unright-eousness . . .'.[6] The first specific charge, providing the main thrust of the whole declaration, was that Boniface was a false pope and usurper of the apostolic see: he was a master of untruths, claiming to be called 'Bonifacius' when he was in every way 'maleficus', entering 'not by the door into the sheepfold' but rather as 'a thief and a robber',[7] deceiving his predecessor, Celestine V, into resigning (in December 1294), laying violent hands upon him and appropriating to himself the Church of Rome. He had been tolerated, for fear of schism, until it could be seen by his fruits[8] whether he had achieved office through the working of the Holy Spirit; now it was clear to all that his fruits were the most noxious. The evil tree 'should be hewn down and cast into the fire'.[9] The central charge, therefore, was that Boniface had no rightful claim to be pope.

The other specific accusations in March were very succinctly stated: that the pope was a manifest heretic; that he was the worst simoniac that the world had ever known; and that his crimes were so great and so manifest that they could no longer be tolerated without subversion of the Church. Some of these manifest crimes were listed: for example, instead of nurturing churches he tore them apart, wickedly squandering the goods of the poor, supporting evil men and taking vengeance on the just, and imposing grievous burdens on the people of God and the leaders of the people. There was, thus, no pulling of punches in Nogaret's declaration; but, at the same time, the accusations were broad rather than precise. With his biblical, indeed theological, ap-proach,[10] Nogaret had certainly established a distinctive and newly relevant case against the pope. His claim was that it had become clear from his actions as pope that he was an impostor and that he had no God-given authority. Although the March statement is a keen and innovative assault upon the pope, in continuing to emphasise Boniface's supposedly illegitimate elevation it was in some ways backward-looking. It was strongly reminiscent, no doubt consciously so, of the charges made against the pope six years earlier by the disaffected cardinals, James and Peter Colonna.[11]

As an appeal to Philip IV to set in motion the convocation of a General Council the March statement was ineffective. No firm decisions were taken. Reasons for delay are suggested by the fact that there was soon a clear change of tactics. By June not only had the list of charges grown extensively but also the emphasis had shifted radically.[12] The old accusations were not abandoned, but the theme now was Boniface the heretic rather than Boniface the usurper. This broke new ground, moving further away from the earlier Colonna charges, though probably influenced by recent information derived in part from Peter Colonna.[13]

Indeed, the June gathering was itself of a distinctly different kind from the earlier meeting of the king's council. In March, for instance, two archbishops and three bishops had been present; now there were five archbishops and twenty-one bishops. Proceedings in June moved successfully to statements of adherence to the process of summoning a Council – statements first by the king and then, with some conditions attached, by the assembled prelates. At this new assembly it was Nogaret's junior accomplice, William de Plaisians, who presented the case against Boniface; and he took an oath to pursue the matter before the planned Council. All the new accusations, twenty-eight of them, were summed up by the initial denunciation that the pope was a thoroughgoing heretic: 'hereticus perfectus'. This charge of heresy had come very largely out of the blue in 1303;[14] and it was at the June assembly that some circumstantial support for the charge was, for the first time, made public and set down in writing. The accusations were now, though certainly not substantiated, at least bolstered with some detail.

In brief the allegations supporting the charge of heresy were as follows. The pope denied the immortality of the soul, transubstantiation, the existence of an afterlife and the efficacy of penance, and he approved of a heretical work by Arnold of Villanova. In addition to these charges which can be associated directly with a common perception, then as now, of heresy, he was accused of fornication, of sodomy, of homicide, of encouraging idolatry by having images of himself erected in churches, of engaging in demonolatry and black magic, of committing simoniacal practices in the trading of ecclesiastical offices, of causing the death of Celestine V, of undermining the college of cardinals and the monastic and mendicant orders, of planning the destruction of the French king and the French people, of being responsible for the loss of the Holy Land, of oppressing Christians and working as an enemy of peace for the perdition of souls and for the destruction of the Church and of the faith. With this outright defamation of Boniface the future pattern of the attacks on the pope was fully established. It was an exposure of his scandalous behaviour as pope and of his scandalous personal morality. In the years that followed there would be further elaborations on these themes. But of special importance, and there can be no doubt about this, was the charge of heresy. Heresy was now the core of the matter.

There has been a tendency to take these accusations at face value, and to believe that they can be individually investigated in order to arrive at a true understanding of the pope's behaviour and attitudes. Although Jean Coste in his recent work adopted a rigorously critical approach to all the evidence, the central intention of his analysis was to discover whether or not the pope was innocent of the charges levelled against him; his meticulously worked out conclusion was, rather predictably, that the precise charges cannot be substantiated, but that the character and behaviour of this pontiff 'sans scrupules' left much to be desired.[15] It is as though the sheer enormity of the accusations continues to make it difficult to see behind them and to set them in context.

The first most important question is not how true the individual charges were, but rather whether they actually represented the reasons for the Franco-papal rift and for the attempt to bring Boniface to trial. Clearly, if we are to understand what kinds of reality lie behind the documents of 1303, we need to construct a secure legal and political context for them. And the starting-point must be the nature of the documents themselves. What were they?

Both documents were notarially attested statements aiming to establish a proper juridical procedure. They are legal documents, in the nature of individual appeals, in March by William de Nogaret and in June by William de Plaisians. These secular lawyers were the key royal agents in the whole affair. Nogaret's statement was, in the first place, a supplication to the king that, having interceded with leading churchmen and laymen, especially the cardinals and prelates, and with the people, he should convoke a General Council, at which this 'most evil' pope would be condemned and the cardinals would provide a new pastor for the Church. It was abundantly clear from the terms in which this procedure was set out that there was no doubt about the intended outcome of the planned trial. Nogaret's statement comprised, in the second place, a supplication that the king and the cardinals should place the pope in custody and appoint a vicar to administer the Church until a new pontiff could be provided, thus avoiding all possibility of a schism and preventing the 'infamous' Boniface from impeding the proceedings.

Plaisians, in June, presented a more developed set of appeals. He appealed at length to the king and to the French prelates, with elaborate statements that he was acting for the good of the Church and the faith. The result was that the king, having given his own formal support, himself appealed to all the prelates who were present to work for a General Council and issued a 'precautionary' appeal against any action that the pope might take. The prelates then formally consented to the summoning of a Council, with the proviso that they were unwilling to be a party in a legal case, and they too issued a 'precautionary' appeal against any papal action.

Thus by a process of appeals was legal procedure initiated. These were not standard ecclesiastical appeals of a common kind, appeals, that is, from one jurisdiction to a higher jurisdiction; even so, these individual petitions of mere laymen were bolstered by royal and ecclesiastical corroboration and endorsement. The French lawyers were carefully presenting their case within the Romano-canonical tradition, which was marked by ample possibilities of supplication. The particular kind of *provocationes* (the 'precautionary' appeals) which completed the initial procedures were entreaties against future harm, and these had come to be employed, not infrequently, in the late thirteenth century in cases with political overtones.[16]

The accusations against the pope were, thus, elements within a jurisprudential framework. They should not be read as though they were elements of a political pamphlet or as though they formed part of some coherent statement of policy or belief. Did the French lawyers, then, have specific juristic precedents to follow in setting out to achieve the deposition of the pope? The advancement of the papal monarchy in the thirteenth century and the prevailing belief in the superiority of the pope's overarching spiritual power[17] were such that it is difficult to see the assault upon Boniface as anything other than extraordinary. It was, after all, a fundamental principle of canon law that the pope could be judged by no man, a claim supported on occasion by a text of St Paul: 'But he that is spiritual judgeth all things, yet he himself is judged of no man.'[18] And it is certainly true that the French lawyers were treading new ground in actually setting in motion the summoning of a General Council to try the supreme pontiff. Nowhere had precise legal processes for the trial of a pope been formulated. Yet, in the world of Realpolitik (and schisms) the position of popes (not only anti-popes) had often been challenged and threatened, and Gratian's Decretum (c. 1140), the sourcebook par excellence of papal superiority, had itself cited cases of popes who had submitted to judgments. More than this, it is clear that in the commentaries of canonists, from c. 1140 onwards, the possibility of papal deposition was both acknowledged and discussed.[19] While this canonistic debate apparently receded for much of the thirteenth century, there can be no doubt that c. 1300 legal principles relating to papal deposition were well known within – and probably also without – ecclesiastical circles. And it should be stressed that the heated question of the resignation of Celestine V had certainly brought to the fore the whole issue of papal suitability.

It seems, in fact, very likely that in the formulation of the appeals of 1303, especially of June 1303, the French lawyers took their lead from the canonists, and especially from the decretists, the commentators on Gratian's Decretum, working from c. 1140 to c. 1220. The text which had demanded elucidation was Gratian's declaration that the pope could be judged by no man 'unless he is shown to have deviated from the faith (*nisi deprehendatur a fide devius*)'[20] – unless, that is, he is considered to be a heretic. Glosses upon this 'dictum', notably those of Huguccio and Teutonicus,[21] could well have been an inspiration, perhaps a direct inspiration, in the shaping of the 1303 appeals. Above all else, there was, of course, the emphasis upon heresy. For the canonists a charge of heresy just had to be the crux of the matter. In addition, the canonists stressed that there should be a common belief in the validity of the charge of heresy; and it is a constant refrain in June 1303, in accusation after accusation, that the pope was 'publicly defamed'. Although there was no consistent canonical theory on what, in the context of a papal condemnation, should or should not constitute heresy, Huguccio had unambiguously claimed that a pope could be condemned of notorious crimes, since to scandalise the Church, by committing, for example, simony or fornication, was itself a heresy; and in 1303 the many accusations of scandalous behaviour and scandalous personal morality were undoubtedly part of the overall charge of heresy. Also, the importance of persistent contumacy had been stressed by the canonists; and the 1303 appeals, in the ninth year of the pontificate, having moved

decisively away from debate on the legality or otherwise of the pope's elevation, derived much of their force from the claim of long-term and continuing
misdemeanours.

Furthermore, it is likely that the canonical influence upon the French
lawyers was immediate and contemporary. The work of the decretists was
being studied anew by canonists active in the late thirteenth and early fourteenth centuries, whether by those critical of the papal monarchy (notably
John Monachus and William Durand the Younger) or by those with the
highest regard for papal authority (notably the outstanding academic jurists
Guy de Baysio and his pupil John Andreae). It is clear that there was a
renewed interest in the question of popes who 'deviated from the faith'.[22] Both
Guy de Baysio and John Andreae took the view that resistance to a pope
suspected of heresy required a criminal indictment and a subsequent trial,
and Guy stated firmly the opinion that a General Council alone was com-
petent to judge a pope. So, it is even possible that some of the inspiration for
the shaping of the assault upon Boniface VIII came from the innermost ranks
of his own learned supporters.

It is, therefore, first and foremost, within a legal context that the form and
content of the 1303 appeals must be understood and judged. But not only in
a legal context. The attack upon Boniface VIII by the French king and court
was, there is no question, a political attack, concerning the nature and the
exercise of papal authority in relation to royal authority. The very accusation of heresy was, of course, charged with deep political significance. It was,
after all, more appropriate that the pope should be a saint. The heresy charge
was an echo of imperial accusations against Gregory VII in the late eleventh
century.[23] And it is surely significant that, in the thirteenth century, it was
the slur of heresy that had become a basic justification for papal actions against
emperors.[24]

Although heresy was the antithesis of sanctity, the two had developed a
symbiotic affinity.[25] In some ways they were understandable, almost even
definable, only because of each other; and during the thirteenth century the
papacy had drawn to itself ultimate and exclusive responsibility for identifying both heretics and saints. There emerged, for the one, earnest inquisitorial
procedures and, for the other, more and more elaborate and protracted canonisation enquiries. Intense political influences pervaded both processes. While
papal control was dominant, in many cases relating to both heresy and sanctity the ascendant authority of the French monarchy had been at stake. Indeed, since the time of the Albigensian crusade early in the century opposition
to heresy had become a key feature of the work of the Capetian dynasty; and
in 1297, at the beginning of a four-and-a-half-year period of alliance between
Boniface and Philip IV, the pope had, with all due ceremony, canonised the
king's grandfather Louis IX, one of whose virtues had been that he had taken
up arms against the enemies of Christendom, including heretics.[26] Thus, it is
clear that the attack upon Boniface as a heretic was a dramatic way, at a time

of bitter crisis with the papacy, of reinforcing the saintly image of the Capetian lineage. And in this climate of polarised and politicised vices and virtues, it comes as no surprise that, after Boniface VIII's death, Philip pressed – and with success – for the canonisation (in 1313) of Celestine V, the hermit pope whose controversial resignation had made way for Boniface's elevation. Boniface's enemies had heresy-hunters and saints among their ranks.

It is striking, too, that this was an age in which major political developments or wrangles might well result in high-profile legal actions. It was an age, in other words, of political trials and attempted political trials, which often displayed a large element of propaganda or political manoeuvring and must thus rank as show trials. Some of these trials, involving spectacular accusations, were (and remain) notorious: for instance, the processes against the Knights Templar between 1307 and 1314 and against Guichard, bishop of Troyes, between 1308 and 1313.[27] Others are less well known. For example, following a rising of the commune of Laon in February 1295 and an assault upon the cathedral church, Boniface VIII had attempted to settle the dispute by initiating legal proceedings against the citizens of Laon, in support of the sentences of excommunication and interdict of local churchmen; in the event, it was only by royal intervention that, in 1298, the church and citizens of Laon became reconciled.[28] Another legal intervention by the pope, this time in England, had also been a dismal failure. Boniface had responded to a plea by John Ferrers, concerning what in fact had been the Crown's expropriation of his father's earldom of Derby, by appointing Robert Winchelsey, archbishop of Canterbury, as papal judge delegate to hear a case against Thomas of Lancaster on the grounds of usury.[29] Proceedings began in St Paul's London between April and June 1301. Since the action turned on contractual arrangements about the fief of an earldom and called into question royal policy relating to the creation of Lancastrian wealth, no one can have been surprised when this extraordinary legal process was suddenly aborted, with the archbishop's commissaries declaring that they did not dare to continue.

Two other legal assaults had been directed at individual bishops, one English and the other French. These cases against churchmen, initiated by laymen, were interesting precursors of the case against the bishop of Rome. The intriguing attack upon Walter Langton, bishop of Coventry and Lichfield and king's treasurer, made by the knight John Lovetot junior, had led to the bishop's suspension and summons to Rome.[30] He cleared his name in 1303. The accusations against the bishop were in many respects similar to those against Boniface, though without any specific mention of heresy: there was the claim of public defamation (*vox fama et publica*) and the mixture of irresponsible ecclesiastical policies (simony and pluralism) with immoral and criminal behaviour (adultery and murder) and consorting with the devil.

The second recent case against a bishop patently foreshadowed the accusations against the pope. Indeed, it was the renowned attack by Philip of France upon Bernard Saisset, bishop of Pamiers, that brought down the full force of papal wrath against the French Crown and precipitated the bitter crisis between king and pope.[31] The Saisset case was 'the first important treason trial of a cleric in later medieval France'.[32] The bishop was seized, held prisoner and tried before the king and council (in October 1301), before being sent to Rome early the following year.[33] The political relationship beween the case against Saisset and the case against Boniface has been frequently acknowledged and yet merits closer study. It must suffice here to point to the nature of the accusations against Saisset: he was accused not only of notoriously scandalous remarks against the king, kingdom, and royal court, and of conspiring time and again against the king, with the count of Foix, the count of Comminges and the king of England, but also of manifest simony, of claiming that fornication with men in holy orders was not a sin and that Pope Boniface was the devil incarnate, and of spreading many heresies, notably in opposition to the sacrament of penitence.[34]

The emergence of the open and personal anti-papal censures in 1303 must thus be seen against a backdrop of high-level, and judicial, lay/clerical tensions. And there is another political context to be considered. The accusations served an immediate and vital political purpose: the marshalling of public opinion. Directly indicative of this aim was the repetition time and again in the June complaints that the pope's scandalous behaviour was well-known: 'on this matter public opinion is working against him (*super hoc laborat publica fama contra ipsum*)', or 'on these matters he is publicly defamed (*super hec est publice diffamatus*)', or 'on this matter there is public outcry (*de hoc est publica vox et fama*)'.[35] In truth, whatever the situation before March and June 1303, the public revelations of the pope's scandalous transgressions were themselves designed to ensure that his vices were notorious. No claims could have been more self-fulfilling. The planned summoning of a General Council at which the pope's trial could take place required widespread support, and the public accusations were the first stage in an elaborate policy of obtaining that support. Within days of the June assembly remarkable procedures were initiated for obtaining dossiers of letters of adherence to the summoning of a Council from nobility, clergy and townspeople throughout the realm.[36] The controlling of public opinion was part of the political, and legal, process. A mere spat between Philip and Boniface would not unseat the pope.

The denunciations need to be seen, therefore, in the context of an appeal to the whole French Church, its lay as well as its clerical members. For this purpose accusations that were very precise and in some way substantiated were unnecessary. Dramatic and general accusations that were difficult to contradict were the order of the day. There was certainly no point in opening up debatable political matters. The censures must serve to carry the Crown's case forward. It was therefore important that the agenda for the planned legal proceedings be at least indicated. In both March and June the appealers declared that the details concerning heresy would be specified in due course in the proper place and at the proper time.

What, then, should we deduce from this survey of the legal and political context of the trial texts of 1303? It is tempting to believe that the carefully formulated charges were the outright inventions of the calculating French lawyers. But this is too simple a conclusion. To carry weight the accusations had to be credible, and there were certainly commonly held views of the kinds of reprehensible behaviour of which churchmen, especially those enmeshed in the political world, were capable. It seems clear that the accusations, however much they were being turned to the advantage of the French Crown, were derived, even at the outset, from common perceptions and from stories with at least some degree of general acceptance. Take, for example, the accusation of homicide. There is evidence which suggests how this charge may have emerged. It can be related to a specific incident. This was the death of fifty or so pilgrims crushed under foot by a great crowd on the occasion of the pope's Jubilee celebrations in 1300.[37] Also, there were cases, it was claimed, of clerks having died after being gaoled at the pope's orders, in some instances as a result of disputing among themselves Celestine V's right of resignation. That clerks had died as an indirect result of papal actions, and perhaps even papal orders, could easily have given rise to the belief that the pope was guilty of homicide, and it is possible that this was quite a widely disseminated story rather than a deliberate and coldly calculating fabrication.

Some truths may be detectable in the charges. Yet, it is certain that there is little or no point in attempting, item by item, to substantiate or deny the scurrilous anti-papal imputations. Their very forcefulness, tied as they were to a political campaign, was derived from the fact that they were not readily open to debate. Neither the real Boniface nor the real ecclesiastical and political world in which he moved can be effectively revealed through an investigation of the claims made in the 1303 trial texts. In respect of the crucial heresy charge, it is fruitless to attempt to find identifiable and specific heretical traits in Boniface's beliefs and behaviour. The accusations of denying the immortality of the soul and the existence of an afterlife have been linked, notably in an article by Wenck almost a century ago,[38] to the heterodox Aristotelianism and materialism of the late thirteenth century. Thus, the possibility that the pope belonged to a new heretical sect was opened up. But here is a profound irony. The papal policies which had given rise to intense animosity in the French court were a defence of the supremacy of the priesthood, which, evidenced especially in the pope's declaration Unam Sanctam, can be seen, altogether plausibly, as a reaction to the newly threatening Aristotelian notions of the discrete validity of temporal rule.[39] Were the pope's accusers aware – amusedly aware perhaps – of the paradox inherent in their accusations? Their 'heretic' was the staunchest of defenders of priestly authority. There is much to indicate that he was, in addition, careless in word and vainglorious in deed. But to argue that he belonged to some kind of heretical sect seems nothing short of ludicrous. A pointer to what the heresy charge truly signified to contemporaries may well lie in a statement by Peter Dubois.[40]

Dubois was a commentator close to the royal court. He wrote a rejoinder to Boniface's bull 'Ausculta fili' of late 1301, with its famous statement that the king was subject to the pope in both spiritual and temporal matters and its conclusion that the pope considered anyone believing otherwise to be a heretic. Dubois responded that a pope capable of making such a claim should himself be considered a heretic. This suggests that for Dubois, and probably many others in France, the charge of heresy was a charge of abject failure in the defence of the Church and thus of the faith.

The details of the portentous Franco-papal rift of 1301 to 1303 have engaged the attention of generations of historians. Yet the reasons for the crisis have aroused little discussion or debate. The main explanation for this is that one seductive interpretation has long held sway. There is a general consensus that this was a clash between a newly emerging secular and national monarchy and a papacy defending the traditional pretensions of the universal Church. This dichotomy between the new and the traditional demands scrutiny. After all, the French monarchy had its own traditional rights over its own Church and, far from having purely secular concerns, claimed repeatedly to be supporting the interests of the universal Church. It is a surprising fact that the political issues at stake in this Franco-papal conflict have yet to be adequately clarified. But our analysis of the charges which emanated from the French court in 1303 demonstrates that the actual lists of accusations are altogether inadequate sources for the study of the reasons for the attack upon the pope. Perhaps it is artless to expect that trial texts concerning those in high – not to say the highest – office might themselves indicate the underlying reasons for the intended trial. Indictments, indeed, may well have a political context which legal documentation serves to hide rather than elucidate. The political issues underpinning the Franco-papal clash must be sought in other sources. Of special interest for a comprehension of the immediate circumstances surrounding the decision to plan for a papal trial are the twelve articles sent by Boniface in late 1302 and the king's twelve responses of February 1303.[41] Here was a dialogue about some major issues, as, for example, the filling of vacant ecclesiastical benefices. Here are some indications of the political causes of bitterness and tension. The French accusations of March and June 1303 need, certainly, to be studied in relation to their own legal and political context, but, in the quest for an understanding of the reasons for the attempted papal indictment, these trial texts are a false trail.

Notes

1 The author gratefully acknowledges that the initial research from which this article has developed was undertaken during his tenure of a British Academy Readership.

2 See T. Schmidt, *Der Bonifaz-Prozess: Verfahren der Papstanklage in der Zeit Bonifaz' VIII und Clemens' V* (Forschungen zur kirchlichen Rechtsgeschichte und zum Kirchenrecht, 19, Cologne and Vienna, 1989), pp. 435–6, and for the continued shadowy existence of the Boniface affair in French historiography, p. 2 n.9.

3 See especially P. Dupuy, *Histoire du differend d'entre le pape Boniface VIII et Philippes le Bel* (Paris, 1665); R. Scholz, *Die Publizistik zur Zeit Philipps des Schönen und Bonifaz' VIII* (Stuttgart, 1903); J. Rivière, *Le Problème de l'église et de l'état au temps de Philippe le Bel* (Louvain and Paris, 1926).

4 J. Coste (ed.) *Boniface VIII en procès: articles d'accusation et dépositions des témoins* (Pubblicazioni della Fondazione Camillo Caetani, Studi e Documenti d'Archivio, 5, Rome, 1995).

5 *Ibid.*, pp. 103–22.

6 II Peter 2, 1–3, 15. Biblical texts are cited here from the Authorized Version.

7 John 10, 1.

8 See Matthew 7, 15–20.

9 Matthew 3, 10.

10 Schmidt, *Bonifaz-Prozess*, pp. 60–1.

11 For the Colonna manifestos see Coste (ed.), *Boniface en procès*, pp. 32–63.

12 *Ibid.*, pp. 122–73.

13 *Ibid.*, pp. 128–31.

14 *Ibid.*, pp. 90–103.

15 See especially *ibid.*, pp. 885–908.

16 N. Adams and C. Donahue (eds), *Select Cases from the Ecclesiastical Courts of the Province of Canterbury c. 1200–1301*, Selden Society, 95, 1978–9, introduction, p. 62 and n. 6, and J. H. Denton, 'Philip the Fair and the ecclesiastical assemblies of 1294–1295', *Transactions of the American Philosophical Society*, 81 pt 1 (1991), 17 and n. 51.

17 See, for example, J. A. Watt, *The Theory of Papal Monarchy in the Thirteenth Century* (London, 1965).

18 I Corinthians 2, 15. See John of Paris, *On Royal Power*, (ed.) J. A. Watt (Toronto, 1971), p. 31.

19 B. Tierney, *Foundations of the Conciliar Theory* (Cambridge, 1955, reprinted 1968), pp. 57–67; J. M. Moynihan, *Papal Immunity and Liability in the Writings of the Medieval Canonists* (Analecta Gregoriana, 120, Rome, 1961), pp. 43–106; E. Peters, *The Shadow King* (New Haven and London, 1970), pp. 220–2; and Schmidt, *Bonifaz-Prozess*, 1, 62.

20 D.40 c. 6 – see E. Friedberg (ed.) *Corpus iuris canonici* (Leipzig, 1922), I, p. 146. For the origins of this 'dictum' see Moynihan, *Papal Immunity*, pp. 27–42.

21 Tierney, *Foundations*, pp. 58–67, 248–50, and Moynihan, *Papal Immunity*, pp. 75–106.

22 Tierney, *Foundations*, pp. 179–96, 212–15, and Moynihan, *Papal Immunity*, pp. 117–19.

23 M. Chazan, *L'Empire et l'histoire universelle de Sigebert de Gembloux à Jean de Saint-Victor (XIIᵉ–XIVᵉ siècle)* (Paris, 1999), pp. 273–5.

24 *Ibid.*, pp. 575–7.

25 For this paragraph see J. H. Denton, 'Heresy and sanctity at the time of Boniface VIII', to be published in *Tolerance and Repression in the Middle Ages* (1998 Conference Papers, Institute of Byzantine Research, Athens).

26 See especially A. Vauchez, *La Sainteté en occident aux derniers siècles du moyen âge*, École française de Rome, 1988, pp. 74n, 214, 265, 415–17, and J. H. Denton, 'Taxation and the conflict between Philip the Fair and Boniface VIII', *French History*, 11 (1997), 249–53.

27 See *inter alia* M. Barber, *The Trial of the Templars* (Cambridge, 1978), and A. Rigault, *Le Procès de Guichard, évêque de Troyes* (Paris, 1896).

28 J. Denton, 'The second uprising at Laon and its aftermath, 1295–98', *Bulletin of the John Rylands University Library of Manchester*, 72: 3 (1990), 79–92.

29 M. Bateson and J. Denton, 'Usury and comital disinheritance. The case of Ferrers versus Lancaster, St Paul's, London 1301', *Journal of Ecclesiastical History*, 43 (1992), 60–96.

30 For the accusations against him see T. Rymer (ed.), *Foedera: conventiones, litterae et cujuscunque generis acta publica* (4 vols in 7, London, 1816–1869), I ii, pp. 956–7. Other primary and secondary sources are cited in J. B. Hughes (ed.) *The Register of Walter Langton, Bishop of Coventry and Lichfield 1296–1321* (Canterbury and York Society, 2001), I, p. xxxv, and J. H. Denton, *Robert Winchelsey and the Crown 1294–1313* (Cambridge, 1980), p. 53 (the statement here of 'intercourse' with the devil meant, of course, communication with the devil: cf Hughes, (ed.), *Register of Langton*, p. xxxv n.115).

31 For the Saisset affair see especially Dupuy, *Histoire du differend*, pp. 621–62; D. de Sainte-Marthe et al. (eds), *Gallia Christiana in provincias ecclesiasticas distributa* (16 vols, Paris, 1715–1865), XIII, instrumenta 107–38; and J.-M.Vidal, *Bernard Saisset* (Toulouse and Paris, 1926), pp. 76–115.

32 S. H. Cuttler, *The Law of Treason and Treason Trials in Later Medieval France* (Cambridge, 1981), p. 73.

33 G. Digard, *Philippe le Bel et le Saint-Siège de 1285 à 1304* (2 vols, Paris, 1936), II, pp. 95–6.

34 Dupuy, *Histoire du differend*, pp. 628, 653–6, and Saint-Marthe et al (eds), *Gallia Christiana*, XIII, instrumenta 110, 116–18.

35 Coste (ed.), *Boniface en procès*, pp. 145, 149–50, 152, 155, 159, 161, 163.

36 See W. J. Courtenay, 'Between pope and king: the Parisian letters of adhesion of 1303', *Speculum*, 71 (1996), 577–605, and S. Menache, 'A propaganda campaign in the reign of Philip the Fair 1302–1303', *French History*, 4 (1990), 427–54.

37 Coste (ed.), *Boniface en procès*, p. 302 n.1.

38 K. Wenck, 'War Bonifaz VIII ein Ketzer?', *Historische Zeitschrift*, 94 (1905), 1–66. See Coste (ed.), *Boniface en procès*, pp. 905–6.

39 W. Ullmann, 'Boniface VIII and his contemporary scholarship', *Journal of Theological Studies*, 27 (1976), 58–87.

40 Coste (ed.), *Boniface en procès*, p. 92.

41 Dupuy, *Histoire du differend*, pp. 90–5; C. Port (ed.)., *Livre de Guillaume le Maire* (Documents inédits de France, Mélanges historiques, vol. 2, 1877), pp. 380–4; and Digard, *Philippe le Bel et le Saint-Siège*, II, pp. 138–45.

7

Reasonable doubt:
defences advanced in early
modern sodomy trials in Geneva

William G. Naphy

There are few charges that can be made against individuals more likely to damage their lives, reputations and futures, than sexual deviance.[1] In the early modern period, the danger was even greater as the crime carried the death penalty. For those faced with the gravest of punishments, one might be inclined to suppose that there was only one sure defensive strategy: outright denial. However, before testing this hypothesis, some general information on the quality of the documentation surviving in the Genevan archives is vital. In addition, something must be said about the understanding of deviance in Geneva's courts.

This chapter will take as its chronological parameters the period 1555–1665.[2] This is because 1555 was the date at which Calvin and the ecclesiastical authorities were able to take control of the administration of morals while 1665 saw the last prosecutions for sodomy for a century. Although one might expect to see intensive involvement by the Church in the prosecutions, the Calvinist Church was noticeable by its absence, confining its interest to adultery and pre-marital sex. Thus, this period gives insight into criminalised, rather than socially unacceptable, sexuality. Moreover, it is lengthy enough to allow for a significant number of trials to be examined in an area of criminality that is, for obvious reasons, not overly common. Just as importantly, it allows for the possibility that the Genevan attitude to this crimes might alter and evolve over the period between the advent of close ecclesiastical discipline of morals and the last sodomy trial in the mid-seventeenth century.[3]

Most cases include six types of documentation: a summary, the sentence, legal advice, medical reports, depositions of witnesses and transcripts of the interrogations. Individuals were asked about themselves, any previous prosecutions and the specific charges against them. The city's prosecuting magistrate, his assistants, the city's secretary and any number of senior magistrates, from none to over twenty, were present. Depositions were taken from prosecution witnesses and, in some cases, witnesses for the defendant. Those giving evidence, regardless of their age, were physically confronted with the accused. The defendant was then asked to respond to the specific accusations being made. If the case involved violent sexual assault, a forensic report would be requested. At least two doctors or barber-surgeons would examine the males (predominately boys and youths) while midwives examined the females (of all ages). Eventually, the case documentation was passed to a university-trained legal expert (who had not been present). His role was to advise on the appropriateness of torture.[4] Later, he might be asked to suggest a final sentence. Once the Lieutenant was satisfied that there was no more information to be gained, he would prepare a summary of the case for the city's supreme magisterial council.[5] The Senate would then draft an official sentence, which would be read out in public. As these cases involved numerous interrogations often spread over weeks, there is a substantial body of material. More importantly, the verbatim nature of the records allows one to watch the case developing and to hear the dialogue between the magistrates, seeking evidence of guilt, and the defendant, striving to avoid a conviction – and death – for sexual deviance.

For the most part, Geneva's authorities used a range of generalised terms for these sexual crimes. However, evidence internal to the cases suggests that they were prosecuting with subtlety and discrimination. This chapter proposes to treat these cases in groupings, which reflect the behaviour of the prosecutors and defendants: adult, same-sex acts; bestiality; lesbianism; child abuse; 'deviant' heterosexuality; pre-adolescent sexual activity; and incest. Each of these terms – save incest – is anachronistic. However the anachronism is not forced. For example, any careful examination of the cases of child abuse shows that there are problems with differentiating between the abuse of boys (sodomy) and that of girls (rape). Cases involving children or minors were prosecuted differently from those involving adults. That is, cases of child abuse have more in common with each other than they do with cases given the same technical and legal name involving adults.

It is important to note that this does not mean that an early modern legal precision is being replaced by alternative modern categories, but rather that a culturally and temporally conditioned use of legal terminology is being substituted with categories based on the internal structure and evidence of the cases themselves. This structure and evidence are then being grouped and described in a manner more in keeping with modern usage. If one were to give an early modern Genevan 'catch-all' description to the cases under discussion it would be 'crimes against nature', a phrase which at times equates solely with sodomy (involving males with other males) but, in certain circumstances, encompasses a whole range of sexual crimes. Indeed, the only generalised and generic label with which Geneva's judges seem comfortable and confident is 'crimes against nature'. Genevans may not have been sure how to categorise diverse manifestations of deviance but they knew which behaviour was deviant and that they did not approve of it. Most importantly, they knew it was unnatural.[6]

It seems appropriate to begin with two unique cases, one of lesbianism and the other of group heterosexuality. For ease of reference, see Table 7.1 for the basic details in the order in which they will be discussed below, as well as Table 7.2 which gives the wider statistical context for the trials treated in this chapter. In 1568, Françoise Morel, an itinerant plague worker, was arrested.[7] She had been accused by a co-worker, Amber, of molesting her one night while they were sharing a bed. Amber had resisted and a violent assault had ensued. Françoise countered by asserting her innocence while admitting she had previously confessed to fornication with a male five years before. It seems clear that at the outset of the trial she was trying to advance a defence designed to protect her from further prosecution. She was readily admitting a criminal act (fornication) and a previous conviction. Either she did so because she thought attempting to avoid this admission was more dangerous or she may have thought that a previous conviction for fornication with a man might throw into doubt the charges currently facing her.

Thus, her first line of defence was to confess a known relationship with a man. A midwifery report confirmed that she was not a virgin. She then made the fatal error of retracting her fornication confession. This allowed torture.[8] She admitted the assault on Amber as well as two previous sexual experiences with women and repeated fornication with men. Despite her dissolute life she was forceful in denying that she had ever taken money for sex. She might have been a rather busy bisexual but the lady was no whore. In addition, she denied that her actions with women were fornication. Although Germain Colladon, the legal adviser, judged her guilty of 'the horrendous and appalling crime of sodomising another woman (*le crime horrible et execrable de sodomie sur une aultre femme*)', he strongly advised that the public statement be vague.[9] Finally, the clergy at her execution recorded that she admitted to additional lesbian acts.[10]

The important considerations arising from this case are that her first line of defence was a previously confessed relationship with a man. It is not clear why she attempted to retract this admission since it was manifestly clear that the magistracy knew about it already. They had used questions about her background in an attempt to catch her in the act of perjury or 'variation', which allowed for torture. In addition, both the amateur magisterial judges and Colladon were keen to hide the exact nature of her crime from the general public. It is not necessarily obvious how the final version was more acceptable than that originally proposed but it is certain that Colladon, at least, considered the first draft wholly inappropriate. Finally, from the magistrates' point of view the trial failed to answer their most persistent question about motive. The court was perplexed as to why Morel would have acted as she did. Morel's only insight was to suggest that she was possessed.[11] Although a dangerously reckless assertion, the judges seem

Table 7.1 Specific Genevan trials mentioned

Defendant(s)	Sixteenth-century terminology	Modern terminology	Trial date(s)	Sentence
Francois[e]-Jean[ne] Morel, plague-worker, daughter of Pierre Morel (naturalised Geneva)	Crime against nature	Lesbianism	16–31 March 1568	Drowned
Claude Crestien, from Nantua, Jaques Molleiz, from Rouz, and (in absentia) Sieur de Vergiez, Pierre Dabaux, André Burnet	Animal lust	Group sex	28 January–1 February 1569	Beaten through the streets and banished
Etienne Taccon, Christobla Sertoux (his niece by marriage) and Pierre Dentant	Incest, perjury, complicity	Incest, perjury, complicity	7–18 November 1556	Banished for 10 years.
Jeanne, daughter of Claude Nicolas, aged 15	Incest, theft, fornication	Incest, theft, fornication	25 January–26 April 1569	Drowned
Pierre, son of Claude Nicolas, aged 23	Incest		5 February–2 March 1569	Beheaded
Pierre de la Rue, aged 46	Highway robbery, bestiality	Highway robbery, bestiality	19 October–14 November 1617	Burned alive
Pyramus Mermilliod, aged 16 or 17	Bestiality	Bestiality	22 May–6 June 1660	Acquitted
François Bosson	Bestiality	Bestiality	28 February–16 March 1663	Not proven
Jaquema Gonet (servant) and Esther, aged 15, and Nicolas, aged 8, Bodineau (siblings)	Sodomy and acts against nature	Child abuse, lesbianism, sex between minors	12–24 October 1559	Acquittal. beaten. executed

Bartholomy Tecia, Theodore-Agrippa, and Emeri Garnier (students aged 15)	Sodomy	Sex between minors	28 May–10 June 1566	Acquitted, executed
Thomas Reancourt and Jaques Beudant	Sodomy	Same-sex acts	4 June–11 July 1561	Banished
Jean de la Rue, aged 80	Sodomy	Solicitation and same-sex acts	5–8 February 1617	Burned
Pierre Canal sodomy ring, 1610				
Pierre Canal (steward of the Senate), Abel Benoit (aged 20, soldier), François Felisat (24, carder), Pierre Gaudy (18, porter), George Plongon (25, Sieur Bellerive), Mathieu Berjon (36, printer), Antoine Artaut (30, carder), Jean Bedeville (23), Paul Berenger (23, tailor), Noel Destelle (25, baker), Jean Maillet (61), Paul André (23), Claude Bodet (45, baker), Jean Buffet (23, tailor) [a]	Sodomy	Same-sex act, especially oral sex	12 January–17 April 1610	Fined, banished, beaten, executed
Hozias Lamotte, tutor	Sodomy	Child abuse	29–31 December 1563	Drowned
Louis Guey (aged 72) and Beatrice George (aged 13)	Sodomy	Child abuse	11–21 September 1568	Decapitated and beaten
Jean Bourgeois (aged 45), Françoise Corbet and her daughter Clauda (aged 10)	Attempted rape	Under-aged marriage	20 August 1600	Jailed and fined

Note:

[a] Numerous others were named but were not prosecuted, presumably because they could not be located. The sexual acts dated back, in some cases, to events over the previous decade.

Table 7.2 *Genevan trials, an overview*

Modern terminology	Total number of trials (dates)	Total number of sexual partners (willing or unwilling)	Sentences or verdicts (no., %)
Lesbianism	1 (1568)	5 (4 females, 1 male)	Executed (1, 100)
Heterosexual group sex	1 (1569)	6 (5 males, 1 female)	Beaten and banished (1, 100)
Incest (by blood or marriage)	13 (1556–1636)	22 (11 males, 11 females)	Not proven (2, 15.4) [a]; incarcerated (2, 15.4); banished (1, 7.7); beaten and banished (2, 15.4); executed (6, 46.2) [b]
Bestiality	7 (1565–1663)	14 (7 males, 2 mares, 4 cows, 1 goat)	Unknown (1, 14.3); not proven (2, 28.6); executed (3, 42.9); acquitted (1, 14.3)
Pre-adult sexual experimentation	5 (1555–1624)	14 (12 males, 2 females)	Beaten and banished (3, 60); executed (2, 40)
Adult, same-sex acts	23 (1561–1662)	55 (all males)	Unknown (1, 4.4); fined (2, 8.7); not proven (7, 30.4); beaten and banished (2, 8.7); executed (11, 47.8)
Child abuse			
Against boys	6 (1555–1633)	19 (all males)	Not proven (1, 16.7); banished and beaten (1, 16.7); executed (4, 66.7)
Against girls	17 (1562–1615)	36 (18 males, 18 females)	Unknown (1, 5.9); not proven (1, 5.9); probation (1, 5.9); incarcerated (1, 5.9); beaten and banished (7, 41.8); executed (6, 35.3)
Totals	73 (1555–1662)	171 (128 males, 36 females, 2 mares, 4 cows, 1 goat)	Acquitted (1, 1.4); not proven (13, 17.8); unknown (3, 4.1); probation (1, 1.4); fined (2, 2.7); incarcerated (3, 4.1); banished (1, 1.4); beaten and banished (16, 21.9); executed (33, 45.2)

Notes:

[a] One was a suicide so the case ended inconclusively.

[b] Of these six, one case also involved infanticide and another an attempted murder.

not to have considered it valid and the case ended unsatisfactorily for the judges.

Almost a year later, Claude Chrestien and Jaques Molliez were arrested for having had sex with a girl along with three other men.[12] Molliez breached Claude's effective wall of silence when he confessed that one night he had found the other four men having sex with the same serving girl. After a confrontation with Chrestien and the threat of torture (advised by Colladon), Molliez confessed. His defence was that he had only ever had sex twice. Both men confessed and begged for mercy. Three issues fascinated the magistrates. Who went first and had the order been agreed in advance? The prisoners reported the same order (that is, Lord Veigiez went first and there had been no previous discussion).[13] Second, had they watched each other? Both admitted their act of fornication but said that, although it sounded like the others had had sex, they were not sure.[14] Third, what had the other four been doing while the fifth was having sex? Three stood idly by, definitely not looking at one another or handling themselves – or one another – while the next in line, as it were, sat ready at the foot of the bed.[15]

The court's understanding of the crimes they were facing is fascinating. Colladon was clear that lesbianism was sodomitical and against nature. However, the group sex, while revolting, was 'normal' fornication.[16] Once the magistrates had established the guilt of the men, they were interested in ensuring that they had not engaged in any contact with one another. That is, the judges were eliminating the additional charge of a crime against nature. Although the group sex disgusted them, the actual activities uncovered in the second case remained within the general category of 'natural sexual acts'. This interest in 'natural' and 'unnatural' is the issue to which this chapter will return.

Let us turn to incest. The most interesting aspect of the statistics is the rate of execution. In the case of incest, 46 per cent of the trials resulted in an execution. If one adds a pre-sentence suicide then defendants died in 54 per cent of these trials. Clearly, this suggests a marked difference from the single case of group sex. Can the statistics provide any more insight into magisterial sensibilities? In those cases involving sexual acts between relatives by marriage the verdicts resulted in sentences of floggings and banishment in two cases, two not-proven verdicts and a single execution (see Table 7.2). However, in the five cases involving close blood relatives, the sentence was always death. One might be inclined to infer from this that sex with relatives by marriage, while incestuous, was not as serious an offence as sex with a close blood relative. Can one hypothesise that the former, like group sex, was disgusting and criminal while the latter, like lesbianism, was unnatural? Also, can the case details give us any further insight?

Two cases of incest are worthy of closer investigation. In 1556, the city was rocked by the scandal of a leading merchant, 'Fat' Etienne Taccon, being accused of getting his niece by marriage, Christobla Sertoux, pregnant and of trying to arrange a marriage between her and Pierre Dentant which would hide the crime and, it seems, allow him to carry on the relationship.[17] What most shocked the magistrates was the cold calculation shown in Taccon's plans, which only went awry when it became clear that Pierre was not willing to allow the incest to continue and was not too keen on accepting the charge of pre-marital fornication, especially as he only became aware of the pregnancy after agreeing to the marriage. Taccon's defence throughout was his innocence and the assertion that Christobla was carrying Dentant's child. Eventually, after confrontations with Sertoux, he admitted that he had had sex with her but said that Dentant had as well and so the child might not be his.

It was left to Colladon to unravel the evidence. He opined that Taccon and Sertoux were clearly guilty of incest. He faulted Dentant for continuing to perjure himself for so long, though he conceded that he had not known the unborn child was Taccon's, having been told that it was the child of another relative by marriage. As Dentant was even younger than the girl, he suggested that the city might want to be lenient. In the end, the city deemed that they were all guilty of attempting to pervert the course of justice in addition to the incest.[18]

The case of the Nicolas siblings was slightly more complex in that their parents had been executed only weeks before on charges of witchcraft and conspiring to spread plague.[19] However, the important element of the case was the line of defence taken by Jeanne and Pierre Nicolas. Jeanne was primarily questioned for theft and possible complicity with her parents. She was also asked about fornication with her fiancé, Martin Leschiere. Her assertion of virginity was quickly disproved by a medical examination. She then admitted to pre-marital sex with Martin. Despite confrontations with her brother who had already confessed to incest, she maintained her innocence until after she was tortured. Two days later she admitted that she had denied the greater charge because it was a capital crime while fornication was a 'lesser' crime.[20]

Undoubtedly, the memory of her parents' burning had left a vivid imprint on her adolescent mind. Pierre had confessed spontaneously. He had been left little choice once he had admitted to sharing a bed with his sister and – he hastened to add – their younger brother (who had slept between them). It seems he tried this line of defence to prove that his sister had had no opportunity to fornicate with Martin. The result was disastrous. Thus, the defensive strategy taken by both was to admit as much of the truth as possible while avoiding any admission of incest.

With bestiality, there was no partial defence. Denial was the only option. However, even this serious crime only resulted in an execution in 43 per cent of the cases and, interestingly, gave rise to a single acquittal. Three cases contain elements worthy of a brief mention. Pierre Delarue, while being investigated for highway robbery in Protestant Geneva, was discovered to have been convicted of bestiality eighteen years before in a nearby Catholic village.[21] This conviction was used as the justification for burning him alive. Therefore, a case that originally started with an investigation into the theft of some salt became much more dramatic when the Lieutenant began examining the defendant's past. It eventually became apparent that he had escaped from gaol before his scheduled execution and had changed his name. When he was convicted of bestiality, he had been known as Jean Boccard (*alias* La Violette).[22]

In 1660, an eyewitness (Danielle Livron, aged thirty) denounced Pyramus Mermilliod.[23] She had seen him in the stable with one hand on his genitals and the other in or about the cow's fundament.[24] Two factors resulted in Mermilliod's acquittal. First, he claimed 'that he was urinating against the cow's fundament to kill off the flies, having heard at Jussy that this was a good remedy (*quil urinoit contre le fondement de la vache pour faire mourir les mouches vaires ayant appris a jussy q[ue] cestoit un bon remede)'.*[25] Secondly, the Lieutenant's assistant (*auditeur*) reported that he had measured the height of the privates of both the cow and Mermilliod and concluded that since the cow was a good French royal foot higher it was unlikely that an act of copulation could have taken place. One can suppose that the judges had little idea if the defence was true. Thus, although they could not prove he was guilty of bestiality, they thought his behaviour suspicious and dubious and therefore banished him from the city, leaving him 'to God's judgment'.

The final case is a dramatic example of the role of circumstantial evidence in Roman Law trials.[26] Despite an eyewitness account, which allowed the legal adviser to recommend torture, Bosson maintained his innocence in the face of this torture.[27] However, he changed minor elements of his testimony (to his detriment). As a result, the court banished him to God's judgment. In effect, they found that there was sufficient circumstantial and eyewitness evidence to question his innocence but not enough to convict – a 'not-proven' verdict.[28] This highlights the importance, in Roman Law, of incontrovertible proof. It was clear that he had altered his testimony. There was no doubt that he had run away from the arresting officer. There was an eye-witness to the events. However, without a second eye-witness or an outright confession, the court could not convict. Hence, he was banished.

In cases of sexual deviance between minors the rate of execution was comparable to that in the foregoing trials, 40 per cent. In most cases, the younger the defendant the more likely the courts would favour a sound thrashing over death. However, two complicated cases are worth consideration for, yet again, bringing to the fore the issue of 'unnatural' acts. In 1559, Jaquema Gonet, a young servant girl, was executed for seducing her master's daughter, Esther.[29] Together, they 'fingered each other's privates (*mettoient le doigt dans le membre lune de lautre)'.*[30] More importantly, they both abused Esther's brother, Nicolas. Nicolas had reported the acts to his mother and, thereby, initiated the case. The magistrates were mainly interested in knowing the girls' motivation. Esther said it started when Jaquema told her that boys could make their members longer.[31] The judges and Colladon struggled with how to label the crime and to word the public sentence. Colladon, after a number of drafts, decided that Jaquema had committed 'abominable acts of sodomy and a sin against nature' while Esther was guilty of incest, an 'act of fornication which was also against nature in view of the extreme youth of the poor small child'.[32] Although Esther knew that she had sinned, Colladon advised that she should be spared but *only* because of her age.[33] Nicolas should be strongly admonished though he was too young to understand his crime.[34] Thus, one sees an attempt to arrive at a judgment based on an understanding of sexual development and moral responsibility. Also, the state was determined to shield the spectators at the public punishment from the actual details of the case. Even the summation avoids clarity.[35]

The trial involving three students, Tecia, Agrippa and Garnier, is of most interest because of the unwillingness of the latter two to report Tecia.[36] It became clear in the trial that Tecia had repeatedly exposed himself and fondled a number of fellow students and even attempted to force himself on Agrippa one night in bed. His behaviour was outrageous.[37] Nevertheless, no one rushed to report him.[38] Tecia quickly made a full confession. He had been abused in Avignon when he was ten and, despite repeated solicitations, had not been able to entice any of his fellow students.[39] What was also clear was his lust for Agrippa and the manipulative lengths he was willing to employ to satiate that desire.[40] He cited the fate of Sodom and Gomorrah and called upon the magistrates to punish him.[41] They obliged within a fortnight.[42]

Since male, adult same-sex crimes are fairly numerous, I will have to summarise the defences taken in these cases. First though, it is important to note that only 48 per cent of the trials resulted in an execution. The defences themselves take a number of forms. First, whenever possible defendants mentioned their previous sexual acts with women.[43] When forced by witnesses, or torture, they often admitted to some fondling and 'horseplay'.[44] In all cases there was a determined effort to resist confessing to two specific acts. First, penetration (whether anally or orally) was denied.[45] If this was confessed, the defendants strongly denied that ejaculation took place.[46] In effect, there was a defence beyond outright denial: previous heterosexual or 'natural' sexual activities. Once same-sex acts were admitted there was clearly a hierarchy of crime. Penetration, or the attempt thereto, was bad, penetration long enough to ejaculate was worse.

Two cases perplexed the magistrates and an examination of these trials will prove useful: those of Reancourt and Beudant (on the one hand) and Delarue (on the other). In both cases, there was more than sufficient evidence to convict: Reancourt and Beudant were caught in the act while Delarue freely confessed his guilt. Reancourt was clearly suffering from mental problems while Beudant was too young (only eighteen) and had been put up to the behaviour as part of a privately run sting operation against Reancourt, whose exhibitionism and fondling (in church) had begun to annoy leading citizens.[47] Reancourt was well known for his behaviour; however, it seemed that the magistracy was unwilling to take any action against him.[48] They both confessed to kissing one another but denied anything else.[49] Reancourt admitted that he knew their behaviour was wrong.[50] The legal advice eventually concluded that nothing 'approximating to the appalling crime of sodomy (*approchans au detestable crime de sodomie*)' occurred, certainly not through the behaviour of Reancourt.[51] However, the lawyers also mentioned the youth of Beudant and the age and marital status of Reancourt as mitigating factors.[52] In the end, these opinions were followed by the State, which banished both men but placed Reancourt under the harsher sentence of 'on pain of death' while qualifying Beudant's banishment 'on pain of flogging'.

Jean Delarue, for his part, fascinated the magistrates because his primary explanation for his life-long sodomy was that it gave him pleasure.[53] His trial was extremely brief – only four days – and resulted in his execution. The summation noted two important features coming from his testimony. First, he confessed 'that for years he had abandoned himself to committing the horrible crime of sodomy, against nature, with many people outwith this city (*que des longues annees il s'est abandonne a commettre l'horrible crime de sodomie contre nature avec plusieurs personnes hors ceste cite*).'[54] Secondly, he had only been caught because 'he had been in an inn in this city a few days ago with a young man [Balthasar] . . . [and] he had made an attempt on the person of that young man, who had resisted and reported [him] to the law (*il y a quelques jours en un logis public en ceste cite avec un jeune homme . . . il auroit attente sur sa personne lequel jeune homme luy resiste et revele a justice*).'[55] Delarue had managed to maintain an active sex life for many years and seemed to have expected that Balthasar would either acquiesce or, at least, simply ignore the advance. However, the most important feature of this trial is the openness of his confession and the forthrightness of his motivation. When asked 'if he committed this horrible crime for pleasure [he] responded for pleasure . . . and [because of] his poverty, he confessed he had done this for pleasure with all those with whom he had committed it (*sil a part commis cest horrible acte p[ar] plaisir R[eponder] par plaisir . . . et p[ar] pauvrete confesse l'avoir faire p[ar] plaisir avec toute ceux quil avec lesquelz il l'a commisery*).'[56]

The most interesting series of cases, however, relates to Pierre Canal.[57] As can be seen from Table 7.1, a substantial body of men was arrested. There are many important points worth consideration. First, the city was immediately suspicious of the close relationships between these men of widely differing socio-economic backgrounds.[58] Second, whenever possible social and marital status were used as a defence.[59] In addition, although everyone had had oral sex with Canal there was a determined effort to deny ejaculation.[60] Worse from the point of view of the judges, there was evidence of partner swapping.[61] Although torture played a part in the trials it seems not to have produced false confessions.[62] Finally, the behaviour, as with the octogenarian

Delarue, had remained hidden for a considerable period of time.[63] Taken together, this series of trials presents impressive proof both of a close-knit group of men engaged in same-sex acts as part of a wider social context as well as the importance of status, evidence of heterosexuality and 'lack of consummation (ejaculation)' as a defence strategy.[64] These men were not only part of a promiscuous group, but also had a reasonably active (and carefully hidden) social life one with another.[65] In addition, they were all well aware of the best means of protecting themselves when caught.[66] While the historian may infer the types of defences advanced, these men clearly knew them as a matter of life or death.[67]

Although these cases are interesting, the most surprising feature is the repeated stress laid by the magistrates and lawyers on natural versus unnatural acts. Moreover, the creeping defence, of admitting some things while denying the greater crimes, is a common strategy as is the plea of previous involvement in natural sexual activities. Finally, the rate of execution is surprisingly constant at 40–50 per cent.

As can be seen from the Tables though, the situation changes dramatically in cases of child abuse, especially in cases involving boys. In these cases, the rate of execution is nearly 67 per cent. Although the rate of execution in cases involving girls is lower, at 45 per cent, these are the cases in which penetration was proven or confessed; the other cases, in effect, involved 'inappropriate touching'. In other words, sexual assault on children produces an overwhelming rate of execution regardless of gender. The horror of the magistrates in these cases comes through repeatedly; they are truly shocked that anyone would want to harm a child.[68] They regularly ask if the child cried and, if so, why the person persisted.[69] In a sense, crimes against children seem to be the most 'unnatural' in the eyes of the magistrates, lawyers and doctors.

Finally, one might highlight a few additional cases. In 1563, Hozias Lamotte, a student and private tutor, was arrested for violating his pupil, Jehan Cherubim.[70] The tale had come out when young Jehan started crying at the supper table and his parents asked what was wrong. His father was particularly incensed because he had explicitly forbidden the tutor to strike his child, since he had assumed that physical abuse might well lead to worse excesses. Five years later in 1568, Louis Guey was executed for having had sex with Beatrice George.[71] Despite her age, she was beaten. This was because twice she had entered his room and initiated sexual relations. That was deemed to be culpable. Finally, in 1600, Jean Bourgeois was accused by the consistory of Gex, a rural parish, of attempting to rape a young girl, Clauda, by becoming engaged to her with her mother's consent.[72]

So, having survived this hasty trawl through Genevan deviance, what tentative conclusions can be advanced? First, outright denial was rarely tried as the sole defence, except in bestiality cases. Usually, the defendants admitted some crimes while denying the worst charges. Also, in cases of same-sex acts, previous contact with women was quite a strong defence. The most successful defence was that identified by the lawyers: youth and diminished mental responsibility. In many cases, the authorities interpreted these categories very broadly indeed. The most interesting overall conclusion from an examination of these trials is the stress laid on activities that are against nature and those that are not. Unnatural acts are punished most severely. More importantly, there seem to be gradations of unnatural acts. For example, incest with a blood relative is more unnatural than sex with a relative by marriage. Sexual acts involving children, because they also cause pain and suffering to an innocent, are seen as especially unnatural. The defensive strategies adopted by the accused seem to bear this conclusion out. Defendants were willing to admit to just about anything 'natural' but constantly maintained their innocence against the charge of 'unnatural' acts. When forced to confess, by opposing testimony or torture, they still had in mind a firm hierarchy of the unnatural acts that were more natural. Thus, ejaculation during penetration was worse than penetration alone; which was worse than simple assault; which was worse than exhibitionism. Throughout these trials, judges, lawyers, doctors, midwives, witnesses, and the defendants, provide evidence of a very subtle and discrete dialogue about deviance in which many diverse levels are apparent. For an age without psychology, sociology and other 'modern' behavioural disciplines, the participants in these trials reveal themselves to be very acute observers of human behaviour and development and, perhaps, surprisingly modern.

Notes

1 For general studies on this topic see K. Gerard, *Pursuit of Sodomy: Male Homosexuality in Renaissance and Enlightenment Europe* (Harrington Park, Pennsylvania, 1987); M. Goodrich, *The Unmentionable Vice: Homosexuality in the later Medieval Period* (no place: Dorset, 1979).

2 For additional information see E. W. Monter, 'La Sodomie à l'époque moderne en Suisse romande', *Annales: Économies, Sociétés, Civilizations*, 4 (1974), 1023–33 and his 'Sodomy and heresy in early modern Switzerland', *Journal of Homosexuality*, 6 (1980–81), 41–55. All manuscript references are from the *Archives d'État de Genève* and its two series of *Procès Criminels* [henceforth as, PC1 or PC2: dossier number (trial dates); accused].

3 Although prosecutions stopped in the mid-seventeenth century, there are four surviving cases thereafter. However, these were handled in a very different way and evidence a dramatic shift both in magisterial and popular opinion. See PC1: 14778 (5–12 December 1785, Louis Caulet, aged forty-seven, watchmaker, for sodomy with a grenadier, fugitive); 14930 (31 July 1786, Jacob Zimmermann, shoemaker, aged twenty-three, for soliciting soldiers, censured and banished); 15178 (2 June–31 July 1787, Jacob Ponçon, for sodomy with, and corruption of, various soldiers, banished); 15711 (20–22 May 1789, Jaques Dombres, aged forty, billiard-hall owner, for sodomy, deprived of his licence).

4 On the place of torture in judicial processes see J. H. Langbein, *Torture and the Law of Proof: Europe and England in the Ancien Regime* (Chicago, 1977); J. Heath, *Torture*

  and English Law: An Administrative and Legal History from the Plantagenets to the Stuarts (Westport, 1982).

5 The Lieutenant was Geneva's chief investigating magistrate (comparable to the Scottish procurator fiscal) who was helped by his four *auditeurs*.

6 For attitudes elsewhere see G. Ruggiero, *The Boundaries of Eros: Sex, Crime and Sexuality in Renaissance Venice* (Oxford, 1985); M. Rocke, *Forbidden Friendships: Homosexuality and Male Culture in Renaissance Florence* (Oxford, 1996).

7 PC1: 1465 (16–31 March 1568): Françoise, daughter of Pierre Morel, *bourgeois*, aged approximately thirty-six. The papers in the individual dossiers are not paginated or foliated but are arranged (for the most part) in a chronological order. Thus, reference will be by date. The Genevan civic structure needs some comment. At the bottom of the social scale were foreigners and *natifs* without civic power. Registered aliens were sworn to protect the city and called *habitants*. Anyone could buy or be given full civic status (though forbidden senatorial and syndical office) as a *bourgeois*. A child born to *bourgeois* parents in Geneva gained the rank of *citoyen* and access to all offices (including those of Senator and Syndic).

8 PC1: 1465 (22 March 1568).

9 Colladon's explicit description was altered in the first draft of the public sentence to 'debauchery and fornication in a manner contrary to nature (*debordement et paillardise contre nature*)'. The final draft replaced this with '[a] detestable crime contrary to nature (*crime detestable contre nature*)'. Colladon's phrase made the sex act clear. The first draft was still explicit (fornication, *paillardise*) while the final form was so vague as to include bestiality. For more on women and crime see U. Rublack, *The Crimes of Women in Early Modern Germany* (Oxford, 1999).

10 Cf. F. Canade-Sautman, *Same Sex Love and Desire among Women in the Middle Ages* (Basingstoke, 2000); J. C. Brown, *Immodest Acts: The Life of a Lesbian Nun in Renaissance Italy* (Oxford, 1986).

11 For the close association of gender, sexuality, and the demonic see L. Roper, *Oedipus and the Devil: Witchcraft, Sexuality and Religion in Early Modern Europe* (London, 1994); D. Elliott, *Fallen Bodies: Pollution, Sexuality, and Demonology in the Middle Ages* (Philadelphia, 1999).

12 PC1: 1517 (28 January–1 February 1569). See also the case of group homosexuality involving three Europeans and three Muslim converts to Calvinism, PC2: 1634 (19–24 February 1590): Girardin Dupuis (from Versoix, aged fifty, acquitted), Jean Chaffrey (from Dauphiné, aged twenty, executed), Etienne Chappuis (*citoyen*, aged fifteen, executed), Tatare Mohamet (from Martara, aged thirty-five, executed), Assan (from Turkey, aged twenty, executed), Ali Arnaud (from Rumania, aged thirty-four, executed).

13 PC1: 1517 (27, 29 January 1569): Claude (son of Claude Chrestien), from Nantua, a mason and Jaques (servant of Claude de Lac, son of Pierre Molliez), from Rouz. The other three men implicated but not prosecuted were the Sieur de Veygiez, Pierre Dabaux (servant, along with the girl, of the Avullier household) and André Burnet (servant of Jean Burnet, mason, from Nantua, and Chrestien's employer as well). The young woman was Pernette Chappuis, niece of André Bonjon. They all lived in the Avullier house.

14 PC1: 1517 (26 January 1569).

15 PC1: 1517 (28 January 1569).

16 His undated advice referred to the acts as '[a] thing completely horrible (*chose tout horrible*)'. The summation said that 'like creatures, wholly shameless and bestial, they had defiled themselves and fornicated together (*comme gens de tout effrontes et brutaux se polluerent et paillarderent tous*)'. The public sentence added the marginal note that they had acted 'like dogs and brute beasts (*comme chiens et bestes brutes*)'.

17 PC2: 1110 (7–18 November 1556): Etienne (son of François Taccon, *bourgeois*, called *Gros Thivent*), Christobla (daughter of Jehan Sertoux, from St-Jullien) and Pierre (son of Pierre Dentant, from Neynier, shepherd).

18 Colladon's opinion, as well as both the summation and sentence, expressly mention the incest and the perjury.

19 PC1: 1516 (25 January–26 April 1569); 1519 (5 February–2 March 1569): Pierre (a wool-carder) and Jeanne Nicolas (aged about fifteen), the children of Claude Nicolas (a lace maker raised as an orphan in the city's *Hôpital Général*) and Claudine l'Hoste, a *citoyenne*. A mother's status did not pass to her children. Thus, they were both *natifs*. Jeanne's fiancé, Martin Leschiere, was banished on pain of death a few months later, see PC1: 1518 (1 February–9 June 1569), PC2: 1311 (1 February 1569).

20 She had been examined and proven not a virgin (29 January 1569). Her explanation of her prevarication came on 20 April.

21 PC1: 2378 (19 October–14 November 1617): Pierre (son of Pierre Delarue) from La-Baume-en-Genevois, aged forty-six.

22 The summation explained the tangled events: in 1609 'While at Baumont, he had abandoned himself to perpetrating that horrible and execrable crime against nature with a mare; having been detained as a prisoner for this in the said place he managed to escape (*estant au lieu de Baumont il se seroit abandonné à commettre l'horrible et execrable crime contre nature avec une jument, pour lequel estât detenu prisonnier dud[ite] lieu il se seroit evadè d'icelles*).' Cf. the use of the phrase '*crime detestable contre nature*' to obfuscate the lesbian case above.

23 PC1: 3696 (22 May–6 June 1660): Pyramus (son of Pierre Mermilliod), from Troinex, aged sixteen or seventeen, servant of Esaia Colladon in Petit-Sacconex.

24 A second witness was Catherine, daughter of Jaques Lebouz, from St-Genys (22 May 1660).

25 That is, 'that he was cleaning [the fundament] (*quil le nettoyent*)' (28 May 1660).

26 PC1: 3777 (28 February–16 March 1663): François (son of Roulet Bosson), from Vernier in Gex, master carpenter, aged thirty.

27 The witness was Estienne (daughter of Hugues Duvillard), *habitant*, servant of Noé Remilly, aged thirty. He was tortured on 7 March 1663.

28 His defence was hampered both by his variations and because he had fled the officer of the court when they had tried to arrest him (28 February 1663).

29 PC1: 862 (12–24 October 1559): Jaqueme (daughter of Bernard Gonet, from La Cluse, labourer), chambermaid of Pierre Tolliet (apothecary); Esther (daughter of Ylaire Bodineau and Nicole Renaud, from Bles, *habitant*, step-daughter of Estienne Batteneau, book-seller and *habitant*), aged fifteen; Nicolas (son of Estienne Batteneau and Nicole Renaud), aged eight or nine.

30 12, 14 October 1559.

31 Jaqueme told Esther 'that she had seen some men who had lengthened [become erect] their penises (*quelle avoit veu des hom[m]es que avoyent leur membres long*)' and boys and girls in the village playing with one another (12, 18 October 1559).

32 The public verdict against Jaqueme is explicitly vague: 'you have committed a detestable crime not to be named and likewise you have been possessed by the Devil (*tu as commys crime detestable qui nest point a nommer et mesmes que tu as este possedee du diable)*'.

33 The final advice comes in a second opinion from Colladon which seems to struggle with the exact wording of the crimes and punishment. The first opinion, by Nicolas des Gallars, Louis Enoch and Colladon, follows a similar line but inclines to a harsher punishment for Esther. Esther's public verdict also says 'you have committed a detestable crime not to be named (*tu as commus crime detestable et que nest point a nomme[r])*'.

34 He is not actually sentenced in an official way. The appeal by their mother, Nicole Renaud, failed to prevent Esther's flogging and banishment on pain of death.

35 Referring to 'obscene and detestable acts that are not fit to be discussed (*actes vilaines et detestables et que ne sont pas dignes destre recitez)*'.

36 PC1: 1359 (28 May–10 June 1566): Bartholomy (son of Bastian Tecia, from Piedmont, *habitant*); Theodore-Agrippa (son of Jehan Daubigny, from Gascony); Emeri (son of Arnaud Garnier, from Gascony). Likewise, Joseph Guarino, when sexually assaulted by Claude Bodet, a *bourgeois*, in 1610 simply discussed the attack with his employer, Martin Anglois. Guarino said that when he had rebuked Bodet, the latter 'trembling, could not reply (*tremblant il ne peult pas repondre)*'. Neither took the matter further (see PC1: 2022, 2 February).

37 Daubigny said that 'an Italian student staying with me tried to bugger him that night about midnight (*ung escoleur Italien demourât chez me le principal le voulut le nuict bougrer environ la muynuit)*'.

38 Hence, both Garnier and Daubigny were initially arrested though they quickly changed from co-defendants into chief witnesses for the prosecution.

39 He confessed on 30 May 1566.

40 Tecia said 'While Agrippa was asleep one night, [Tecia] tried to force him to realise his desire to place his member inside [Agrippa] (*Agrippa dormât une nuyt il se voulut efforcir daccomplir son desire cest de mettre son membre dand[it] luy)*' (31 May 1566).

41 See 30 May 1566.

42 Colladon made it clear that Tecia 'cannot be excused because of being too young and ignorant (*ne peut estre excuse de trop grande jeneusse et ignorâce)*' because of the manipulative nature of his acts 'to incite him [Garnier] into consenting to all those totally abominable acts (*pour le [Garnier] inciter a le consentir tous lesquelz actes sont du tout abominables)*'.

43 Jean Buffet was willing to admit to his extramarital fornication but was vehement in denying he had had any sexual contact with another man (PC1: 2031, 10 April 1610). Cf. Pierre du Four's assertion that he was so far from being a sodomite that he had already fornicated (aged nineteen or twenty) and that his father knew it (PC1: 1818, 5–15 November 1600).

44 See the case of Tecia above.

45 See the discussion about the cases revolving around Canal below.

46 Again, see the Canal affair below.

47 PC1: 957 (4 June–11 July 1561): Thomas (son of Michel de Reancourt, from Normandy), goldsmith, *habitant*); Jacques (son of Pierre Beudant, from Nîmes), draper, servant, aged eighteen.

48 A string of depositions (on 4, 6, 9, 11, 28 June and 12 July 1561).

49 See Beudant's confession (17 June 1561) that 'he had also put his tongue in [the other man's] mouth *(luy passant aussi sa langue entre ses levres)*'. Reancourt denied that the kiss was intimate (6 June 1561).

50 His plea was that the behaviour was innocent in intent: 'it was only in play, with no wicked intent *(qua plus en se jouant non pas a mal)*' (12 June 1561).

51 See the sentence.

52 One said that 'in the first place and without any doubt, the said Thomas is, in age, a legal adult having a wife and children *(en p[re]mier lieu et sans aucung doubte q[ue] led[it] Thomas estat en aage dhom[m]e p[ar]faict ayât femme et enfans)*'.

53 PC1: 2350 (5–8 February 1617): Jean (son of Jaques Delarue, from Passeri), aged eighty.

54 See the summation.

55 See the summation.

56 See 7 February 1617.

57 All the trials took place in 1610. PC1: 2013 (12 January–2 February, Canal, executed); 2014 (20 January–13 March, Jean Maillet, *citoyen*, spying and murder); 2016 (31 January–24 February, Plongon, *citoyen*, fined 200 écus); 2017 (31 January–25 February, Boniot; Felisat; Gaudy; sodomy, all executed); 2018 (31 January–3 March, Berjon, *citoyen*, banished); 2019 (31 January–3 March, Artaut; Bedeville; André; Destalle; sodomy); 2022 (1 February–17 April, Bodet, *bourgeois*, sodomy, fined 1,000 écus); 2031 (30 March–10 April, Buffet, fornication and sodomy, banished).

58 See Table 7.1 for details on status and profession.

59 Canal made it clear that he had not had oral or anal sex with his wife although he had taken the active and passive roles in both with other men, see PC1: 2013 (31 January 1610). Bergeron was specifically asked if he was married and had to admit that he was not married at the time of his first sexual relations with Canal (PC1: 2018, 3 February). Despite confessing to frottage, intercrural sex, and mutual masturbation with Canal and Destalle (and at least six other youths) at various times in the previous thirteen or fourteen years, Bodet was only fined (PC1: 2022, 1 February).

60 Bonoit admitted that Canal had 'eaten his member' but that ejaculation had not occurred 'except one time' (PC1: 2017, 19 February 1610); despite torture, he maintained the distinction (23, 26 February). Felisat confessed to frottage and mutual masturbation only (31 January). Despite repeated torture, Artaut would only admit to mutual masturbation and that Canal had orally stimulated him but denied he had ejaculated in Canal's mouth or that he had ever performed oral sex on Canal (PC1: 2019, 3, 19, 26 February).

61 Plongon was accused (PC1: 2016, 23 February 1610) of having allowed his hand to wander while sharing a bed with Hugonin Challon (aged thirty-six) three weeks before the trial. Bodet admitted to fondling Destalle (PC1: 2019, 1 February).

62 See for example PC1: 2014 (20 January–13 March 1610), Maillet, who resisted extreme applications of torture and whose piteous pleas are preserved. He was acquitted. Canal was so badly tortured at one point that he could not speak and 'had trouble breathing' (PC1: 2013, 27 January). Two surgeons reported that Bergeron's arms had been badly damaged by torture (PC1: 2018, 1 March).

63 Pierre Guaict (aged twenty-six) said that men had been calling Canal a 'bugger' in public for the previous eight years, see PC1: 2013 (29 January 1610). Bergeron

145

admitted that Canal had molested him seven or eight years before the trial when Bergeron was in his late twenties and that he had not reported it (PC1: 2018, 31 January). Bedeville said his relationship with Canal had started five years before (PC1: 2019, 31 January). Destalle said that Canal had tried to molest him while he was still a student (in 1602, aged seventeen or eighteen); this was not reported nor did it end their friendship (PC1: 2019, 31 January).

64 One of the more creative defences was produced by Destalle who said that he had discussed masturbation with the minister De la Faye, who had told him it was wrong, although a number of other prominent youths had told him that masturbation (even mutual masturbation) was not a sin (PC1: 2019, 19 February 1610).

65 Plongon admitted (PC1: 2016, 31 January 1610) that he had slept over at Canal's house when he was about twenty-one but denied any acts of oral sex. The judges specifically wanted to know why André kept visiting Canal's house if he was always having to rebuff unwanted sexual advances (PC1: 2019, 2 March); André simply denied that anything had actually happened.

66 Felisat (PC1: 2017, 19 February 1610) defended himself by saying he 'intended no evil but knew that Canal was a man of reputation (i.e., socially prominent and powerful)'. Gaudy also took a similar line saying Canal forced himself upon the unwilling Gaudy (19 February).

67 Gaudy's father (also Pierre), after his son's appeal as a citizen to the *Conseil des Deux Cents* failed to overturn the sentence of death, presented a lengthy appeal (PC1: 2017, 28 February 1610) that argued for lenience on a number of grounds: the youth's age, the length of the detention during the trial, the cold in the prison, the harshness of the torture and the untrustworthiness of a convicted traitor, spy, and sodomite (Canal). Bergeron's wife and lawyer tried a similar appeal (PC1: 2018, 2 March).

68 E.g., PC1: 1147 (16–19 August 1563): Claude Barbel, a schoolteacher, was sacked for striking three of his pupils in the mouth with a rod. Cf. L. Haas, *The Renaissance Man and his Children: Childbirth and Early Childhood in Florence 1300–1600* (Basingstoke, 1998); B. A Hanawalt, *Growing up in Medieval London: The Experience of Childhood in History* (Oxford, 1993).

69 E.g., PC1: 3768 (9–24 December 1662): Col. Alphonse Crotto (from Lucca, aged forty-four) and Jean Chabaud (from Avignon, aged thirteen). Crotto was executed and Chabaud beaten.

70 PC1: 1167 (29–31 December 1563): Hozias Lamotte (from Anduze, student) and Jean (son of Jean Cherubim).

71 PC1: 1494 (11–21 September 1568): Louis Guey (*habitant*, from Aosta, aged seventy-two) and Beatrice (daughter of Nicolas George, merchant, from Piedmont), aged twelve.

72 PC2: 1932 (20 August 1600): Jean Bourgeois (from Vernier, aged forty-five), Françoise Corbet (mother of Clauda, from Chevrier), Clauda (daughter of Mauris Roget and Françoise Corbet, aged ten), Bernard Roch (Clauda's uncle). It appeared that this was an attempt to spirit the child across Lake Geneva from Protestant Gex to the re-Catholicised southern shore.

8

Testifying to the self: nuns' narratives in early modern Venice

Mary Laven

In the summer of 1614, scandal erupted at San Zaccaria, the oldest and most aristocratic of the Venetian convents. Laura Querini, a noble nun in her mid-forties, was found guilty of having had sexual intercourse, repeatedly, with a young nobleman in a store-room situated on the edge of the nunnery. Testifying before Patriarch Francesco Vendramin, the head of the Venetian Church, Laura Querini told her story from the very beginning:

> I came to this convent as a little girl during the time of plague [1575–77] . . . ; and then I was sent as a boarding-girl to another convent, San Vido on the island of Burano, where I stayed for five or six years until I was accepted as a nun back at this convent – I must have been about fifteen years old. I took my initial vows at the ceremony of clothing; then I made my profession; but I spoke with my mouth and not with my heart. I have always been tempted by the Devil to break my own neck.[1]

Laura revealed that she first met her lover – whom she called by the pseudonym of Zuanne Cocco – six years before her fall into scandal. He was introduced to her by a woman called Donna Cipriana, who over the years had supplied the noble nun with a series of 'friendships'. Laura stated that, during the course of these liaisons, 'I never did anything wicked, that is, I never lost my virginity'.[2] But with Zuanne, a young man about twenty years her junior, things were different. Not satisfied by their occasional meetings in the convent parlour, Laura pursued Zuanne with absolute determination:

> I fell in love with him, and I induced him to love me. I used every means to make him love me, including diabolical methods, that is, spells and superstitious prayers invoking devils, and I paid Donna Cipriana to provide me with these things.[3]

Young Zuanne, however, was wary of the risks that he ran. Less than a decade earlier, in 1605, the Venetian government had passed a stern new law, which prescribed capital punishment for any man found guilty of visiting a nun illegally.[4]

Dangerous as the situation was, Laura devised a plan which would enable the lovers to consummate their relationship. She identified a small store-room on the canal side of the convent, and – with the help of another nun, Suor Zaccaria – set about bashing a hole in the wall. The nuns were committed and resourceful. They wrenched a piece of iron from the window-grille of Laura's cell, and used it as a crowbar. It took them more than a month to break their way through the wall, which was six stones deep.[5] In order to obscure the gaping hole they had made, the nuns pulled a large stone across the outside and smeared it with terra cotta; on the inside, they used black and white lime to fill in the cavity.[6] At last, the two nuns achieved their goal. Zuanne Cocco arrived, accompanied by his cousin Zorzi, who would be Zaccaria's lover:

> The two men came in a boat, and put a plank across. We unblocked the hole, and they entered through it, and they stayed with us for two or three hours, while they had intercourse with us.[7]

Underlining the supremely sacrilegious nature of this encounter was the fact that it took place in Lent, the time of year expressly designated by the Catholic church for fasting and sexual abstinence. Using language heavy with sexual overtones, Laura told of how Zuanne had returned alone, after Easter, to penetrate the convent once more:

> The said Cocco entered through the same hole, and he concealed himself within the store-room for ten or twelve days, nor did he ever leave that place; meanwhile, I went around the public spaces of the convent, ensuring that I was seen by the other nuns; and then when everyone was asleep, I went alone to be with him. Nor did I ever take lunch or dinner with him, except on just one occasion, but of course I brought him his food.[8]

With almost gratuitous honesty, Laura added: 'And all those nights that Cocco stayed in the nunnery, he had intercourse with me.'[9] This rich piece of first-person testimony, laden with autobiographical and cultural detail, was spoken in the vernacular. Laura Querini was on trial for her transgressions, yet she seems to have been determined to confess the full enormity of her errors. The drama of the unfolding narrative, and the highly personal nature of Laura's revelations, make for compelling reading. It is qualities such as these which have made trial records a favourite source among social and cultural historians – early modernists in particular. Some of the most renowned examples, such as Carlo Ginzburg's *The Cheese and the Worms*, Natalie Zemon Davis's *The Return of Martin Guerre*, and Judith Brown's *Immodest Acts*, are microhistories, studies which throw an intense spotlight on a particular person, event, or place, in order to reveal broader truths about the society and culture in which they were situated.[10] Trials have also provided the evidence for more macro-historical studies, for example Laura Gowing's *Domestic Dangers* (a study of gender in early modern London, based on defamation suits), or Stephen Haliczer's *Sexuality in the Confessional* (based on the trials of Spanish confessors brought before the Inquisition for soliciting penitents).[11] Both kinds of history have used trial records to recover voices from the past, from the whole spectrum of social and educational backgrounds, voices which would often otherwise be lost to oblivion.[12]

Colourful and copious as this kind of evidence is for the early modern period, an era of rapid expansion in the activity of the law-courts, it has proved to be a methodological minefield for the incautious historian. Among the objections commonly articulated, and relating particularly to the records of criminal trials, the most basic (and the most readily dispatched) can be summarised as follows:

1   Trial records are factually unreliable, because witnesses are prone to lie in order to protect themselves.
2   They focus on the transgressive and so do not tell us about general experience.
3   (And this is a hardline view) they do not, in fact, tell us about the history of crime or the transgressors who appear before the courts, but can only be used to reveal the history of criminal justice, that is the workings, policies and personnel of the courts. This position has been elegantly contested in a published debate between the two Italian historians, Mario Sbriccoli and Edoardo Grendi. While Sbriccoli argues that it is an illusion to believe that we can learn anything from criminal records beyond the history of legal institutions, Grendi insists that they shed light on the social practices which the magistrates seek to discipline.[13]

Interestingly, these problems seem to have been more troubling in the late 1980s than at the time of writing this chapter. All three have been met and countered by influential historians who have set themselves up as the champions of trial evidence. The defence has been carried out most conspicuously from the ranks of cultural historians, who have self-consciously shifted the goal-posts of archival research, rendering those problems which I have outlined pretty much irrelevant. Firstly, they have argued that values, perceptions and strategies may be uncovered from the testimony of court witnesses, regardless of their factual accuracy. Secondly, they have pointed out that a clear sense of what is considered transgressive or deviant enables us to draw the boundaries of the normal. And, thirdly, in so doing they have taken criminal records beyond the domain of criminal history, using trials to reveal more general truths about the society and culture which gave rise to them. A manifesto along these lines was presented by Natalie Zemon Davis in her book, *Fiction in the Archives*.[14] Davis took the use of court records beyond the conventional realms of criminal and judicial history. At the same time, she tackled the problem of unreliability in court records, articulating a new strategy for coping with the partialities which inevitably characterise trial evidence. Embracing forensic fictions, half-truths and lies, her fascination was with 'how sixteenth-century people told stories . . . , what they thought a good story was, how they accounted for motive, and how through narrative they made sense of the unexpected and built coherence into immediate experience'.[15]

But just when we thought the problems were behind us, a new set of criticisms has emerged, engaging the cultural historians more squarely on their own terms. Thomas Kuehn has criticised the microhistorians' reading of narrative representations in trial records, arguing that they are inclined to familiarise the past, 'making the Other into the Same'. His attack is focused upon Gene Brucker's study, *Giovanni and Lusanna*, subtitled *Love and Marriage in Renaissance Florence*.[16] That book aspires to reconstruct the 'history of a relationship' between a young Florentine male of high social standing and his older mistress of artisan stock. It is based on the trial which ensued when in 1455 Lusanna brought a suit against Giovanni for failure to honour his promises to her. Kuehn's point is that these records do not provide us with the 'history of a relationship'; rather, they provide us with the 'narrative of a trial'. He baulks, for example, at the way in which Brucker mines the testimony of witnesses for personal details about the central couple. Lusanna is described by witnesses on her side as 'strikingly beautiful', but then she would be (claims Kuehn), for Lusanna's legal representative would have suggested such terms to them as supporting her suit.[17] Moreover, Brucker's assertion that Lusanna was 'an extraordinary woman . . . of strong passions . . . prepared to risk dishonour to follow the dictates of her heart', takes no account of the prominent role of her brother, Antonio, in pursuing her suit. In Kuehn's view, the family's desire for revenge and financial compensation may have motivated the case quite as much as the dictates of Lusanna's heart.[18] Kuehn takes these weaknesses of *Giovanni and Lusanna* to be typical of microhistories, perhaps unfairly, since other works in the genre are more alert to the distortions wrought by legal procedures. However, his review article does draw attention to the more general problem of whether or not we can attempt to deduce the character or personality of early modern people from their representations in the courtroom (or come to that anywhere else). In Kuehn's view, microhistorians are particularly guilty of reductiveness in their characterisation of individuals. Thus Arnaud du Tilh (of *The Return of Martin Guerre*) becomes an imposter, Benedetta Carlini (the nun of *Immodest Acts*) becomes a lesbian, Menocchio (*The Cheese and the Worms*) is styled as 'bearer of popular illiterate culture', Lusanna becomes 'a lover' and Giovanni 'a typically exploitative young male'.

The problem has surely arisen precisely because trial testimonies are so seductive, and because the protagonists in long-forgotten courtroom dramas have a continuing ability to engage our sympathies. But then Kuehn is right:

we need to be careful about over-familiarising our historical subjects and effacing the contexts in which they speak. To quote Thomas and Elizabeth Cohen, the editors of an anthology of trial documents from early modern Rome:

> . . . we social historians, in reading vivid documents such as these trials, walk a narrow causeway. On one side yawns an abyss of bafflement, while on the other side there gapes a chasm of complacency.[19]

One early modern historian who has been charged with just such complacency is Miranda Chaytor, author of an article on narratives of rape in seventeenth-century England.[20] In a published response, Garthine Walker took Chaytor to task over many of her assumptions.[21] The most basic accusation is that Chaytor, who is informed by psychoanalysis, imposes modern readings on early modern accounts of rape. Walker insists that 'accounts of subjective, personal experiences are produced and made sense of within available collective, cultural meanings'.[22] In the context of the courtroom, first-person narratives are shaped by the constraints of legality, by the demands of the audience (in this case, the male officials presiding) and by a concern with reputation (what other people – for example, family members or neighbours – will think). According to Walker, 'accounts of rape found among early modern legal records ought not, therefore, to be analysed as if they were tales told about the self which provided access to a person's repressed memories or their most intimate experiences'.[23]

From Florence to the Northern Circuit, there is a new unease about the ways in which we read and understand court testimonies. The new worries are preoccupied not so much with the issues of reliability and typicality (factual distortions and the focus on deviance); they turn instead on our responses to narrative and self-expression, the two concerns of this chapter. Fuelled by the historical vogue for using the methods of psychoanalysis to interpret the past, recent debates are not limited to the uses and abuses of trial records as historical evidence. They reflect upon the more general question of whether – and how – the historian can gain access to subjectivities.[24] How does our perspective on the narrative of Laura Querini – a character who may be in some danger of taking up her place in Thomas Kuehn's gallery of microhistorical types as 'the desirous woman' – change when we turn to explore the various contexts in which she presents herself to us?

First of all, taking heed of the admonitions of Kuehn and Walker, we need to consider the legal context. Laura's transgression fell under the jurisdiction of the highest authority of the Venetian Church, the patriarch. The crime of her lover, on the other hand, fell under secular jurisdiction, and was tried by the Provveditori sopra Monasteri – the Venetian state magistrates, first appointed in 1521, with special responsibility for affairs relating to the city's numerous convents.[25] Laura was interrogated by both authorities, firstly as defendant, secondly as witness. Uncommonly, transcripts from both trials – amounting to nearly one hundred pages – have survived, preserved within the archives of the Provveditori.[26] We are therefore able to contrast Laura's forthcoming, confessional mode before the patriarch with her more reticent testimony in the trial carried out by the Provveditori. For Laura was hoping to protect the identity of the young men who had been the nuns' lovers, and of the lay accomplices who had helped to bring about the sinful events in the store-room. When she finally admitted the true name of her lover, Andrea Foscarini, she begged the Provveditori to forgive her for having refused to name him previously, 'because I did not want to be his ruin'.[27]

While the two authorities of church and state were trying different individuals, they were trying the same crime, or at least investigating the same events, and we need to be sure about how those events were construed as criminal. Clearly, Laura and her lover had committed a heinous deed of sacrilege. Indeed, given Laura's status as Christ's bride, her lover's conduct might be interpreted as cuckolding God himself.[28] But if this dimension to the crime was understood, it was not prominent in the rhetoric of either the secular or religious authorities. In the preamble to the trial, the patriarch held forth at some length about the damage wrought by the nuns upon a wall which was six stones deep, before finally revealing that one of the men (Foscarini) had stayed within the convent 'for ten to twelve days eating and drinking wine, and [that] he had carnal commerce with Suor Laura'.[29] The patriarch's central concern was with the breach of conventual enclosure which had occurred at San Zaccaria, and his remarks about the sexual transgressions which had taken place as a result of that breach appear almost marginal. This preoccupation with walls echoed those Counter-Reformation directives which had emanated from the Council of Trent and from Rome in the 1560s, subjecting all nunneries to strict enclosure, whatever the nature of their rule or customary rights. The same rulings pronounced anathema on anyone who dared to traverse the holy boundaries of enclosure, in either direction, without episcopal permission.[30]

Surprisingly, perhaps, considering the customary intransigence of the Venetian republic in response to the dictates of Rome, the State lent its secular arm to the Church in support of the drive to enclose female religious houses. Since the early sixteenth century, the government had busied itself increasingly with matters of conventual discipline. By the time of Laura Querini's trial, the secular legislation on nunneries had reached its zenith. In 1605, the Venetian Council of Ten produced its toughest law to date against unauthorised intruders, for the first time prescribing the death penalty. The wording was as follows: 'And if in future anyone . . . is found [unlawfully] inside any convent, or is accused of having entered, day or night, even if he is not convicted of carnal commerce, once he has been arrested and the truth established, let him be beheaded.'[31] Unlawful entry to a convent was now punishable by death, regardless of whether 'carnal commerce' had taken place. Engagement in sexual relations with a nun was, in terms of the secular law, an irrelevance.

When we review Laura's apparently open and honest testimony in the context of these legal conditions, we now see why she could afford to be so self-revealing. For she must have been aware that the authorities of Church and State were, above all, concerned to track down her lover and his friend, who – wisely, given the potential severity of the sentence that they would incur – had fled the city. In the event, the two men were sentenced – in absentia – to perpetual banishment, not just from Venice but from the entire Venetian dominion; if they were caught within the confines of the territory from which they were banned, they were to be brought back to the city and decapitated on the scaffold in St Mark's Square.[32]

Although there was a clear jurisdictional divide between the patriarch and the Provveditori, there is extensive evidence of cooperation in this case. And while church officials insisted on their unique right to try the nuns, and controlled access of the Provveditori to the nuns, they were also extremely keen to assist in bringing Foscarini and friend to justice. So while Laura refused to name her lover during the course of a month and a half of interrogations, eventually complying under threat of torture, she spoke freely of her own errors, including her claim to have seduced Foscarini with love magic, safe in the knowledge that it was largely irrelevant to the investigation. Also irrelevant was the fact – willingly disclosed – that Laura and her lover had had sexual intercourse repeatedly during his stay at San Zaccaria. Of course her own fate was yet to be decided; but the range of punishments to which female religious could be subjected was very limited. In-house imprisonment, a diet of bread and water, deprivation from the chapter and from the convent parlours were the most common penalties. Given that Laura's guilt was not in dispute, honesty was a tactic which any defence lawyer might have counselled.

That said, honesty is not a neutral commodity, and Laura's confessions are by no means free from artifice. The details which she supplied about her childhood and her unwilling entry to the religious life were clearly designed to win the sympathy of the court. They served to mitigate her errors, placing them in the context of a social problem which was all too familiar to the authorities in Venice: the high incidence of forced vocations. For it was a matter of considerable embarrassment for the Counter-Reformation Church (and a certain amount of discomfort for the government too) that convents played a highly expedient role in the economic strategies of noble families, which – determined to prevent the patrimony being frittered away on costly marriage dowries – dispatched their superfluous daughters to take the veil.[33] Laura's assertion that she made her profession with her mouth and not her heart was something of a cliché among the testimonies of unhappy nuns, and was an inversion of the customary response elicited from female religious during patriarchal visitations: 'I made my profession voluntarily and have always remained content.'[34] Nor was there anything original about Laura's suicidal urges, a familiar topos of forced vocation narratives.[35] So, in making her testimony, Laura not only took account of the legal construction of her crime, in an effort to protect her lover; she also emphasised certain aspects of the social context of her transgression, playing upon contemporary anxieties about forced vocations and their disciplinary consequences.

As we would expect from a defendant, Laura's testimony was governed by a desire not to incriminate (a concern which applied more to her lay accomplices than it did to herself). She was also driven by a wish to acquit and explain herself in the eyes of society – a matter of honour and reputation rather than of guilt or innocence in a legal sense. But her narrative is not simply about defending and justifying the actions of herself and others. She says far too much for that to be the case. The confidence and eloquence of her testimony (as well as the content of what she says) indicate a keenness above all to speak and to be heard. When we situate Laura within the specific conditions of the Counter-Reformation convent, we must remember how few opportunities she would have had to express herself. For enclosure meant more than the confinement of nuns within impenetrable compounds. It aspired to isolate nuns culturally and emotionally, as well as physically. Endless regulations were issued in the effort to control nuns' contacts with outsiders – neighbours and employees, priests and doctors, family and friends. All correspondence in which nuns participated was to be strictly censored by the abbess; the nuns were not allowed to keep pen, ink, or paper in their cells. Reading as well as writing was restricted, and the inspection of convent libraries was a standard feature of every visitation. As for music, an area which had traditionally offered nuns opportunities for creative expression, the picture was similarly bleak. There was a crack-down on the employment of lay music-teachers to instruct nuns, and female religious were generally discouraged from singing and music-making in church, particularly in the presence of a lay congregation. Ideally nuns were to be rendered inaudible as well as invisible.[36]

In accordance with the enclosure regulations, Laura's testimony before the authorities of church and state did not take place in an ordinary courtroom. Although the Provveditori applied to the patriarch for permission to remove her to a secular court, their request was denied. And so the judicial authorities of Church and State were brought into the parlour of San Zaccaria, where Laura Querini testified across an iron grille. While the rituals of the confessional had doubtless schooled Laura in the art of presenting her sins, the trial situation presented this noble nun with a rare chance to have her say before the patriarch and the Provveditori, fellow members of the Venetian ruling class. At a time when reformers aspired to block every channel of communication, drastically curtailing nuns' scope for self-expression, female religious developed new strategies for making themselves heard. The space of the trial provided nuns with an opportunity to speak to the outside world; their responses were often strikingly loquacious.

In that last respect, the case of Suor Laura Querini recalls that of Menocchio, the protagonist of Ginzburg's *Cheese and the Worms*. Just as the Friulian miller apparently relished the opportunity of rehearsing his heretical beliefs in front of an audience of inquisitors, so the Venetian nun enthusiastically regaled the city authorities with her sexual errors. Menocchio paid for his frankness with his life. The legal context in which Laura testified meant that her confessions carried fewer risks. Notwithstanding the differences, these two cases from the early modern period draw attention to the possibilities of the trial as a forum for self-expression.

Such possibilities are, as we have seen, constrained by the conventions and practices of particular courts. And in situations where the courtroom leaves defendants and other witnesses the freedom to say what they want to say, their words may nevertheless be tampered with in the process of transcription. In early modern tribunals, witness statements were sometimes paraphrased, translated into Latin, or formalised in some other way. The trial records examined in this chapter are especially vivid, for they appear to have been transcribed in full, retaining the linguistic peculiarities of the local vernacular. As a means of gaining access to the voices of nuns these documents are precious, since the Counter-Reformation restrictions on female religious recounting their experiences in writing mean that letters or diaries are as elusive for these elite women as they would be for the lowliest members of society.

For Venetian nuns, shut up in convents from their infancy and barred from communication with the outside world, trials afforded a rare opportunity to speak out. Their words cannot be taken to be artless effusions of individual character (whatever that may be). In the case of Laura Querini, we have witnessed the entanglement of the individual in her cultural contexts, the complicated balance between the personal and the rhetorical, the constraints and procedures which conditioned a narrative. And yet it is in the artificiality of her testimony that we find evidence of Laura's determination and purpose. Fashioned to the demands of her audience, Laura's story enabled her to control both the record and, to a certain extent, the result of the trial. Her testimony was an artefact, a creation, not a reflection of her self.

Notes

I am grateful to Jason Scott-Warren, who read and commented upon earlier drafts of this chapter.

1 Archivio di Stato di Venezia (hereafter ASV), *Provveditori sopra Monasteri* (hereafter *PSM*), busta 265, S. Zaccaria, 1614, fol. 9r–v: 'Io venni in questo Monasterio putta piccola in tempo del contaggio . . . ; et poi fui messa a spese nel Monasterio di San Vido di Buran dove stetti cinque in sei anni fino che fui accettata Monaca in questo Monasterio, che potevo haver intorno quindese anni, et fui vestita, et feci poi la professione con la bocca, ma non col core. Io son stata sempre tentata dal Demonio di rompermi il collo'.

2 *Ibid.*, fol. 9r–v: 'et sempre ho havuto per il tempo passato diverse amicitie propostemi, et messemi per le mani da Donna Cipriana, ch'è morta, ma con queste amicitie io non hò mai fatto cosa cattiva, cioe non ho perso la mia virginità'.

3 *Ibid.*, fol. 9v: 'et finalmente già sei anni mi fu fatto vedere da detta Donna Cipriana, che all'hora viveva, un Zuanne Cocco giovane all'hora de XX anni in circa il quale è venuto qualche volta à vedermi nascosamente alli parlatorii in maniera, che io mi inamorai in lui, et lo indussi ad'amarmi, et usai ogni arte etiam diabolici per indurlo ad'amarmi cioè scongiuri et orationi superstitiose, invocando diavoli, et hebbi queste cose da detta Donna Cipriana, per forza de danari'.

4 ASV, *PSM*, bu. 1, fols 39r–41v: decree of the Council of Ten, 7 February 1604. The date given in the records conforms to the Venetian style of dating, in which the new calendar year began on 1 March. In the text, I have converted the year to 1605, in accordance with the modern calendar.

5 ASV, *PSM*, bu. 265, 1614, S. Zaccaria, fol. 3v.

6 *Ibid.*, fol. 5v.

7 *Ibid.*, fol. 10r: 'Vennero tutti due in un copano con una tavola à traverso, et noi sbloccassimo il buso, et loro entrarono dentro per esso, et essendo stati due ò tre hore insieme hebbero commercio carnale il Cocco con me, et la detta suor Zaccaria col Zorzi, in detto luogo separatamente.'

8 *Ibid.*, fol. 10r: 'il detto Cocco entrò per il buso medesmo, et si fermò in detto luogo diese in dodese giorni ne mai è uscito di quel luogo mentre io me ne andavo per li publici luoghi del Monasterio per farmi vedere; et poi come tutte erano à dormire io andavo à star con esso mi sola nè mai ho disnato, et cenato con lui altro che una sola volta, ma ben gli hò portato il suo vivere'.

9 *Ibid.*, fol. 10v: 'et tutte quelle notti, che esso Cocco stette in Monasterio, egli hebbe da far con me'.

10 C. Ginzburg, *The Cheese and the Worms: The Cosmos of a Sixteenth-Century Miller*, trans. J. and A. Tedeschi (Baltimore and London, 1980); N. Z. Davis, *The Return of Martin Guerre* (Cambridge, Massachusetts, 1983); J. Brown, *Immodest Acts: The Life of a Lesbian Nun in Renaissance Italy* (Oxford, 1986).

11 L. Gowing, *Domestic Dangers: Women, Words, and Sex in Early Modern London* (Oxford, 1996); S. Haliczer, *Sexuality in the Confessional: A Sacrament Profaned* (New York, 1996).

12 On the importance of trial records as a means of recovering lost voices, see T. Cohen and E. Cohen, *Words and Deeds in Renaissance Rome: Trials before the Papal Magistrates* (Toronto, 1993), p. 4; U. Rublack, *The Crimes of Women in Early Modern Germany* (Oxford, 1999), p. 3.

13 M. Sbriccoli, 'Fonti giudiziarie e fonti giuridiche. Riflessioni sulla fase attuale degli studi di storia del crimine e della giustizia criminale', *Studi storici*, 29 (1988) 491–501; E. Grendi, 'Sulla "storia criminale": risposta a Mario Sbriccoli', *Quaderni storici*, 73 (1990), 267–75.

14 N. Z. Davis, *Fiction in the Archives: Pardon Tales and their Tellers in Sixteenth-Century France* (Princeton, 1988). Among those who have been influenced by the approach of Davis, see G. Ruggiero, *Binding Passions: Tales of Magic, Marriage, and Power at the End of the Renaissance* (New York, 1993), pp. 18–19, and Gowing, *Domestic Dangers*, pp. 52–3.

15 Davis, *Fiction*, p. 4.

16 G. Brucker, *Giovanni and Lusanna: Love and Marriage in Renaissance Florence* (Berkeley, 1986); T. Kuehn, 'Reading microhistory: the example of *Giovanni and Lusanna*', *Journal of Modern History* 61 (1989), 512–34.

17 Brucker, *Giovanni and Lusanna*, p. 15; Kuehn, 'Reading microhistory', 519–20.

18 Brucker, *Giovanni and Lusanna*, p. 84; Kuehn, 'Reading microhistory', 514–15.

19 Cohen and Cohen, *Words and Deeds*, p. 6.

20 M. Chaytor, 'Husband(ry): narratives of rape in the seventeenth century', *Gender and History*, 7 (1995), 378–407.

21 G. Walker, 'Rereading rape and sexual violence in early modern England', *Gender and History*, 10 (1998), 1–25.

22 *Ibid.*, 3.

23 *Ibid.*, 4–5.

24 For a validation of the use of psychoanalytic theory in the interpretation of early modern subjectivities, see L. Roper, *Oedipus and the Devil* (London, 1994); some reservations are offered by S. Greenblatt, 'Psychoanalysis and renaissance culture', in P. Parker and D. Quint (eds), *Literary Theory / Renaissance Texts* (Baltimore, 1986), pp. 210–24.

25 I. Giuliani, 'Genesi e primo sec. di vita del Magistrato Sopra Monasteri, Venezia, 1519–1620', *Le Venezie Francescane: Rivista storica artistica letteraria illustrata*, 28 (1961), 42–68, 106–69.

26 The patriarchal records of investigations into the 'crimes of nuns' were lost during the nineteenth century, and all that remains at the Archivio della Curia Patriarcale di Venezia is an index, entitled 'repertorium criminalium monialium'.

27 ASV, *PSM*, bu. 265, S. Zaccaria, 1614, fol. 39v: 'Questo è stato Andrea Foscarini . . . et la prego à perdonarmi, se non l'ho nominato innanzi; perche non volevo esser la sua ruina'.

28 For an elaboration of this interpretation of sexual crimes involving nuns, based on legal discourses in fourteenth- and fifteenth-century Venice, see G. Ruggiero, *The Boundaries of Eros: Sex Crime and Sexuality in Renaissance Venice* (New York, 1985), pp. 70–88.

29 ASV, *PSM*, bu. 265, S. Zaccaria, 1614: fol. 3v: 'che vi si fermò 10 in 12 giorni, magnando, e bevendo vini, et hebbe commertio con S. Laura'.

30 The tridentine ruling, passed in 1563 at the twenty-fifth and final session of the Council, reenacted the 1298 bull *Periculoso* of Boniface VIII, insisting on the maintenance of enclosure or its reintroduction 'where it has been breached (*ubi violata fuerit*)', and forbidding professed nuns to leave the convent 'save for some lawful reason which must be approved by the bishop (*nisi ex aliqua legitima causa, ab ipso episcopo approbanda*)'; J. Alberigo et al. (eds), *Conciliorum oecumenicorum decreta*, II (Freiburg, 1962), pp. 777–8. With the bull *Circa pastoralis* of 29 May 1566, Pius V confirmed and clarified the universal application of the Council's decree, asserting that all professed nuns, by virtue of their profession, were bound to strict enclosure, regardless of their customary rights or dispensations; *Bullarium diplomatum et privilegiorum sanctorum romanorum pontificum*, (24 vols, Turin, 1857–85), VII, pp. 447–50. For a full discussion of these measures and their implications, see R. Creytens, 'La riforma dei monasteri femminili dopo i decreti tridentini', in *Il concilio di Trento e la riformatione* (Rome, 1965), pp. 45–84.

31 ASV, *PSM*, bu. 1, fos 39r–41v: decree of the Council of Ten, 7 February 1604 Venetian style, Consilio X: 'Et se alcuno nell'avenire . . . , sarà trovato dentro di alcun Monasterio, ovvero sarà accusato di esservi stato, così di giorno, come di notte, etiam che non fusse convinto di comertio carnale, essendo retento, et giustificata la verità, gli sia tagliata la testa, si che si separi dal busto, et muora'.

32 ASV, PSM, bu. 265, S. Zaccaria, 1614; decree of the Council of Ten, 22 August 1614.

33 On the social causes of forced vocations in renaissance and early modern Venice, see P. Paschini, 'I monasteri femminili in Italia nel Cinquecento', in *Problemi di vita religiosa in Italia nel 500* (1960), p. 58; G. Spinelli, 'I religiosi e le religiose', in B. Bertoli (ed.), *La chiesa di Venezia nel Seicento* (Venice, 1992), p. 194; S. Chojnacki, 'Dowries and kinsmen in early renaissance Venice', *Journal of Interdisciplinary History*, 5 (1975), 576; V. Hunecke, 'Kindbett oder Kloster. Lebeswege venezianischer Patrizierinnen im 17. und 18. Jahrhundert', *Geschichte und Gesellschaft*, 18 (1992), 460–1.

34 See, for example, the responses of the nuns at Santi Biagio e Castaldo in the patriarchal visitation of 1593; ACPV, *Visite pastorali*, 1452–1730.

35 For other examples of nuns claiming suicidal urges, see the cases of two escapee nuns: Suor Crestina Dolfin, who ran away from Spirito Santo in 1561 (ASV, PSM, bu. 263), and Suor Faustina, who escaped from San Giovanni Lateran in 1555 (ASV, PSM, bu. 263).

36 For the proliferation of ecclesiastical rules and regulations regarding the enclosure of Venetian convents, see Lorenzo Priuli, *Ordini & avvertimenti, che si devono osservare ne'Monasteri di Monache di Venetia, sopra le visite et clausura* (Venice, 1591), and Antonio Grimani, *Constitutioni et decreti approvati nella sinodo diocesana, sopra la retta disciplina monacale* (Venice, 1592). On the restriction of nuns' musical activities, see C. Monson, *Disembodied Voices: Music and Culture in an Early Modern Italian Convent* (Berkeley, 1995) and R. Kendrick, *Celestial Sirens: Nuns and their Music in Early Modern Milan* (Oxford, 1996).

9

The trial of Giorgio Moreto before the Inquisition in Venice, 1589

Brian Pullan

Since the 1960s, historians of the great continental inquisitions of Rome, Spain and Portugal have divided into schools and put their documents to different uses.[1] Some of them incline to the belief that court records are efficient only at performing the task of showing how courts proceeded, and that they can afford only a sectional view, taken from a peculiar angle, of the prisoners and witnesses who came before the courts to undergo interrogation. Historians who hold this opinion have therefore concentrated on the structure and functions of the inquisitions themselves; on the mentality, aims and methods of their judges, officials and supporters; on the political struggles and personal rivalries that arose within the institutions; and on the relationship between inquisitions and diocesan and lay authorities in the states which accommodated them.

Other scholars, quite the other way, have turned to the prisoners rather than the judicial panels, and have looked to the trial records to provide a key to the mind and conduct of independent thinkers and rebels against ecclesiastical orthodoxy. Some have used the transcripts to examine systematic heresies formally condemned by papal bulls or conciliar pronouncements. Some have explored the ways in which inquisitions advanced or discouraged the process by which popular magic began to be perceived as diabolical witchcraft and prosecuted as apostasy from the Christian faith. Several writers, in search of the typical rather than the spectacular, have examined the routine cases which accounted for the bulk of the proceedings conducted by the Spanish and Roman Inquisitions. They have shown how, after the first few decades of the inquisitions' existence, when the Spanish Inquisition was no longer pursuing judaisers or the Roman Inquisition 'Lutherans' and Anabaptists, the judges' concern was mostly with lesser offences: how they pursued and corrected speeches or acts which amounted, not to fully fledged heresies, but merely to 'heretical propositions', to abuses of sacraments, to displays of 'scandalous' ignorance, to superstitious rituals rather than truly diabolical practices.

Certain indefatigable researchers have proved themselves as 'historians of great numbers', undaunted by the prospect of analysing statistically the 44,000 cases which were examined by the Spanish Inquisition between the mid-sixteenth and the early eighteenth centuries and described in the *relaciones de causas* drawn up by the inquisitors and their assistants.[2] Some, by nature project managers, have organised collective enterprises designed to compile more accurate and consistent inventories of the proceedings conducted by the many local tribunals of the Roman Inquisition in Italy. Their ambition is to make international comparisons and to plot the great trends in the institution's history, by identifying changes in the concerns of judges and prosecutors.[3] Other scholars, the miniaturists of the discipline, fascinated by the peculiar qualities of particular cases, have striven to 'see a world in a grain of sand', to uncover the hidden culture of obscure people by paying close attention to particular trials or to groups of trials which illustrate a theme. Trial transcripts have enabled them to write compelling studies of ordinary–extraordinary folk in the firm belief that these have as much right to biography as do people of status. Individualists, persons of modest social rank but heterodox opinions and eccentric behaviour, emerge vividly from the records if the inquisitors allow them to speak freely, as they give the floor to Domenico Scandella, the Friulian miller, or ask for written memoirs, as they do of Cecilia Ferrazzi, the pretended saint of seventeenth-century Venice.[4]

This chapter has the modest aim of illustrating the day-to-day workings of one tribunal, in the hope that readers will draw their own conclusions about the judges, the prisoner and the society in which they were placed. It will present in English translation the record of the trial of an obscure person who was arrested in April 1589 by the Inquisition (otherwise the Holy Office) in Venice. The transcript will perhaps throw light on the procedures and concerns of members of the court. It exemplifies the kind of story that inquisition records can tell about the way of life of people in casual employment, who lived by their wits rather than their skills as craftsmen: about the manners and customs of those who generally left no documentary traces apart from bald statements about their births, marriages and deaths in parish registers and necrologies.

The tribunal which inquired into the misconduct of Giorgio Moreto, 'Swarthy George', was one of some forty Italian branches of the Roman Inquisition, responsible to the Holy Office created in 1542 and the Congregation of the Index of 1571. The ecclesiastical judges of the Inquisition functioned with the collaboration, sometimes grudgingly and sometimes enthusiastically given, of the lay authorities in the states and cities which housed their tribunals.[5] Giorgio was a ribald Venetian sailor, ordinary rather than ordinary-extraordinary, who attracted attention by creating scandal and ignoring the barriers which the Catholic Church and the Venetian State were seeking to maintain between Christians and Jews. Perhaps he was desperate for entertainment during Lent, the Christian season of intensified self-denial, or perhaps it was a natural sociability which drew him to the ghetto. He was not an isolated figure. Several Venetian youths shared his taste for unleavened bread and his pleasure in wearing a Jewish hat for a joke, although they did not stand trial with him. Giorgio's was one of seventy-five cases involving Jews and judaising, some with several defendants, which are known to have come before this tribunal in the second half of the sixteenth century. In one respect it was unusual. Most charges of judaising were levelled at baptised Christians of Jewish stock, many of whom had once been practising Jews themselves, and were now suspected of betraying their baptism by returning to or taking up the law of the Jews. Giorgio Moreto, however, apparently had no Jewish blood. He was a Venetian who hailed from the parish of the Madonna dell' Orto, in the district of Cannaregio, close to the ghetto. His crime was to haunt the Jewish quarter, particularly at night, in such a manner as to arouse suspicion that he was flirting with Judaism, and enjoying the company of Jews if not sharing their beliefs.

Giorgio's trial was briskly and decisively conducted. It involved the elements of an inquisition *processo*, without any frills – a denunciation; an inquiry or *processo informativo* based on information provided by the author of the denunciation, and directed not by police officers but by judges, who took sworn testimony by word of mouth and had it recorded, seemingly verbatim, by the court notary; arraignment and examination of the prisoner; a verdict and sentence. The judges acted both as examining magistrates and as the magistrates who pronounced judgment and sentence. Certain procedures, less vital to the make-up of a trial, were absent. The court did not draw up a written indictment. Nor did it formally invite the prisoner to make his defences, though under interrogation he put his own side of the case. No advocates were appointed for the prosecution or the defence. No formal abjuration was required of Giorgio and no spiritual penance was imposed upon him. All these things might well have been done in a more complicated process, on which – had there been any question of using torture or imposing a death sentence – judges in Venice would probably have sought advice from Rome.

In the absence of a formal indictment, it was not entirely clear what the charges were, or which the judges took most seriously. Apostasy, turning Jew in order to marry a Jewish sweetheart, was the gravest crime contemplated, but it was not the offence which eventually earned the culprit a sentence of harsh imprisonment. Several lesser crimes were mentioned and probably regarded as more susceptible of proof – breaking the Church's dietary laws, uttering heretical blasphemies, and disobeying the Inquisition itself by defying its injunction to stay away from the ghetto. Rejection of the Church's authority was an important component of heresy, though Giorgio, however disrespectful in his behaviour, never uttered any profound intellectual statements or devised any outlandish theories.

Presented here is a translation made from the monumental edition, by Pier Cesare Ioly Zorattini of the University of Udine, of all surviving trials of Jews and judaisers conducted by the Inquisition in Venice between 1548 and 1734.[6] The court record has been fully rendered save that the translation does not repeat all the standard formulae used at the start and finish of each witness's testimony. They differ little from those employed with regard to the first Jewish witness examined (Jacob, son of David) and the first Christian witness (Alessandro, son of Innocenzo). The translation gives only the final version of the text drawn up by the court notary, and does not include the words he crossed out, either to correct his own errors or to introduce emendations requested by witnesses. The endnotes refer to one or two, but not all, of the marginal notes made by somebody going through the text and highlighting incriminating statements, perhaps with a view to drawing up a list of charges or of points on which the suspect was to be interrogated. Most of these notes merely state the obvious by repeating phrases used in the record, but occasionally they help to clarify obscure issues. Very likely, the texts which survive in the state archives, as this one does, are transcripts supplied to the Venetian noblemen who attended the court. They purport to give a complete account of the Inquisition's proceedings. However, the dialogue they record may not have been wholly spontaneous and some unrecorded events may have occurred off stage, for it is known that inquisitors sometimes approached witnesses beforehand or coached prisoners in the art of showing repentance.[7]

In fact, if not in canon law, the court which judged Giorgio Moreto was a mixed tribunal composed of clerical and lay members. Only clerics could pronounce sentences and only laymen could enforce them and enable the Inquisition to impose anything other than spiritual penances. In Venice, as in Genoa, or Savoy, or Ferrara, or Florence, the Holy Office could not make itself sufficiently feared without the magistrate's support.[8] The constitution of the Venetian Inquisition was intended to bind together three authorities which shared an interest in the suppression of heresy and to enable them to act in unison, even though the possibility of jurisdictional conflict and mutual jealousy was latent in their relationship. Papal authority was represented firstly by the nuncio, who was not merely a diplomat but also a legate endowed with the powers of an inquisitorial judge, and secondly by the Dominican inquisitor, whose authority was delegated to him by apostolic brief. The 'ordinary', as distinct from delegated, authority of the patriarch of Venice was important to the tribunal, although it had not always been essential. In the words of the canonist Francisco Peña, writing in the late 1570s, 'There are two kinds of judges in matters of faith, the first being ordinaries, such as the supreme pontiff of Rome and the bishops of the various places, who receive power and jurisdiction over heretics by divine right when they are ordained or consecrated.' As the record of this trial shows, the patriarch usually delegated the task of hearing routine cases to his vicar, even as the nuncio entrusted some of his own responsibility to an assistant known as an auditor. Since the early fourteenth century, canon law had enjoined the ordinary and the inquisitor to act together when imprisoning a suspect, authorising torture or pronouncing sentence. They had not always done so in sixteenth-century Venice and, on occasion, the patriarch and his vicar-general had proved to be more aggressive than the inquisitor himself.[9]

Formal sessions of the tribunal were attended by at least one of the three senior Venetian magistrates known as the Tre Savii sopra l'Eresia, who acted as the eyes and ears of the Venetian State if not as its mouthpiece. They represented the Republic's legitimate interest in the pursuit of heresy. In Venice, as in most states and societies, heresy was associated with disorder and sub-version, especially if the suspected heretics were Venetians, Venetian subjects, or other Italians. Venetian authorities showed less enthusiasm for pursuing Germans, Flemings or Frenchmen denounced for heresy while visiting or sojourning in Venice. Baptised Jews from Spain or Portugal who came to Venice as approved Jewish traders received guarantees against prosecution for heresy in and after the year of Giorgio's trial, 1589.[10] As a native Venetian, Giorgio himself could plead no privilege and it could be said that his bad behaviour violated the laws of the State as much as those of the Church, for the Venetian Senate had created the Venetian ghetto and Venetian magis-trates regulated it.

The Tre Savii existed both to spur the Inquisition on and to prevent it from acting against the State's commercial or political interests or trespassing on its jurisdiction. In Italy generally, complaints that the Inquisition was tepid and ineffective were as common as charges that it was breaking its bounds.[11] Fierce controversy had arisen, especially between the Republic and Pope Julius III in 1550–1, over the precise role of lay judges in tribunals of the inquisi-tion. Were they to be fully-fledged inquisitors themselves, or mere collateral judges and consultants, or simply coadjutors who supplied the force of the secular arm when called upon to do so? The State would have had them be judges; the pope threatened excommunication for laymen who infringed the jurisdiction of the Church.[12]

It seems clear that in 1589 the Savii were, as they had always been, more than mere executors of clerical decisions; they almost certainly took part in deliberations of the court, although in the past the State had been anxious that their interventions should not be recorded.[13] Appointments to their posi-tions were generally, until the mid-1590s, of a conciliatory nature, since most of the Savii were pious, elderly men unlikely to pick unnecessary quarrels with their ecclesiastical colleagues. They had almost invariably served as mem-bers of the Council of Ten, Venice's permanent committee of public safety; indeed, in the course of at least one trial, they had been said to represent the Ten in the Inquisition.[14] Of the laymen who attended the Moreto trial, Giovanni Battista Querini, seventy-nine years of age, was serving his sixth term as a Savio; Andrea Bernardo, aged seventy-one and a former governor of Padua, his third term; and Federico Contarini, a new recruit, was a mere baby of fifty-one. He had risen with unnatural speed through Venice's gerontocratic pol-itical system because he had been able, in 1571, to purchase an honourable office, that of procurator (i.e. advocate or protector) of the church of St Mark's. This had given him access at an early age to the Ten and its attached committee, the Zonta. His pro-papal zeal and enthusiasm for the Jesuits were said to be so strong that, had the full extent of his Roman sympathies become known, his reputation in Venice would probably have been ruined.[15] He was hardly the man to restrain the Inquisition from acting against the irreverent and disorderly Moreto.

It was the task of the Inquisition to pursue heresy, even in its inchoate forms, and even where it seemed to arise out of ignorance or frivolity rather than from a resolution to defy the Church and question its teachings. Should people allegedly speak, act, or neglect their religious duties in such a way as to give rise to suspicion of heresy, the court could justifiably call on them to prove their faith and to confess, acknowledge and repent of errors. In Venice the Inquisition had no business with religious offences such as improperly entering convents or simple blasphemy, which, since they raised no subtle theological issues, could properly be dealt with by lay magistrates.[16] It seems likely that Giorgio Moreto first fell into the hands of a Venetian police magistracy which suspected him of disorderly conduct and breaking the state's rules concerning the ghetto, but handed him over to the Inquisition when it became clear that his behaviour also bordered on the heretical because he was violating Lent and courting a Jewish girl.

Since the Savii sopra l'Eresia were active members of the court, the Inquisition was calling on representatives of what appeared to be very different legal systems, one based on professional and the other on amateur judges. The inquisitor and some of his colleagues were trained in theology or canon law or both these disciplines, and could read procedural manuals designed to take them through every step of the trial.[17] On the other hand, Venice's republican political system was based on a brisk rotation of offices among members of a legally defined ruling order, a hereditary, untitled, urban nobility often called a patriciate. No distinction was made between judicial posts and fiscal or administrative offices, and no professional qualifications were required in order to fill any of them. As judges Venetian noblemen were expected to pay attention to equity and to exercise discretion and common sense in passing sentences. Venetians, jealous of their sovereignty, were well known for their refusal formally to acknowledge Roman and canon law, which they were believed to dismiss as unacceptable symbols of papal and imperial dominion. Many inquisition cases, however, involved straightforward questions of fact as much as theological issues, and the Moreto case was one of these, though it also raised questions about the intentions which lay behind the words and deeds attributed to the prisoner. The lay members of the court would have had something to contribute to the case's resolution, which dispensed entirely with spiritual ceremonies and penalties.[18]

The scene of Giorgio's crimes was the Venetian ghetto. This had originated in a disused copper foundry, on a site which had happened to be available in

1516 when the voices of preachers, inveighing against intimacy between Christians and Jews, had become so strident that the government was disposed to pay them heed. Ghettoisation made it possible for Jews to live in Venice but not be of it, in a crowded enclave which was to some degree self-governing. In 1589 the ghetto consisted of two districts, the large Ghetto Nuovo originally intended for the so-called 'Germanic' Jews (many of whom were really Italians) and the small Ghetto Vecchio. Theoretically at least, the Ghetto Vecchio, which had been enclosed and reserved for Jewish occupation in 1541, was for 'Levantine' Jews who were, or had been, or could claim to be, subjects of the Ottoman Empire.[19]

Venice agreed to the presence of the Jews, partly because they served the economy by performing specialised functions, as Germanic and Italian Jews provided pawn offices and Spanish and Portuguese Jews promoted trade with the Levant; partly because they gave employment to Christians and consumed their products; and partly, too, because they were potential converts to Christianity. Since the mid-sixteenth century the city had maintained a house of converts, the Pia Casa dei Catecumeni, in which a small number of Jews and Muslims who had professed interest in turning to Christianity were instructed in the essentials of the Catholic faith. It was often argued that unless Jews lived in some place close to Christian society, they would never change their ways and beliefs. But in the view of authority, both ecclesiastical and lay, it was vital to maintain a hierarchical relationship between Christian and Jew, to demonstrate the superiority of Catholic Christianity to Judaism. It ought to be unthinkable that Christians should contemplate turning to Judaism, and it was scandalous that Giorgio Moreto should boast that he had thought of doing so. Proximity must not lead to intimacy, or business dealings to social relations: Christians were not to mingle with Jews on equal terms, to sit at their tables, to sleep under their roofs, or to share their beds. Levantine Jews bore turbans, but others were generally obliged to wear yellow or red hats, intended to forestall familiarity by contrasting garishly with the black hats of the Christian laity. As the trial record shows, frivolous disrespect for this badge of religious allegiance contributed to Giorgio Moreto's downfall.[20]

Separation between Christians and Jews was not intended to be total. The day was for business transactions; crowds of Christian customers flowed into the ghetto, bent on pledging or redeeming at the pawn offices, or on making purchases or sales at the second-hand shops. Giorgio Moreto described himself as doing 'a bit of brokering'. Indeed, the economic activities of Jews were liable, in Venice and other cities, to generate middlemen who dealt on behalf of clients with pawnbrokers and second-hand dealers, supervised and recorded transactions, and used their know-how to bring buyers and sellers together. In the late sixteenth century there were at least sixteen officially recognised brokers in the Venetian ghetto (twelve Christians and four Jews), and they were evidently concerned both with the second-hand trade conducted by the Germanic Jews and with the transactions of Levantine Jewish merchants.[21]

Three Christian brokers were summoned to give evidence in the Moreto case. It is unlikely that Giorgio himself, scraping a living by his wits, had any official status or paid the government's brokerage tax. But his trade gave him reason to be on the streets by day.

Giorgio was on much shakier ground when he ventured into houses by night. A curfew was imposed on Jews, from an hour or two after sundown, and enforced by the warders on duty at the gate. In March 1589 a decree of the magistrates in charge of the ghetto permitted Christians to remain in the place, at least in winter, until the fourth hour of the night, but only if they were performing recognised services for the Jews.[22] Giorgio Moreto's enthusiastic participation in Jewish festivities would scarcely have met with official approval. Like the brokers, the warders on the ghetto gate were expected to be reliable and well-informed witnesses to occurrences in the Jewish quarter, and two of them were summoned by the Inquisition to testify in Moreto's case. One was the elderly Domenico Spadini, called 'the Gobbo', otherwise 'the hunchback'; the other was his son, Antonio, whom Giorgio accused of bearing false witness against him. Did Shakespeare get to hear of them, transform them into Lancelot and his gravel-blind father, 'Old Gobbo', and include through them an oblique reference to the ghetto in *The Merchant of Venice?* The story of Giorgio and his Jewish girl, Rachel, reads a little like a plebeian version of the tale of Lorenzo and Jessica, but without a happy ending. However, two of the main protagonists of Giorgio's story – Rachel and her father, Isaac the Deaf, – are tantalisingly absent from the list of witnesses examined by the Inquisition.[23]

By definition trials are concerned with improper behaviour and tell us about those alleged to have overstepped a mark. However, by studying deviance one comes to know what was considered correct, or at least what was expected by the authorities represented by the judges. Giorgio's offence was to challenge, perhaps unthinkingly, the orderly scheme which authorities, both clerical and lay, were seeking to impose upon Venice as upon other Catholic cities. Since all human beings were sinners, good and evil, fidelity and infidelity, chastity and fornication could all have their places in a Christian society. Indeed, institutionalised 'lesser evils' such as licensed prostitution and usurious moneylending could be justified on the grounds that they were practised by outcasts in such a way as to prevent them from corrupting respectable Christians. But right order had to be expressed visibly by reserving spaces for particular purposes and making attempts to separate good physically from evil, purity from impurity, the sacred from the profane. This end had to be achieved not only by means of the ghetto, but also through such measures as the separation of prostitutes' dwellings from sacred places and the ban on whores visiting churches at certain times; the protection of nunneries from violation; the removal of beggars from streets and churches and their consignment to the hospital of the Mendicanti, established in the 1590s.[24] It seemed shocking to Giorgio's delator that he should mix up things that ought to be kept apart – not only that he should confuse Carnival and Lent, but also that, having scourged himself one day in honour of Christ's passion, he should venture the next day into the ghetto, the territory of Christ's enemies. No doubt the Roman Inquisition bore cases like his in mind when it decreed in 1598 that 'Christians attending Jewish circumcisions, accepting breakfasts [*ientacula*] or unleavened bread, serving in the houses of Jews, conversing with them in a familiar vein, or discussing matters of faith with them shall be punished, together with those very Jews, by the Holy Office.'[25]

Up to a point Giorgio's conduct was ambiguous: his presence at Jewish festivities could conceivably be explained as part of a devious scheme to woo a Jewish girl and, by converting her, to win a soul for Christ. Even so, he had not informed or involved the officials of Venice's house of converts, the Pia Casa dei Catecumeni, and by failing to do so he was taking a grave risk. In the end, when he ignored the Holy Office's injunction to avoid the ghetto, there could be no doubt of his disobedience, whether drunk at the time or not, to authority and its explicit commands.

The Record of Proceedings Against Giorgio Moreto

Thursday 6 April 1589
Against Giorgio, called Moreto, otherwise the mariner. Presented by Don Jacopo, son of Pietro Malosso, deputy constable of the Five Lords Justices of the Peace.[26]
My lords of the Holy Office. I, your unnamed informant, being a Christian and your most loyal servant, do not wish to conceal from you the wicked ways pursued by Giorgio, known as Moreto, mariner, who shows no respect for the holy ordinances you have posted in Santi Giovanni e Paolo, or for the justice of God. For he, in contempt of the holy decrees of mother Church, habitually eats with Jews and associates with them at all times of the year, and he eats and goes masked and makes merry in such a manner as to make no distinction between Lent and Carnival, a thing that is not to be tolerated by your most excellent lordships.

The first point is that on 22 March, at the nuptials of the Jew Solomon Maestro, he [Giorgio], being in attendance with a lighted torch in his hand, invited the Jewish people in and received them in the manner of Jews, and then, when they were assembled, repaired to the house of the Jew Jacob di Oresi, where was the oven at which they cooked capons and other roast meats which are forbidden to us Christians at that season, and he pulled a capon off a spit which they had removed from the oven, and tore it apart and ate it. Present were the said Jacob di Oresi, and Jacob, son of David Bichele, and the man who works pasta for Jacob, and his baker, who are both Christians, whom Jacob will name.

Likewise, concerning the nuptials of Moses Moresco, a Jew, during this same Lent, Tonin, son of the Gobbo [hunchback], warder of the ghetto, had occasion to say to Messer Alvise Minotto, who disposes of a wardership of the ghetto, that this Giorgio eats meat and is worse than a Jew.[27] When the Jews are holding vigils over new born boys in order to circumcise them he goes along and attends all vigils until daybreak together with the Jews, as is their custom, and when there are feasts and dances he attends them and is forever inviting and leading other Christians to them, and he goes masked during Lent. Witnesses are the warders of the ghetto, and Abram Levi, servant to the Jacobi di Mezo, and Benedict, son of Orso Scocho, a Jewish mercer from Padua.

And the said Giorgio is courting a Jewish girl, the daughter of Isaac the Deaf, and because her father the Jew and her relatives and others reproved him and threatened not to give him the girl, it was said that he wanted her at any price, even if he had to think of becoming a Jew. Witnesses are David Medici, and Samson, son of Vital, butcher, his father and uncle to the girl.[28]

On Good Friday he was heard to say in the ghetto that he wanted to scourge himself, and on Easter Saturday when any passer-by touched him he cried: 'Oy, don't touch me, I've been beating myself.' And he said those words in the middle of the house of that Jewish woman that we are building, in the presence of the Jewess Michiela Capagia. Furthermore, by examining the Christian warders and the Jews it will be found that he, Giorgio, is in the ghetto at all hours of the day and night, and this I have made known to your lordships so that, having had the truth, you may give me something to help me live and support my family, and I commend myself to your favour.[29]

Saturday 8th April 1589

With the noble lords Giovanni Battista Querini and Andrea Bernardo in attendance, and before the reverend master Stefano Guaraldo of Cento, inquisitor, and the reverend lords Anteo Claudo, auditor to the papal nuncio and Desiderio Guidone, vicar to the patriarch, there appeared in answer to a summons Jacob, son of David, a Jew dwelling at present in the Ghetto Vecchio, and the oath was administered to him, which he swore upon a pen, in the manner of the Jews.[30]

Asked if he knew one Giorgio, called Moreto, mariner, how he knew him and for how long, he replied: 'I have known this Giorgio for perhaps six to eight months.'

Asked upon what occasion, he answered: 'This Giorgio frequents the ghetto by day and by night, and it is said that he is courting a young woman, the daughter of Isaac the Deaf.'

Asked how he knew that this man was courting the Jewish girl, he answered: 'I know it because Giorgio has told me on many occasions that he is courting her and that if he could lead her away he would.'

Asked if he had seen Giorgio eating in the ghetto, at what time and on how many occasions, he answered: 'I have seen him do so many times, mostly on the street in the ghetto, and I have seen him eat buns [*focaccie*] and cottage cheeses [*puine*], and he snatched the cheeses from the vendors, and it all happened during this Lent just past, but I have not seen him eat meat or capons.'

Asked if he had seen Giorgio at the nuptials which were celebrated in the ghetto, and at other festivals, he answered: 'I have seen him at festivals in the ghetto and seen him dance at those festivals, and this carnival I myself arranged two or three feasts in the house of one of my masters, and Giorgio came there to dance.'

It was said to him: 'With whom did the said Giorgio dance and in what manner?'

He answered: 'He danced with our Jewish women and I have seen the said Giorgio go to dance at all the celebrations in the ghetto, for you cannot hold a ball without he goes to it.'

The witness was asked if he had seen the said Giorgio at the wedding of one Solomon, a Jew, and he answered: 'No, my lord, I did not see him.'

Duly examined as to personal details, he gave his age as forty years. He confirmed his testimony after it was read over to him and silence was imposed on him upon a penalty to be determined at the court's discretion.[31]

Benedict, aged seventeen, son of Orso dalla Mano, a Jew dwelling in the Ghetto Nuovo.
Asked if he knew one Giorgio Moreto, mariner, he answered: 'Yes, my lord.'

Told to say for how long, and on what occasion, he answered: 'Giorgio has frequented the ghetto for perhaps nine years. I have seen him speak with Jews. He used to make a lot of noise, and I have seen him take fruit and eat it.'

Asked if he knew or had heard tell that the said Giorgio has fallen in love in the ghetto, he answered: 'I have heard it said that he is in love with a Jewish girl, the daughter of Isaac the Deaf, a cook.'

Asked if he knew or had seen or heard tell that the said Giorgio had often eaten in the houses of Jews, especially meat or capons, he answered: 'No, my lord, I have not seen him, nor have I heard that said.'

And in response to a question he said: 'I have seen him several times at Jewish festivities, dancing with Jewish women.'

In reply to a question he said: 'I did not see him at the wedding of the Jew Solomon Maestro, because I was not present at that wedding, and I know no more of this matter.'

He confirmed his testimony and added: 'Since you swore me to tell the truth, I have heard from the warders of the ghetto, who are Christians, that this Giorgio sometimes spends the whole night in the ghetto and gives them great trouble in opening and closing it. Their names are Giovanni Maria Razzer and Giacomo Zotto [the lame man], a Friulian, and I do not know the surname of the second man, but he is the son-in-law of Giovanni Maria Razzer.' And he added again: 'I heard this said by certain Jews, who had it from the warders themselves.'

Abraham Levit, son of Vivian, aged twenty-nine, a Jew of the Ghetto Nuovo.
To an apposite question, he replied: 'I have known this Giorgio by sight for seven or eight months and have seen him at a ball disguised in a *bautta* [a little cloak used in masquerades]. When he came they suspected that it was he, and the maidens withdrew and there was no dancing. It happened during our last Carnival and the Christian Lent. There is a Jewish maiden and it is said that Giorgio is courting her, and that was why they departed.'

To an apposite question he replied: 'I have not seen him eat in the houses of Jews and have heard nothing of such things, but I have certainly seen him eat some of our matzos, which are made of flour and cold water, in the street last Lent. I have heard the warders complain that he lingered in the ghetto until the fourth and fifth hours after sundown.'

Before the same gentlemen there appeared in answer to a summons Alessandro, son of Innocenzo, dwelling in the parish of Santa Maria Formosa, and the oath to tell the truth was administered to him, which he swore on the holy gospels of God.
To an apposite question he answered: 'This year and last I have been to the ghetto to cook their matzos, and at this oven the Jews cook capons, pigeons, veal and several other things, mostly on Friday for Saturday, and in the evening they put the pots in the oven for the sabbath morning.'

Asked if he knew one Giorgio, called the Moreto, mariner, he replied: 'I know one Giorgio, who had himself called by that name throughout the ghetto. He has a pointed beard and is taller than me, a young man of some twenty-two or twenty-three years.'

To an apposite question, he said: 'This past Lent, when a couple of Jewish weddings were held in the ghetto (Levantines, I think), after the matzos had been baked they brought capons, doves and tarts to the oven to be cooked, and those who were celebrating the weddings, either the masters or the servants who had brought the stuff to be cooked, said the Jew who owns the bake house where I was doing the cooking, "Take one of the very best capons for your offering!" So the owner of the bake house took a capon out of the pan, and this Giorgio tore a leg or a wing off this capon which had been cooked, and he ate it, and he smeared some of it on me, and the Jew who owns the bake house, whose name is Gneccole, burst out laughing. I don't remember the exact day, but it was one day last Lent.'

And to an apposite question he said: 'I did not see this Giorgio eat with Jews, but I did see that when the Jews were eating at their celebrations the said Giorgio stood by with a torch in hand to give them light.'

It was said to him: 'Who was present when Giorgio ate the wing or leg of the capon?'

He answered: 'Gneccole and I were present, and so were other Jews, but I do not know them, and when Giorgio held the torch for the Jews the porter who is son of Gobbo and a Christian was also present.'

Duly examined as to personal details, he gave his age as twenty-five years. He confirmed his testimony when it was read over to him.

Antonio, son of Domenico Spadini, aged twenty-four, warder of the ghetto.
In answer to an apposite question he said: 'I know this Giorgio, called the Moreto, mariner, a young man of some twenty-eight years, with a little black beard, of swarthy complexion and my own height, and I have known him since Carnival, for he is forever in the ghetto by day and by night, and gives much trouble in opening and closing the ghetto. And my father remonstrated with him and he swore: "*Al cospettazzo de Dio, putanazza de Dio,* you are my foe and give me as much displeasure as you can!"[32]

Asked if he knew or had heard tell or seen that the said Giorgio had eaten meat by day or by night in the ghetto and at what time, he replied: 'Last Lent I saw the said Giorgio eat meat, for there were hens, capons and meat in the Ghetto Nuovo in the house of a banker's servant. The servant is called Moses, his master the banker Samuel, and Moses had taken a wife and was celebrating his wedding, and Giorgio ate on his feet, and eating at the table were the Jews Sosilo, Baruch the tailor, Auromene, Ezekiel, and others who saw when Giorgio ate meat.'

To a question he replied: 'I have seen him many times in the ghetto making a great deal of noise. This Giorgio was in love with a daughter of Isaac the Deaf, and he goes to the festivities in the ghetto, and at night he goes in disguise with a mask on, and he gave me his masks and false beard and cap for safe keeping, and I know nothing more.'

Tuesday 11 April 1589
Before the illustrious and reverend lord archbishop of Ragusa [Hieronimo Matteucci], papal nuncio, the reverend father inquisitor, and the reverend Don Desiderio Guidone, vicar to the patriarch, with the noble lords Giovanni Battista Querini and Andrea Bernardo in attendance, there appeared in answer to a summons Samson, son of Vital, a Jewish butcher dwelling

in the Ghetto Vecchio, and the oath to tell the truth was administered to him, which he swore upon a pen, in the manner of the Jews.

Asked if he knew one Giorgio, called the Moreto, mariner, and for how long and upon what occasion, he answered: 'I have known him for about a year, since he arrived on a ship with certain Jews.'

Asked if he knew or had seen or heard that the said Giorgio frequented the ghetto and for what purpose, he replied: 'This Giorgio spends almost the entire day in the ghetto and is there at night up to the sixth or seventh hour after sundown, in and out of the usual hours, and hence he stays at a house, because he is courting a Jewish girl, the daughter of Isaac the Deaf.'

Asked if he knew or had heard tell that the said Giorgio had said anything about the said girl, he replied: 'This Giorgio has had occasion to say several times that he wants to lead this girl away, and if he cannot, then to have her he is willing to become a Jew, and I have heard this several times from his own lips. I do not remember who was present at the time. And because I am a butcher in the ghetto this Giorgio has come several times to plague me at my stall and take chops and other meat to eat in company with Jews. To get rid of him I had an order drawn up by an Avogador, but I do not remember who he was, for he did not come to my stall.'[33]

In reply to an apposite question, he said: 'These last few days, Giorgio was wounded in the ghetto by certain Christians, on account of the matzos (or so they say) which Giorgio was going round the houses and collecting and was unwilling to give to those young men.'

To a question he said: 'I do not know that this Giorgio ate meat in the ghetto on days forbidden to Christians and I know nothing else of this matter.'

Duly examined as to personal details, he gave his age as forty-three years. He confirmed his testimony when it was read over to him.

Joseph Zozzoli, Jew, son of Salvadio, aged forty-four.
In answer to an apposite question, he said: 'I have known this Giorgio, called Moreto, mariner, for about two years, for he sometimes enters the ghetto and does a little brokering.'

At this point there arrived the noble lord Federico Contarini, procurator of St Mark's.

'I see him almost all the day in the ghetto, for he is courting a Jewish girl, the Deaf Man's daughter.'

He was asked if he knew or had heard tell that the said Giorgio had eaten meat in the ghetto on days forbidden to Christians, and answered: 'I have neither seen nor heard such things.'

He was asked if he knew or had heard anything else concerning the person of the Deaf Man's daughter, and replied: 'I have heard nothing else, save that he is fond of her, and I know nothing more.'

The Jew Benedict the Roman, son of Donato, aged forty-five.
In answer to an apposite question, he said: 'I know one who goes about the ghetto, and his name is Giorgio. I do not know that he is a mariner, but he is known as the Moreto and may be about twenty-five years of age. He has little beard, is not very tall, and seems almost always to be in the ghetto during the day. At night I do not look and have heard nothing; I have no knowledge of his being in love in the ghetto, and I have never seen him eat meat there, for I have no acquaintance with him and do not seek his company.'

The Jew Abraham, son of Salvadio, aged twenty-six, dwelling in the Ghetto Vecchio.
In answer to an apposite question, he said: 'I have known this Giorgio for some ten to twelve months, and he walks up and down in the ghetto and does some brokering in the ghetto and generally frequents the place; I have seen him around, but have never seen him eat anything save a matzo or two.'

The Jew David Medici, aged twenty-five, dwelling in the Ghetto Vecchio.
In answer to an appropriate question, he said: 'I know this Giorgio, who is a Christian, and I have known him for about a year. He frequents the ghetto and goes to-and-fro all day on the street.'

He was asked if he knew or had heard tell that Giorgio had fallen in love in the ghetto, and answered: 'The crowd in the ghetto say that he is in love and is courting a Jewish girl, the daughter of a deaf Jew called the Steward [Scalco].'

To a question he replied: 'I have never seen him eat or take a meal in the ghetto, nor have I heard of him doing either.'

To a question he replied: 'I never heard tell that Giorgio had occasion to say that if he could not have the Jewish girl he would wish to become a Jew.'

The Jew Jacob, son of Servadio, aged about twenty-eight, dwelling in the Ghetto Vecchio.
To an apposite question he replied: 'I have known this Giorgio for one or two years, and he goes to-and-fro in the ghetto and does a bit of brokering, and I have not heard tell that Giorgio fell in love in the ghetto. I do not know, and I have not seen or heard it said that Giorgio ate in the ghetto by day or by night.'

Thursday 13 April 1589
With the lord procurator Federico Contarini in attendance, and before the very reverend father, Master Stefano da Cento, inquisitor, the reverend lords Anteo Claudo, auditor of the lord papal nuncio, and Desiderio Guidone, vicar to the patriarch of Venice, the man named below was brought from prison and sworn to tell the truth.
Asked his name, surname, country and occupation, he answered: 'My name is Giorgio Moreto of Venice, and I have had different occupations, for I have been a trader and am now a mariner.'

Asked if he was accustomed to frequent the ghetto and to live there by day and night, and for what reason, he replied: 'It is my habit to frequent the ghetto during the day because I go about and do a bit of brokering, and have sometimes been there at night, when I have gone to celebrations and to eat with Jews and things of that kind.'

To a question he said: 'I have been at many Jewish festivities and do not remember any in particular, but there was one in the house of the Jew Scocco, another in that of Abraham Boaf, and various others which were held at night, and I went to their banquets and ate with them, but never ate any forbidden foods, because they have their feasting at the time of our Lent, and I ate bread, olives and fruits and danced unmasked at their balls upon several occasions, and I danced with the Jewish women, and the Jews ate meat at their meals, but I did not eat at their tables and kept apart, so that even if they were only eating fish I did not have it, but ate only fruit, bread and some of their matzos.'

To a question he said: 'I danced with the Jewish women, both the wives and the maids, and they took me for partner and I them. I have frequented the ghetto ever since I was born, because I live nearby at the Madonna dell' Orto, although I have been closely connected with it only for the last sixteen months, of which I spent six or seven in Alexandria, and the rest of the time I have been often in the ghetto.'

He added, in response to another question: 'I would remain in the ghetto until about the fourth, fifth or sixth hour after sundown, but I have never slept there, and if you find out that I did your lordships must do as you please. I could not tell you how many times I ate in the ghetto, but it might have been thirty, forty or a hundred – I do not remember.'

Asked whether he ever ate meat or the products of dairies in that place during Lent, he replied: 'No, my lord. I never did.'

Admonished to tell the truth, he replied: 'I am here to tell the truth, and I trust in God and the Mother of Grace that they will help me to speak it.'

Asked whether he was in love with any Jewish maiden, and if so with whom, he answered: 'I am courting a Jewish maiden, the daughter of those who brought this suit against me, who are not only persecuting me in this place but have pursued me through all the tribunals of Venice. By the grace of God they have never succeeded in harming me, and I do not believe they will do so here.'

To a question he replied: 'Those who brought suit and are persecuting me are the brothers Samuel and Isaac Semchà and their sons and all their relatives; and one Solomon, a Jewish butcher, who is my enemy. Other enemies I do not have, to my knowledge.'

To a question he replied: 'This Jewish girl whom I am courting bears the name of Rachel and I have been wooing her for sixteen months, since I began visiting the ghetto so often.'

Asked if he thought of taking her to wife or had had her in some other way, he answered: 'If the said Rachel had been willing to come with me as she promised, I would have had her baptised and taken her to wife, and I would have done so willingly, and I hope in God that she may still resolve to convert! It is true that I boasted and bragged to many people that I wanted to lead the said Rachel away, but I always meant to do so with her consent, because she promised to come with me, as I said. And because her relatives became aware of this they stopped up the doors and balconies and hatched a thousand plots and wanted to injure me.'[14]

Asked whether he had ever had occasion to say or had thought in his heart that if he could not lead this Rachel away he would want her on any terms, even if he thought of becoming a Jew, he answered with a smile: 'I never said or thought or imagined such a thing. I'd have had to be out of my mind!'

On being told that he must resolve to speak the truth, because witnesses have been examined and deposed that he said such things, he answered: 'I never said anything of the sort, and if any false witness has said so, I do not intend to be punished, because it must be some enemy of mine.'

Asked if he had ever blasphemed, by way of intimidating the warders of the ghetto who did not want to open the door for him, he replied: 'No, my lord.'

To a question, he replied: 'The reason for my enmity towards Samson the butcher is that he is the trading partner of Samuel Semchà and that one day I went to ask him for meat and he would not give it to me, and I threatened him, saying that one day I'd get it, for which reason he took out a court order against me at the Avogaria.'

He was told that he must resolve to tell the truth as to whether he ate meat during Lent or at other forbidden times, because there were three witnesses who said that they saw him do so and had not been named by him as enemies, and he answered: 'If they say that they saw me eating meat they must be false witnesses, and if one of them was Tonin, son of the Gobbo, a warder in the ghetto, who is a Christian, then I challenge him as a false witness, because he has been declared such by the Criminal Court of the Forty. If another was Benedict Baruc, a Roman Jew, I say the same of him, because he too has been declared a perjurer, and so have one Capon, a Jew, and one Polenta – they are all false witnesses, and have been declared such.'

He was asked if he had other enemies – but he must be truthful – and he replied: 'I have told the truth.'

He was asked if he thought it good, as a Christian, to court Jewish women and seek to lead them astray, and answered: 'Yes, my lord, I do think it good, because I have my conscience, and there have been others who have been led away and been baptised, and so I hope to do with her and have her convert and be baptised, and these things are in my heart and my intentions.'

Asked if there is any Christian baker who is his enemy, he answered: 'I am not aware of having any baker as an enemy.'

In answer to a question, he added: 'Nor any innkeepers, shopkeepers, or others.'[35]

Asked if he was ever in a place where meat was cooked, such as capons, roasts, or things of that kind, he answered: 'I was at the bake house of the Jew Jacob di Oresi this last Lent, and I do not know what day it was that, when certain meat was in the oven that the Benini, who are Jews, had had cooked, I took a chicken bone and the whole leg came away, and I said "I too want to eat meat", and I pretended to put it in my mouth but in fact I threw it over my shoulders to a dog, and I did not eat it. If I had eaten it I would tell you, because I would hope for mercy.'

Asked if he would resolve to tell the truth, he replied: 'I have told the truth.'
At this point he was returned to his place. He confirmed his testimony when it was read over to him.

Saturday 15th April 1589

Before the very reverend father inquisitor and the reverend auditor to the papal nuncio and the vicar to the patriarch, with the noble lord Giovanni Battista Querini in attendance, there appeared in answer to a summons the Jew Aaron Macchioro, son of Abraham, dwelling in the Ghetto Vecchio, and swore the oath in the manner of the Jews.

In reply to an apposite question he said: 'I have known this Giorgio Moreto for some fourteen to sixteen months, and I made his acquaintance in the ghetto, and for five or six months he has often been in the place, ever since he returned from Cairo in the Levant. This last Lent in the Christian calendar I went about the ghetto and was on my way home, and when I was in the doorway of Samson the butcher I saw a servant of Solomon Maestro (I could not recall his name) who was preparing the food for the wedding of his son, and this man had a plateful of meat and other things, and I saw Giorgio take a piece of *melina* stuffed with meat and put it in his mouth and eat it.'[36]

He was asked: 'Since it was night-time, how did you see this, and how far were you from him?'

He answered: 'About an arm's length from him, indeed rather less, because it was a narrow place, and I saw him because Giorgio had a lighted torch in hand, since he was going along with the Jews to fetch the stuff from the oven. Because weddings in the ghetto are always held on Wednesdays, this must have been a Wednesday evening according to the Christian calendar with Thursday coming on, and there was nobody present but myself and that servant, whose name I do not know, and I have not seen Giorgio eat meat on other occasions.'

Duly examined as to personal details, he gave his age as about twenty years.

With the noble lords Giovanni Battista Querini and Federico Contarini in attendance, the holy tribunal of the Inquisition of Venice, having seen and pondered the record of the present proceedings, have for the time being, for the purpose of avoiding scandal, decreed that the said Giorgio shall be forbidden any further contact with either the Ghetto Vecchio or the Ghetto Nuovo of the Jews, and that on no account shall he venture by day or by night to enter the Ghetto Vecchio or Ghetto Nuovo, nor shall he loiter near their gates, upon pain of being consigned to the galleys to row in chains for a period of three years, and that any person who accuses him of or reports such a transgression shall receive a reward of one hundred *lire di piccoli*, to be taken from Giorgio's possessions.[37]

Saturday 10 June 1589

The constable Girolamo Verier [Hieronimus Vitriarius], who serves the Holy Office, reported as follows. 'Yesterday Giacomo Malosso, deputy constable of the Five Lords Justices of the Peace, escorted Giorgio Moreto, mariner, to the prisons of the Holy Office because he had seen and found him in the ghetto on several occasions, even though he has been forbidden to enter the ghetto by a judgment of this Holy Office, on pain of a fine of 100 lire should he disobey. Furthermore, Giorgio, servant to the Holy Office, has seen Giorgio Moreto at the Aseo bridge [near the ghetto] with a Jewish hat upon his head, and the said Giorgio Moreto, now in prison, admitted to me yesterday that he, together with certain butchers, wore a yellow hat upon his head.'

Before the reverend lord papal nuncio, the very reverend father inquisitor and the reverend auditor to the papal nuncio, with the noble lord Giovanni Battista Querini and the procurator Federico Contarini in attendance, there appeared Ser Giorgio, son of Battista of Tarvisio, servant to the Holy Office of the Inquisition in Venice, and the oath to tell the truth was administered to him.

To an apposite question he replied: 'About a month ago, on my way to the parish of the Servites to summon certain witnesses on the orders of this Holy Office, I saw in a little boat [*fesolera*] that Giorgio who was imprisoned here on the orders of the Holy Office, and with him were three others whom I did not recognise, and Giorgio and the three others all had yellow hats upon their heads, etc.'

Ser Domenico called the Gobbo, warder of the ghetto, aged fifty-six.

To an apposite question, he said upon oath: 'I know Giorgio Moreto, mariner, and on Thursday morning (not yesterday, but last week), when I was in the Ghetto Nuovo selling from my baskets of greenery, he touched my beard and said: "Old man, you'll yet be examined on my account." I said to him: "I rejoice that you are out of trouble!" I never saw him save on that occasion.'

Don Pietro Volpato, son of Don Volpe of Venice, aged thirty-six, broker in the ghetto.

To an apposite question, he replied: 'I know this Giorgio, and he used to be often in the ghetto, and whenever I saw him passing through the Ghetto Vecchio he always said: "I'm going out, I'm going away." I have not seen him since he was imprisoned here at the Holy Office.'

Ser Pantaleone, son of Don Giuseppe of Venice, aged forty, broker in the ghetto.
To an apposite question he replied: 'I know this Giorgio Moreto, and not yesterday but the other day I saw him pass through the ghetto from the Cannaregio gate to go towards the Ghetto Nuovo.'

Don Albino, son of Francesco, a Grison, aged forty, broker in the ghetto.
On being questioned he said: 'I know this Giorgio Moreto and I saw him last Thursday passing through the ghetto at a run and he was saying: "I'm going away", and he entered from the gate of the Ghetto Nuovo and ran towards the gate of the Ghetto Vecchio, and I saw him only that day.'

The aforesaid Giorgio was brought from prison and arraigned before the said gentlemen and sworn to tell the truth.
Asked if he knew the reason for his arrest, he replied: 'No, my lord, I do not know, because I was taken at the Two Bridges [at Santi Ermagora e Fortunato in Cannaregio] by the officers of the Five Justices of the Peace.'

He was asked: 'Have you in the last few days, since you were released from the prisons of the Holy Office, been in a boat with other men, wearing a Jew's hat upon your head?'

He answered: 'It is more than twenty days since I went to Murano for a joke with two others who are butchers, and one is called Bortolo and the other Giacomo. And for a jest we wore the yellow hats of Jews on the way out and on the way back, and one of those young butchers went to pick the hats up from the ghetto, and I stayed in the boat there at the Beco bridge [at San Giovanni in Bragora, in Castello], and this is two or three cannon-shots away from the ghetto, and we were carrying some carpets which were in the house of one of the butchers, and we bore them to the nunnery of San Matteo [on the island of Mazzorbo], where the man's sister is a nun, and we wore the yellow hats for a joke, not realising that there would be any objection.'

Asked whether this last Thursday he was within the ghetto of the Jews of Venice and if so for what purpose, he answered: 'On Thursday, when I was here at St Mark's, I hailed some young men and we went to a tavern at San Girolamo and ate and drank there, and being tipsy with the wine the young men said: "We want to go down through the ghetto!" I said to them: "Let's go." And so I passed through the ghetto, and I went in by the gate of the Ghetto Nuovo and out through the gates of the Ghetto Vecchio, and with me were Fabio, silk-mercer, and Luca, tailor.'

It was said to him: 'Did you not know that when you were released by the Holy Office a month or two ago you were charged and warned not to enter the ghetto and forbidden even to approach it? You have treated this order with contempt, and have indeed made so bold as to go out in public in a boat, wearing upon your head the yellow hat of a Jew.'

He answered: 'I knew it, I was always aware of it, and to extricate myself from this affair I wanted to join up with the captain of the gunners. This is the first time I have been at fault, I ask for your pardon and mercy, the wine was my undoing.'

At this point the holy tribunal, having seen and heard the aforesaid evidence, ordered the said Giorgio to be sent to row in the galleys of the Venetian state for a spell of three years, in accordance with the decree drawn up on the fifteenth day of April just past, and 100 lire from his possessions shall be given in accordance with the aforesaid decree.[38]

Notes

1 On the historiography of the Inquisition see, for example, G. Henningsen and J. Tedeschi with C. Amiel (eds), *The Inquisition in Early Modern Europe: Studies on Sources and Methods* (Dekalb, Illinois, 1986); A. Del Col and G. Paolin (eds), *L'Inquisizione Romana in Italia nell' età moderna. Archivi, problemi di metodo e nuove ricerche* (Rome, 1991).

2 See J. Contreras and G. Henningsen, 'Forty-four thousand cases of the Spanish Inquisition (1540–1700): analysis of a historical data bank', in Henningsen and Tedeschi with Amiel (eds), *The Inquisition*, pp. 100–29.

3 For proposals see A. Del Col, 'L'inventariazione degli atti processuali dell' Inquisizione Romana', in Del Col and Paolin (eds), *L'Inquisizione*, pp. 87–116; A. Del Col, 'Strumenti di ricerca per le fonti inquisitoriali in Italia nell' età moderna', *Società e storia*, 20 (1997), 143–67, 417–24.

4 See C. Ginzburg, *The Cheese and the Worms: the Cosmos of a Sixteenth-Century Miller*, trans. J. and A. Tedeschi (Baltimore-London, 1980); Cecilia Ferrazzi, *Autobiography of an Aspiring Saint*, (ed.) and trans. A. J. Schutte (Chicago, 1996).

5 For a useful list of the forty-two tribunals of the Roman Inquisition which were active in the second half of the seventeenth century, see Del Col, 'Strumenti', 153. On the Roman Inquisition in Malta, see F. Ciappara, *Society and the Inquisition in Early Modern Malta* (San Gwann, Malta, 2001). For the reform of the Roman Inquisition, see for example A. Prosperi, 'Per la storia dell' Inquisizione romana', in Del Col and Paolin (eds), *L'Inquisizione*, pp. 40–1; A. Prosperi, *Tribunali della coscienza. Inquisitori, confessori, missionari* (Turin, 1996), pp. 38–40.

6 See P. C. Ioly Zorattini (ed.), *Processi del Sant' Uffizio di Venezia contro ebrei e giudaizzanti, 1548–1734* (14 vols, including *Appendici* and *Indici Generali*, Florence, 1980–1999). For the Moreto case, see VIII (1587–1598), pp. 81–98. For a brief account of the case, dependent on the manuscript in Archivio di Stato, Venice, Sant' Uffizio, processi, busta 64, see B. Pullan, *The Jews of Europe and the Inquisition of Venice, 1550–1670* (Oxford, 1983; reprint, London, 1997), pp. 164–6.

7 See N. S. Davidson, 'The Inquisition in Venice and its documents: some problems of method and analysis', in Del Col and Paolin (eds), *L'Inquisizione*, pp. 119, 122–4.

8 Prosperi, 'Per la storia', p. 61; Prosperi, *Tribunali*, pp. 59, 75–8, 87–8.

9 On the composition and operation of the Venetian tribunal, see P. Grendler, *The Roman Inquisition and the Venetian Press 1540–1605* (Princeton, 1977), pp. 39–49; Pullan, *Jews of Europe*, pp. 26–44; R. Canosa, *Storia dell' Inquisizione in Italia dalla metà del Cinquecento alla fine del Settecento* (5 vols, Rome, 1986–90), II, pp. 10–14, 168–80; A. Del Col, 'Organizzazione, composizione e giurisdizione dei tribunali dell' Inquisizione Romana nella Repubblica di Venezia (1500–1550)', *Critica Storica*, 25 (1988), 244–94; A. Del Col, 'L'Inquisizione Romana e il potere politico nella Repubblica di Venezia (1540–60)', *Critica Storica*, 28 (1991), 189–250; Prosperi, *Tribunali*, pp. 83–103.

10 See J. Martin, 'Per un analisi quantitativa dell' Inquisizione Veneziana', in Del Col and Paolin (eds), *L'Inquisizione*, p. 151; also Pullan, *Jews of Europe*, pp. 186–98. Cf. J. Martin, *Venice's Hidden Enemies: Italian Heretics in a Renaissance City* (Berkeley, Los Angeles and London, 1993), pp. 161–5, 189, 191.

11 For examples see Prosperi, 'L'Inquisizione', p. 52, 58, 61; Prosperi, *Tribunali*, p. 90.

12 Del Col, 'Organizzazione', 293–4; Del Col, 'L'Inquisizione', 211–13.
13 Del Col, 'L'Inquisizione', 219.
14 See the records of the trial of Abram Righetto, 29 May 1572, in Ioly Zorattini (ed.), *Processi*, III (1570–72), p. 128.
15 For all three, see P. Grendler, 'The *Tre Savii sopra Eresia* 1547–1605: a prosopographical study', *Studi Veneziani*, new series, 3 (1979), 325–31; for Contarini, G. Cozzi, 'Federico Contarini: un antiquario veneziano tra Rinascimento e Controriforma', *Bollettino dell' Istituto di Storia della Società e dello Stato Veneziano*, 3 (1961), 190–220, and Grendler, *Roman Inquisition*, pp. 220–1.
16 For the lay magistracy responsible for convents see the chapter by Mary Laven in this volume. For blasphemy and related offences, see R. Derosas, 'Moralità e giustizia a Venezia nel '500-'600. Gli Esecutori contro la Bestemmia', in G. Cozzi (ed.), *Stato, società e giustizia nella Repubblica Veneta (sec. XV–XVIII)* (2 vols, Rome, 1980–85), I, pp. 431–528; G. Cozzi, 'Religione, moralità e giustizia a Venezia: vicende della magistratura degli Esecutori contro la Bestemmia (secoli XVI–XVII)', *Ateneo Veneto*, new series, 29 (1991), 7–95.
17 For example, by that of the embattled fourteenth-century Catalan inquisitor Eymeric, which had recently been reissued with extensive notes and commentary by the Spanish canonist Francisco Peña: N. Eymeric, *Directorium inquisitorum, cum scholiis seu annotationibus eruditissimis D. Francisci Pegnae Hispani, S. Theologiae et Iuris Utriusque Doctoris* (Rome, 1578). There were several subsequent editions. See A. Borromeo, 'A proposito del *Directorium inquisitorum* di Nicolás Eymerich e delle sue edizioni cinquecentesche', *Critica storica*, 20 (1983), 499–547; J. Tedeschi, 'Inquisitorial sources and their uses', in his *The Prosecution of Heresy. Collected Studies on the Inquisition in Early Modern Italy* (Binghamton, New York, 1991), pp. 51–5.
18 See G. Cozzi, 'La politica del diritto nella Repubblica di Venezia', in Cozzi (ed.), *Stato, società e giustizia*, I, pp. 15–152; G. Ruggiero, *Violence in Early Renaissance Venice* (New Brunswick, New Jersey, 1980), pp. 40–4; G. Ruggiero, *The Boundaries of Eros: Sex Crime and Sexuality in Renaissance Venice* (New York and Oxford, 1985), pp. 4–5; G. Cozzi, M. Knapton and G. Scarabello, *La Repubblica di Venezia nell' età moderna* (2 vols, Turin, 1986–1992), I, pp. 113–14, II, pp. 104–5; the texts translated in D. Chambers and B. Pullan (eds), *Venice: A Documentary History 1450–1630* (Oxford, 1992), pp. 102–4.
19 For the Venetian ghetto and the Jewish economy, see B. Pullan, *Rich and Poor in Renaissance Venice: The Social Institutions of a Catholic State, to 1620* (Oxford, 1971), pp. 486–8, 538–78; R. Finlay, 'The foundation of the ghetto: Venice, the Jews and the War of the League of Cambrai', *Proceedings of the American Philosophical Society*, 126 (1982), 140–54; B. Ravid, 'The religious, economic and social background and context of the establishment of the ghetti of Venice', in G. Cozzi (ed.), *Gli ebrei e Venezia (secoli XIV–XVIII)* (Milan, 1987), pp. 211–59; D. Malkiel, *A Separate Republic. The Mechanics and Dynamics of Venetian Jewish Self-Government, 1607–1624* (Jerusalem, 1991).
20 Cf. Pullan, *Jews of Europe*, pp. 145–67, 243–74.
21 Pullan, *Rich and Poor*, pp. 549–51; G. Vercellin, 'Mercanti turchi e sensali a Venezia', *Studi Veneziani*, new series, 4 (1980), 60–1, 68–9. By about 1674–75 there were twenty-four officially recognised brokers in the ghetto.
22 See B. Ravid, 'Curfew time in the ghetto of Venice', in E. E. Kittell and T. F. Madden (eds), *Medieval and Renaissance Venice* (Urbana and Chicago, 1999), pp. 251–2.

23 For this theme see B. Pullan, 'Shakespeare's Shylock: evidence from Venice', in B. Garvin and B. Cooperman (eds), *The Jews of Italy: Memory and Identity* (Bethesda, Maryland, 2000), pp. 193–208.

24 See Chambers and Pullan (eds), *Venice*, pp. 122–3, 126–7; on the Mendicanti, Pullan, *Rich and Poor*, pp. 362–70. For breaches of cloister, see chapter 8 by Mary Laven in this volume.

25 Quoted in S. W. Baron, *A Social and Religious History of the Jews* (second edition, 18 vols, London, New York and Philadelphia, 1962–80), XIV, pp. 121–2.

26 The Cinque alla Pace were a minor Venetian magistracy responsible for law and order. It is possible that, although this version of the denunciation is clearly addressed to the Inquisition, an earlier version had been submitted to the Cinque alla Pace, who, noting its religious implications, had urged the delator to resubmit it to the Inquisition. Note the remark later made by Giorgio Moreto to the effect that his enemies had 'pursued him through all the tribunals of Venice' and the fact that he was arrested on 9 June by an officer of the Cinque alla Pace, who were evidently still taking an interest in the case.

27 The noble family of Minotto owned at least some of the houses in the ghetto (see Pullan, *Jews of Europe*, p. 158). The warderships of the ghetto, like many such positions in Venice, were probably paid offices which could be assigned to persons who exercised them through nominated substitutes.

28 The original text differs from the published version and reads: 'Et il dito fa l'amor con una ebrea fiol de Isach dito il Sordo et perché suo padre di esa ebreo et li suoi parenti et altri l'ano represo, li ano manaciati di darli et auto a dir che la vol a tute foze si'l credese a farsi ebreo.' I am grateful to Professor Ioly Zorattini for pointing this out. The wording remains somewhat obscure. There is a note in the margin of the delation: 'He wants a Jewish girl, with whom he is in love, even if he had to think of becoming a Jew'.

29 The informant is not technically an accuser but a delator. He does not personally undertake to prove the case and suffer penalties if he fails to do so. Rather, he hands the case over to the Inquisition, which chooses to investigate it. It would also have been open to the Inquisition to investigate the matter *per viam inquisitionis*, that is, without a particular delator, but on the strength of reports or rumours, *fama* or *clamor*, reaching the judges' ears. See Eymeric, *Directorium*, pp. 283–4; Peña's notes (separately paginated), pp. 124–6.

30 The practice of swearing an oath on the pen of the court notary was widespread among Italian Jewish communities, and had the same value for Jews as swearing with a sacred object in the hand – see Ioly Zorattini (ed.), *Processi*, I (1548–1560), p. 157, n.11.

31 For the importance attached to evidence that a suspect had eaten meat or poultry or fat at forbidden times, during Lent or on Fridays and Saturdays without a licence from a parish priest, compare the case of the Venetian mercer Giovanni Zonca in 1582 – see V. Rossato, 'Religione e moralità in un merciaio veneziano del Cinquecento', *Studi Veneziani*, new series, 13 (1987), 204–5, 208–9, 212–13, 228–31. Itself an offence against ecclesiastical discipline, the violation of Lent aroused suspicion of heretical tendencies.

32 There is a note in the margin, 'Heretical blasphemies'. 'Al cospetto' or 'al cospettazzo de Dio' was a euphemism for 'al dispetto de Dio' or 'in defiance of God' and implicitly denied God's omnipotence; 'putanazza de Dio', a reference to 'God's whore',

denied the goodness of God. See Pullan, *Jews of Europe*, pp. 80–2; Canosa, *Storia dell' Inquisizione*, V, p. 213; Cozzi, 'Religione, moralità e giustizia', pp. 27–8.

33 The Avogadori di Comun were the attorneys-general or chief law officers of Venice; among much else they acted as examining magistrates and prosecuted in the higher criminal courts.

34 On campaigns for the conversion of Jews to Christianity in Italy, see Pullan, *Jews of Europe*, pp. 243–312; B. Pullan, 'The conversion of the Jews: the style of Italy', *Bulletin of the John Rylands University Library of Manchester*, 70 (1988), 53–70, reprinted as Item XI in B. Pullan, *Poverty and Charity: Europe, Italy, Venice, 1400–1700* (Aldershot, 1994).

35 None of the witnesses called had been examined in Giorgio's presence and their names were concealed from him. This was almost universal practice in inquisition cases and was designed to protect witnesses against retaliation. Suspects could of course try to deduce the names of witnesses from the court's questions at their own examination. There were other ways of finding out – some years later a priest under investigation for solicitation in the confessional sent a boy to hang around the door of the Holy Office and see who went in to be interviewed (C. Madricardo, 'Sesso e religione nel Seicento a Venezia: la sollecitazione in confessionale', *Studi Veneziani*, new series, 16 (1988), 134–5). The prisoner was always asked to name any personal enemies as part of his defence. Should he do so, and give convincing reasons for their enmity, less attention would be paid to their testimony: only evidence of 'mortal enmity', *inimicitia capitalis*, would disqualify them completely, according to Eymeric's manual – see his *Directorium*, pp. 295–6.

36 A dish named after the Yiddish *melen* or the German *Mehl*, meaning 'flour' – see Ioly Zorattini's note 27, p. 93, to the text of the trial.

37 The Inquisition had not, apparently, reached any firm conclusions as to Giorgio's guilt. He had admitted attending Jewish festivities, eating unleavened bread and being in the ghetto until all hours of the night, but not eating meat during Lent or sleeping in the ghetto, still less having any serious intention to become a Jew. The evidence against him may have seemed inconclusive. In a more complex case the prisoner might well have been provided with a written document summarising the evidence against him, been provided with an advocate, and even put to the torture with a view to obtaining a full confession on the grounds that the case against him was half-proved but not fully so. However, Eymeric's manual states that 'in cases concerning the faith one proceeds concisely, simply and smoothly [*summarie, simpliciter et de plano*] and without the fuss of advocates and judgments . . . it is not necessary to offer a written statement [*libellum*] or to contest the case; groundless appeals are not to be entertained . . .' (Eymeric, *Directorium*, p. 285). The Moreto case shows how that principle could be applied. The Inquisition's first concern was to reform Giorgio's behaviour rather than to punish him – or perhaps they had decided to give him the liberty to convict himself.

38 The Council of Ten had decreed in 1559 that heretics were not to be condemned to the penal galleys for fear that they might disseminate their subversive ideas in all-too-receptive surroundings (Del Col, 'L'Inquisizione', 220). In 1568, however, a rigorous papal nuncio, Facchinetti, had succeeded in getting the law changed so that 'those who deserve it' could now be sent to the galleys (A. Stella, (ed.), *Nunziature di Venezia*, VIII, Rome, 1963, p. 455). On the penal galleys see A. Viaro, 'La pena della galera: la condizione dei condannati a bordo delle galere veneziane',

in Cozzi (ed.), *Stato, società e giustizia*, I, pp. 379–430. In practice a sentence to the galleys was likely to prove far harsher than a sentence of perpetual imprisonment imposed on a more systematic but socially superior offender, who, if he gave evidence of contrition, might be pardoned within a few months, whereas many oarsmen in the penal galleys failed to obtain a prompt release on the expiry of their sentences (see Borromeo, 'A proposito', 542; J. Tedeschi, 'The organisation and procedures of the Roman Inquisition: a sketch', in his *The Prosecution*, pp. 147–51; the example of the mercer Giovanni Zonca in Rossato, 'Religione', pp. 246–7).

Index

Note: 'n.' after a page reference indicates the number of a note on that page.

Lightning Source UK Ltd.
Milton Keynes UK
UKOW021145180212

187494UK00001B/24/P